THE

ENTREPRENEURIAL

MINDSET

THE

ENTREPRENEURIAL

MINDSET

Strategies for Continuously Creating Opportunity in

an Age of Uncertainty

Rita Gunther McGrath

and

Ian MacMillan

HARVARD BUSINESS SCHOOL PRESS
BOSTON, MASSACHUSETTS

08 07 06   11 10

978-0-87584-834-1 (ISBN 13)
Library of Congress Cataloging-in-Publication Data
McGrath, Rita Gunther.
   The entrepreneurial mindset : strategies for continuously creating oppor-
tunity in an age of uncertainty / Rita Gunther McGrath and Ian MacMillan.
     p. cm.
   Includes bibliographical references and index.
   ISBN 0-87584-834-6 (alk. paper)
    1. Entrepreneurship. 2. Leadership. I. MacMillan, Ian C., 1940– II. Title.

HB615 .M3735 2000
658.4'21—dc21   00-033514

There was homework and hockey and horseback riding
And the book
There was ballet and swimming and baseball
And the book
There was family and music and travel
And the book
There were friends and gossip and dishes
And the book
For Anne, John, and Matt,
Who good-naturedly lived with a book in the midst of our
    domestic bliss

RITA GUNTHER MCGRATH

To Jean, whose sacrifices of time and whose emotional
investment to make this book happen cannot be measured.

IAN MACMILLAN

CONTENTS

PREFACE

THIS BOOK SUMMARIZES THE PRACTICAL IMPLICATIONS OF OUR
accumulation of experience, research studies, and active teaching
and working with business organizations attempting to deal with
uncertainty and with entrepreneurs learning to launch and grow
their businesses. MacMillan's early interest in entrepreneurship
stemmed from his experience as an entrepreneur, when he worked
with John Foggitt to create a global travel business based on novel
travel concepts. McGrath also spent time as an entrepreneur, creating first a political consulting business, then a prototype of what one
might recognize as a Kinkos type of operation called Unworried
Words. Neither venture proved sufficiently attractive to stick with
for the long haul, although they were great learning experiences.
She began her academic career after closing these businesses to pursue an exciting opportunity in the world of information technology
design.

   We thought that you, our readers, might be interested in the
origins of some of the ideas in this book. The primary thrust of the

book—that uncertainty can yield tremendous opportunity when looked at in the right way—has long been a topic at the heart of the academic study of entrepreneurship.[1]

Chapter 2 stems from our experiences with teaching entrepreneurship and helping would-be entrepreneurs. One of our most consistent challenges was to get entrepreneurial wanna-bes to make sure that their proposed venture ideas were worthwhile. Accepting proposals for any old venture inevitably generated lists of viable, but basically boring businesses (like dog-walking services). So, we challenged them to think of business concepts that would be worthwhile in comparison with the opportunities they could have working for a large company. Without further ado, the insufficiently profitable ideas vanished. The business equivalent is to make sure at the outset that your ideas have the potential at maturity to contribute in a worthwhile way to your company. This is what we call framing the business.

In chapters 3 and 4 we examine ways of seeing existing product and service offerings in a new light. The material is extensively drawn from fieldwork in which we have analyzed patterns of opportunity recognition by independent entrepreneurs and by managers pursuing corporate ventures. We are particularly fortunate to have worked with Citibank (now Citigroup), Chubb & Son, American Reinsurance, DuPont, and other companies that showed us how new opportunities emerged and how these organizations used them as the basis for new business models.[2] By new business models, we mean the way an organization organizes inputs, converts these into valuable outputs, and gets customers to pay for them. A business model, in other words, is how a business is designed to generate profits.

Chapter 5 builds on research in which we worked with managers of established companies to try to understand their competitive terrain and identify breakthrough opportunities they might otherwise have missed. This work was largely driven by McGrath's deep interest in real options reasoning as an approach to strategizing under conditions of uncertainty. As the name suggests, new businesses often begin as options—small, uncertain investments that can later prove worthy of further investment. Early experiments can be immensely important later on. Evaluating new technologies as options has been used at global companies such as Merck, Matsushita, and DuPont. DuPont recently sponsored a collaboration in which McGrath was the principal investigator and concluded that the approach gave them a new way to explore opportunities.[3]

Chapters 6 and 11 draw largely on research based on McGrath's Ph.D. dissertation, which involved both extensive fieldwork and survey/analysis of new businesses involving new products, new technologies, or new markets begun by established firms. The tools presented in chapter 11 have been used to diagnose the progress of more than one thousand such new business development projects of strategic importance to managers involved in our executive education and research programs.[4]

The insights into the composition of a company's portfolio of business initiatives and the importance of achieving strategic focus and making trade-offs between attractive projects are presented in chapters 7 and 8. These chapters draw largely on our observations of many companies and their corporate venturing programs. Our observations included a four-year engagement by MacMillan in the General Electric Work Out program and more than a decade of interactions with GE managers in the company's Crotonville, New York, facility. We also drew on some of the earliest empirical work on strategy, taking a statistical approach to assessing commonly held assumptions in the strategy arena. One early article, for instance, challenged the widely held belief that businesses classified as "dogs" in the famous Boston Consulting Group's product/portfolio matrix were inherently unprofitable.[5]

Entry strategies for new markets, the focus of chapter 9, formed a considerable part of MacMillan's work on competitive dynamics and were a major thrust of his research in the late 1980s, as the effects of hypercompetition began to become evident to managers of even the most staid businesses. McGrath became involved in applying traditional ideas from competitive dynamics to highly uncertain business environments.[6]

Chapter 10 presents discovery-driven planning, an approach we devised to help managers plan under highly uncertain circumstances. Originating from joint work with Zenas Block, a co-author of MacMillan's and a multiple-venture entrepreneur, the concept of discovery-driven planning departs dramatically from conventional strategic planning but is no less disciplined. The concepts underlying it were distilled from Block and MacMillan's experiences working with habitual entrepreneurs—people who make a habit of detecting and exploiting the business opportunities that arise from uncertainty. An article on discovery-driven planning was the first of several jointly authored pieces McGrath and MacMillan published in the *Harvard Business Review*. The methodology is now being actively used by companies such as Intel, Hewlett-Packard, Fluor Daniel, Matsushita, and Sonera.[7]

Chapter 12, a distillation of the practices of entrepreneurial leadership, is based on massive amounts of fieldwork. Our first projects compared the behavior of managers of highly successful corporate venture divisions with that of managers in similar circumstances who appeared unable to create new business opportunities for their firms. Later work drew on our corporate venturing studies, such as the Citiventures project we worked on in the early 1990s.[8] We refer you to other research studies that we use and build on throughout the text as appropriate.

Throughout this book, we have provided figures and tables that allow readers to generate scores and derive conclusions. These materials are all based on considerable theoretical and empirical research. Readers should be aware, however, that the way we suggest that managers might use them to inform their decision making should not be confused with a rigorous empirical methodology. By necessity, we have simplified the tools and omitted additional variables that might be used to assess bias, reliability, and generalizability in the interests of helping practitioners gain some insights into "roughly right" solutions.

The following box provides a more general overview of how this book fits into scholarly perspectives on strategy.

THEORIES OF STRATEGIC MANAGEMENT UNDER UNCERTAINTY

Problems of planning and leading under uncertain conditions are pervasive in the life of any manager, but have not always been central to the theory of strategic management. Neoclassical economists, for instance, finesse the issue of disruptive change by focusing on seeking the conditions under which equilibrium will emerge. Drawing from the neoclassical tradition, strategic management scholars in the 1940s and 1950s tried to identify the regular patterns that would be amenable to predictive theorizing.

An early and still useful framework that adopted this approach was known as the structure-conduct-performance paradigm. The essential argument was that certain market structures, such as markets spread across geographic regions, demanded specific organizational responses (such as the creation of a multidivisional, or M-form, firm to permit greater local discretion than a headquarters-controlled bureaucracy). Appropriate conduct by the management of a firm given this market structure would then lead to higher performance. Uncertainty in the structure-conduct-performance paradigm had to do primarily with ascertaining which features of the competitive landscape one should pay attention to. Changes in this landscape were treated as fairly slow-moving and infrequent.[a] Strategies, similarly, were seen as relatively stable for a given firm over time.[b]

This perspective gained enormous influence with the publication of Michael Porter's *Competitive Strategy* in 1980, a book that gave us a parsimonious five-forces model with considerable explanatory power.[c] The emphasis was on relatively stable features of the landscape and how these could be influenced in one's favor. For instance, a strategist might discover how barriers to entry could be created to limit rivalry. At about this time, consultants also began to explore the practical implications of relatively stable industry structures and to develop tools to help managers identify what the main features of the competitive landscape were, in order to make informed choices. From about this period onward, for instance, findings regarding strong linkages between market share and profitability influenced many managers to seek businesses characterized by high growth and the potential to achieve large share positions.[d]

Parallel to this line of thinking was a point of view on strategy that emphasized the internal capacities and capabilities of firms. The focus in this view was on change, evolution, and path-dependent progress rather than on stability, and on internal resources rather than environmental or competitive characteristics.[e] Pioneering economists Richard Nelson and Sidney Winter introduced the idea of *evolutionary economics* as part of this tradition in 1982. Among their insights was the idea that firms develop valuable path-dependent routines but that these are difficult to change. Uncertainty thus presents a major challenge, because the best resource combination may only be clear after the fact. The insight stemming from this perspective is that adaptation, new competence creation, and learning are crucial components of strategic management.[f]

Uncertainty, idiosyncrasy, and the unexpected had always featured prominently in the work of scholars studying entrepreneurship.[g] Uncertainty was seen as essential to the capture of profits from creating new combinations of productive resources, because profit came from an entrepreneur's perceiving an opportunity not obvious to others and then investing to capitalize on it.[h] Moreover, those individuals and organizations able to create new models for doing business could replace less effective older models, in the course of what Josef Schumpeter famously called "gales of creative destruction."[i]

The now-familiar list of factors leading to instability in industries and company strategies (globalization, deregulation, technological change, information intensity, etc.) are forcing managers today to cope with the kind of rapid, unexpected change that has long been central to the theory of entrepreneurship. We believe that the time is consequently right for a new integration of entrepreneurship and strategic management. The successful future strategists will exploit an entrepreneurial mindset, melding the best of what the older models have to tell us with the ability to rapidly sense, act, and mobilize, even under highly uncertain conditions.[j]

a. Bain (1959); Chandler (1962).

b. Miles and Snow (1978).

c. Porter (1980); Porter (1985); Porter (1990).

d. One of the most famous frameworks is the Boston Consulting Group's product-portfolio matrix, which used insights on experience curve effects and industry growth patterns to inform portfolio and investment decisions (Henderson 1980).

e. Selznick (1947); Penrose (1959); Nelson and Winter (1982); Wernerfelt (1984); Barney (1991); Dierickx and Cool (1989); Amit and Schoemaker (1993); Teece, Pisano and Shuen (1997).

f. March (1991); Levitt and March (1988); Levinthal and March (1993); Cohen and Levinthal (1990); Cohen and Levinthal (1994); Levinthal (1997); Henderson and Cockburn (1994); Leonard-Barton (1992).

g. Indeed, Hebert and Link's (1988) research finds the earliest use of the term *entrepreneur* in the work of Richard Cantillon, who in 1755 used the term to describe someone who "exercises business judgment in the face of uncertainty."

h. Knight (1921); Schumpeter (1950); Kirzner (1997); see also Rumelt (1987); Venkataraman (1997).

i. Schumpeter (1950).

j. McGrath (forthcoming); see also Brown and Eisenhardt (1998); Christensen (1997); and Slywotzky and Morison (1997) for other books that are consistent with this point of view.

CHAPTER 1

NEEDED

An Entrepreneurial

Mindset

YOU CAN'T PICK UP A BUSINESS BOOK THESE DAYS WITHOUT reading about how dramatic increases in competitiveness and technological turbulence have introduced a pervasive sense of uncertainty to everyday managerial life. This is hardly news. What we hope will be new to you in this book is that uncertainty can be used to your benefit if you create and deploy an entrepreneurial mindset—a way of thinking about your business that captures the benefits of uncertainty. Once entrepreneurial thinking becomes second nature, you will be able to continuously identify uncertain yet high-potential business opportunities, and exploit these opportunities with speed and confidence. Uncertainty becomes your ally instead of your enemy.

There are three ways in which *The Entrepreneurial Mindset* is different from other business books. First, since successful entrepreneurs are action-oriented, so is this book. Each chapter is intended to give you ideas that you can put to work immediately, even if your situation is uncertain. Second, we've made the concepts we describe simple to use. When you are moving fast, complexity only creates confusion and delay. A huge part of becoming an entrepreneurial leader is learning to simplify complexity, so that your co-workers can act with self-confidence. The ideas you will encounter here have helped others to gain confidence, and we think they can help you, too. Third, the book is intended to grow with you. We start off simply, then add to the level of challenge as the book moves on.

How will you know that the entrepreneurial mindset has taken hold? You'll know when you begin to think and act like the unusual people we call *habitual entrepreneurs*. Habitual entrepreneurs have made careers out of starting businesses, some working within existing businesses and some in independent start-ups. They have in common finely honed skills in forging opportunity from uncertainty.

This book distills our observations of habitual entrepreneurs. The point is to show you how they think, how they behave, and exactly what it is that they do so well. They capitalize on uncertainty rather than avoid it, they create simplicity where others see complexity, and they embrace the learning that comes from taking calculated risks. They recognize that when opportunities are fleeting, it is sometimes more expensive to be slow than to be wrong. As a consequence, they will find solutions that are "roughly right" rather than consume time developing an analytically correct, but slow, answer.[1] This special group has an immense amount of insight and experience to offer you.[2] Whether you are a manager or an executive, or an entrepreneur yourself, we believe that you can learn a lot from habitual entrepreneurs. Throughout the book, we'll show you how to apply the ideas to your domain, whether that is a division, a unit, or an entire company—small or large, your own or someone else's. We'll refer to this domain as your business or your organization.

DEFINING CHARACTERISTICS OF THE ENTREPRENEURIAL MINDSET

Habitual entrepreneurs have five characteristics in common.

1.   They passionately seek new opportunities. Habitual entrepreneurs stay alert, always looking for the chance to profit from change and disruption in the way business is done. Their greatest impact occurs when they create entirely new business mod-

els. New business models revolutionize how revenues are made, costs are incurred, or operations are conducted, sometimes throughout an entire industry. One reason that the emergence of the Internet as a new medium of business has been accompanied by dizzyingly high company valuations is that investors perceive its potential to profitably transform virtually every aspect of economic life.

2. They pursue opportunities with enormous discipline. Habitual entrepreneurs not only are alert enough to spot opportunities, but make sure that they act on them. Most maintain some form of inventory, or register, of unexploited opportunities. They make sure that they revisit their inventory of ideas often but they take action only when it is required. They make investments only if the competitive arena is attractive and the opportunity is ripe.

3. They pursue only the very best opportunities and avoid exhausting themselves and their organizations by chasing after every option. Even though many habitual entrepreneurs are wealthy, the most successful remain ruthlessly disciplined about limiting the number of projects they pursue. They go after a tightly controlled portfolio of opportunities in different stages of development. They tightly link their strategy with their choice of projects, rather than diluting their efforts too broadly.

4. They focus on execution—specifically, adaptive execution. Both words are important. People with an entrepreneurial mindset execute—that is, they get on with it instead of analyzing new ideas to death. Yet they are also adaptive—able to change directions as the real opportunity, and the best way to exploit it, evolves.

5. They engage the energies of everyone in their domain. Habitual entrepreneurs involve many people—both inside and outside the organization—in their pursuit of an opportunity. They create and sustain networks of relationships rather than going it alone, making the most of the intellectual and other resources people have to offer and helping those people to achieve their goals as well.

ESSENTIALS OF ENTREPRENEURIAL STRATEGY (AND THIS BOOK)

We have used the essential components of entrepreneurial strategy—which we have distilled over years of observation—to guide our development and organization of this book. These components are briefly described below and summarized in figure 1-1.

Creating the Entrepreneurial Frame

The basic objective is to define, in advance, the criteria that would make a business opportunity worthwhile for you to pursue. The way you do this is to articulate challenging objectives for how much value an opportunity should add to your piece of the business. The idea is to improve not only profits, but profitability as well. Your goal should be, in other words, to get into businesses with ever better margins and profits than those you are in today. The trick is to come up with realistic yet challenging targets. What you are after is not just the probable but a stretch to the possible. We'll touch on how you get started on this in chapter 2.

Stocking the Opportunity Register

In chapter 3, we begin describing the techniques for creating an opportunity register for your organization. The opportunity register is like the habitual entrepreneurs' inventory of opportunities. It's a list of your ideas for improving, or even completely reinventing, your current business model or for going into entirely new opportunity spaces. It is meant to be a work in progress, one that you constantly add to and review. We describe techniques that we have seen used to capture five categories of opportunity:

- Redesign products or services (using a methodology called attribute mapping, discussed in chapter 3).

- Redifferentiate products or services (using consumption chain analysis and the quizzing process, both presented in chapter 4).

- Resegment the market (by behavioral segmentation, as described in chapter 5).

FIGURE 1-1

The Structure of the Book

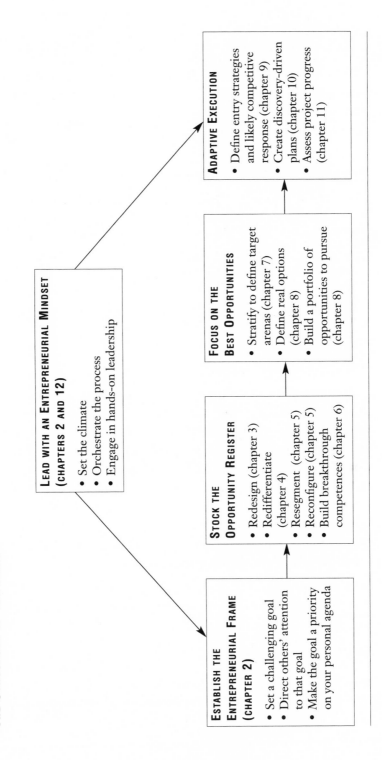

Lead with an Entrepreneurial Mindset (chapters 2 and 12)

- Set the climate
- Orchestrate the process
- Engage in hands-on leadership

Establish the Entrepreneurial Frame (chapter 2)

- Set a challenging goal
- Direct others' attention to that goal
- Make the goal a priority on your personal agenda

Stock the Opportunity Register

- Redesign (chapter 3)
- Redifferentiate (chapter 4)
- Resegment (chapter 5)
- Reconfigure (chapter 5)
- Build breakthrough competences (chapter 6)

Focus on the Best Opportunities

- Stratify to define target arenas (chapter 7)
- Define real options (chapter 8)
- Build a portfolio of opportunities to pursue (chapter 8)

Adaptive Execution

- Define entry strategies and likely competitive response (chapter 9)
- Create discovery-driven plans (chapter 10)
- Assess project progress (chapter 11)

- Completely reconfigure the market (by shifting the boundaries that keep the current markets as they are, also discussed in chapter 5).

- Develop breakthrough competences, or areas of competitive strength, that create new competitive advantages (discussed in chapter 6).

Targeting the Best Opportunities

Armed with a well-stocked opportunity register, your next challenge is to focus on only the best ideas for inclusion in your portfolio of initiatives. This requires making trade-offs that can sometimes be difficult, but that are essential if you are to avoid spreading yourself and your organization too thin. We'll show you how to establish your strategy and structure an opportunity portfolio that matches and supports it. Chapter 7 covers the use of stratification mapping to define a set of target arenas in which you want to compete.

Chapter 8 shows you how to apply real options reasoning to the different opportunities you consider. Options reasoning is key to entrepreneurial investment patterns, because it allows you to control the potential for downside losses while preserving your upside potential. We'll show you how different kinds of options are useful, depending on whether you are facing technical uncertainty, market uncertainty, or some combination. We offer suggestions on how to manage the different types of options to maximize the strategic benefits to you.

Employing Adaptive Execution

Once you have selected your areas of focus, your next challenge is adaptive execution. By this, we mean capturing the opportunity without falling prey to many of the pitfalls of high uncertainty. The key concern is that new and changing business models imply new customers, competitors, and competences. These will force you to operate with a much higher ratio of assumptions to knowledge than you may be accustomed to. The chapters in this part of the book show you where the greatest dangers lie, and offer techniques you can use to avoid them.

In chapter 9, we describe important considerations for market entry. We start by analyzing which market segments, or niches, you will target first. We then consider competitive responses.

Next, recognizing that nothing turns out exactly as planned, we introduce you to a technique for planning even when you can't accurately anticipate the outcomes. This will allow you to adapt your course of action as the real opportunity becomes clear. This technique, discovery-driven planning, is discussed in chapter 10.

Finally, we consider the problem of monitoring whether a competitive advantage is actually emerging from your investment in new initiatives. Chapter 11 describes a simple diagnostic tool, based on a set of surveys, that can help you make this judgment.

Exercising Entrepreneurial Leadership

The last part of the book focuses on your role as an entrepreneurial leader in your organization. In chapter 12, we show you how leaders create an atmosphere in which everyone plays, that is, an atmosphere in which everyone comes to work in the morning eager and able to help you continue to identify ways to reconfigure your business models and create advantage out of uncertainty.

Chapter 13 is a short conclusion to the book. In this final chapter, we look at the growing intersection between the world of the entrepreneur and the world of the strategist, and bring the book full circle.

DIRECTED DISCOVERY

The techniques we recommend are low risk. We make it a point to caution you against precipitously launching costly, demoralizing actions such as downsizing, reengineering, reorganizing, or introducing other traumatic, systemic changes. You may, of course, ultimately decide that one or some of these actions are necessary, but they are not our focus here. At the heart of our philosophy is directed discovery—plotting a direction into the uncertain future and redirecting as reality unfolds. This calls for speed, the capacity for rapid response, and insight. We need speed because opportunities are fleeting, and insight because people have to act on inadequate, sketchy information. An organization in which people take speed for granted and constantly generate new insights has the capacity to become a formidable entrepreneurial competitor.

We hope that this book provides you with some quick hits: modest ideas that you will find useful right away and a good many more that you will revisit when you need them. As you go through the chapters, you will also start to see indications of major opportunities for your business that can form the cornerstones of a genuine breakthrough strategy for your firm.

In a world of uncertainty, our guiding philosophy is: Take charge. If nobody knows what the future will hold, your vision of how to navigate it is as good as anyone's. The future may as well belong to you.

FRAMING

THE

CHALLENGE

YOUR FIRST OBJECTIVE IN CREATING AN ENTREPRENEURIAL mindset is to make sure that you have clearly established what your business needs to do to make the effort worthwhile. You must create a mindset that pushes you and your team beyond mere incremental improvement to entrepreneurial actions that really make a difference. In other words, you should frame what you must do to create a genuine win for your organization in terms of growth in both profits and profitability. It may sound obvious, but stop right now and think about whether you and your co-workers are truly clear about which results from your efforts would make these efforts good investments for your shareholders. People can be surprisingly vague on this point. This has lots of negative consequences, among them a temptation to be complacent and a tendency to look for incremental improvements rather than major wins.

A vivid demonstration of this tendency toward vagueness constantly crops up in the Wharton Small Business Development Center, which helps hundreds of would-be entrepreneurs each year. Our first assignment to would-be entrepreneurs requires these potential entrepreneurs to describe their new business idea in terms of profit potential. Today, we typically get ideas like creating communities on the Internet for consumers of natural skin-care products. The problem is that these are customarily not businesses that would offer a competitive risk-adjusted return compared to the wanna-be's current secure salary. We force them to think through the profit implications of the idea instead of just focusing on the revenue component and their (natural) tendency to incrementally expand on their current income.

Then we ask the aspiring entrepreneurs to go out and look only for business opportunities with the potential to generate twice as much income for themselves (when the venture is mature) as they would earn if they continued to work in their present position. Sometimes our participants are at firms like GE or major banks and insurance companies, or professors from the engineering or life sciences faculties, or MBA students with job offers from Goldman Sachs or McKinsey & Company. As a result, the standard is quite high. We insist that they double this amount to earn them a premium for taking on the task of starting a business. Then we insist that they design a business to get them there within two to three years.

The results are almost always fascinating. The entrepreneurs leave behind the easy-to-do businesses and get creative with ideas that may not be as quantifiable, but that are usually far more interesting and potentially profitable than the first batch. Setting forth a clear and unambiguous standard for what the business must deliver galvanizes their effort, gives them a force for focus, and helps them get on with it. Notice that we didn't do anything more than tell them how good the idea had to be. Once they knew that, they could do the rest.

SETTING CHALLENGING GOALS

So, how do you get started? The best way to begin is with a hard-nosed look at your business's current performance. Ask yourself, If I were to do something in the next three to five years that I, my boss, and my company's investors would regard as a major win, what would this performance record have to look like? The answer will help you to create what we call the entrepreneurial frame. This is a specific, measurable challenge to enhance the value of your piece of the business. The frame provides focus and creates a sense of urgency for you and those you work with.

The entrepreneurial frame has two components. First, you should be clear on the minimum amount of additional profits you need from a new venture (at maturity) to make a difference to your business. You should stress profits, or bottom-line growth, not merely growth in sales revenues. Second, you need to specify what increase in profitability (meaning return on assets or equivalent number for your industry) your new opportunities need to achieve as well. Opportunities less profitable than your existing businesses are hardly likely to get anyone excited and are poor candidates for investment of either your time or your money. The exception to this general principle is in the case of *disruptive technologies*, which represent potentially important new solutions that don't seem that way at first.[1] More on these in chapter 4.

Note that this thinking doesn't just apply to people who run profit centers. Even if you are running a cost center, you can still develop an entrepreneurial frame. In this case, you specify how to significantly reduce the costs and increase the asset productivity of your operation.

Try to make your goal a stretch, without making it ludicrous. If firms in your industry are growing profits at a rate of 5 percent a year, then expecting 10 percent growth from a new initiative may be reasonable. You decide what is possible—the main thing is to hone in on a number that will frame the challenge. Your job as a leader is to set challenges that push your fellow workers to the limits of their abilities without pushing them beyond those limits—a theme we will revisit several times.

Establishing a frame helps people to realize exactly what is expected of them. It can also begin to create a sense of urgency about becoming more entrepreneurial. For instance, we did some work with Hewlett-Packard in which we speculated on what a frame for HP might look like. Table 2-1 provides some baseline data.

TABLE 2-1

HP's FRAMING CHALLENGE (BASED ON 1998 PERFORMANCE)

Total sales	$47 billion
Net income	$2.9 billion
Net profit margin	6.3 percent

CREATING AN ENTREPRENEURIAL FRAME

As you can see, to add 10 percent to the company's profits at current profitability levels, a new business would have to generate $4–5 billion in sales! Not many brand new businesses are this big, which implies that HP would have to grow by developing multiple new businesses. At the same time, since HP is well positioned in a rapidly growing set of markets, has deep managerial and technical skills, and is able to form strong alliances with other firms, it is not unrealistic to think that the company could meet such a significant growth challenge.

The exercise in Table 2-2 will get you started on creating a working frame for your business. It's meant to be a start; you will almost certainly want to elaborate on this as your ideas develop. This is the business equivalent of asking the MBA to find a business to start that will pay at least twice as well as getting a job on Wall Street. The major difference is that we are asking you to define how well your new business must perform to make a substantive contribution to what you are already doing.

Begin by finding out what your organization's profits were for the last full year, and enter these in cell 1. Then enter your return on sales (profit margin) for the same period in cell 2. This should then allow you to calculate the revenues you needed to generate last year's profits, by dividing profit by return on sales (cell 1/cell 2). Put this result in cell 3. Next, put your return on assets for the same period in cell 4. You can then calculate the assets you required to create last year's profits by dividing profit by return on assets (cell 1/cell 4). Put this result in cell 5. What you now have is a very concise description of the performance that today's business model is delivering.

TABLE 2-2

WORKSHEET: MAKING THE ENTREPRENEURIAL FRAME SPECIFIC

	CURRENT PERFORMANCE		DESIRED PERFORMANCE	
Last year's profits	Cell 1	200	Cell 6 = Cell 1 × 110%	220
Return on sales (profit margin)	Cell 2	10%	Cell 7 = Cell 2 × 105%	10.5
Revenues required to produce profits	Cell 3	2,000	Cell 8 = Cell 6 ÷ Cell 7	2,095
Return on assets	Cell 4	15%	Cell 9 = Cell 4 × 110%	16.5%
Assets required to produce profits	Cell 5	1,333	Cell 10 = Cell 6 ÷ Cell 9	1,333

The next step is to specify how you need to improve on this performance by taking entrepreneurial action. To do this, specify the magnitude of additional profits that your business needs to deliver to achieve a compelling business result. Start off with, say, a 10 percent increase in profits. You can calculate this easily by multiplying the cell 1 figure by 110 percent and entering it in cell 6. Since your new businesses should be more profitable than your existing activities, specify a level of enhancement to return on sales that you require. Again, for illustrative purposes, let's say that it's a 5 percent improvement. As before, you can calculate this by multiplying cell 2 by 105 percent, and entering the result in cell 7. This will then allow you to calculate the revenues you'll need to achieve that level of performance, by dividing cell 6 by cell 7. To reflect your need to improve your return on assets, the calculation would go into cell 9. You can then specify the assets allowed by dividing cell 6 by cell 9.

Simple though this exercise is, it can have a surprising amount of impact. If all the growth is going to have to come from new businesses, you can see how big they need to be (see chapter 9). If instead you need to perk up your existing operations, this gives you a sense for how significant the challenges are. Manufacturing or production people, for instance, can be asked whether improvements in asset utilization would allow you to achieve a better return on asset number. The sales and marketing groups can contribute their views on what it would take to improve sales revenues (and maintain profitability).

It isn't enough, of course, just to specify a number and leave the subject. Turning this entrepreneurial frame into a living goal requires that you use it to direct the attention and manage the agendas of everyone in the organization. As a leader, your guidelines are straightforward: People pay attention to what you pay attention to, and to how this links to success and rewards in their careers.

Here's a simple rule of thumb: If the activities that you decide are linked to achieving your goals are not among the first five issues on your personal agenda at every meeting you attend, in every conversation you have, and in every performance review you conduct, people will pretty quickly get the message that you don't care all that much about them. On the other hand, if you are persistent (even boringly repetitive) and follow through with actions that reinforce your verbal commitment, soon people will understand that you mean it. From this belief, it is a small step toward getting them mobilized to do something about it.

Your entrepreneurial frame articulates the outcome of your strategy. It allows you to communicate your ambitions to others and allows them to understand the direction in which you are all taking the business. A robust frame will be particularly important to those who finance your undertaking, whether they are venture capitalists or shareholders. They will judge the value of your stock on their estimate of your prospects for adding value and on their judgment of your ability to execute your plans.

So far we have not urged you to declare a vision, a statement of mission, or other such grandiose thing. This is done quite purposefully. Developing a robust vision for a business is hard, time-consuming work that calls for real insight. If you are just getting started building an entrepreneurial mindset in your organization, you are probably better served by holding off.[2] Rushing the process all too often results only in the production of one of those meaningless vision statements that gets laminated and bolted to the wall. We've all seen them—vapid phrases that fail to tap the company's potential for entrepreneurial thought and action because they reflect neither its core capacities nor its real values.

A good example of the wisdom of not rushing the process—and of how to initiate entrepreneurial leadership—is Henry Schacht and Rich McGinn's decision to take some time to sort out the entrepreneurial vision for Lucent Technologies early in the company's development. In the fall of 1995 Schacht and McGinn were put in charge of managing Lucent's divestiture from AT&T and its emergence as an independent company. As chief executive officer and chief operating officer, respectively, Schacht and McGinn faced the challenge of figuring out what the brand new company would be like. Schacht was a relative outsider, faced with a longtime AT&T management team. An initial public offering (IPO) was scheduled for April 1, 1996 (six months out). Worst of all, the workforce consisted of "143,000 terrified people," who were wondering whether they still had jobs. What did Schacht and McGinn do? They made a conscious decision not to pronounce a strategy and vision at that time, as Schacht described recently to a class of McGrath's.

> What we decided to do was to do nothing. By that I mean that what we said to the 143,000 people was "Go back to work. We're going to need some time to sort the issues out. We have a profit plan to deliver to AT&T, our owner, between now and the end of the year. If we don't get that done, we're not going to have anything to say with respect to the IPO."
>
> Next, we moved to stabilize all the required stakeholders. We quickly put together a group of sixteen people and told them, "You are our management team. We're going to figure out where we are going and how we get there, without going outside the organization for talent. Until you prove you can't do it, we'll assume you can."
>
> We took those sixteen people and put them in a room and said, "We're going to spend every Monday morning together and define for ourselves what our values are, and what our mission is going to be." They were furious to be dragged into this when they had "real work" to do. We got a lot of foot dragging, a lot of cell phones going off in the meeting. They thought it was silly stuff and fought the process initially. We ended up going off campus and banning cell phones and long bathroom breaks. We stuck with it for the better part of two and a half months. Gradually, the team began to come together.

Simultaneously, Carly Fiorina (now CEO of Hewlett-Packard) led a team benchmarking the very best in our industry; we wanted the group of sixteen to understand the metrics that defined the standards of performance in high-tech companies. Carly and her team reported back their findings to the group as they were developed.

It became apparent to the gang of sixteen that Lucent was a low-growth, underperforming company operating in a high-growth, high-performance industry. The group's mission development activities produced a statement describing aspirations to become a high-performance growth company delivering superior sustained shareholder value.

Carly's benchmarking team provided the quantitative metrics of just what that meant; these became known as the Five Simultaneous Equations and brought specific performance measures to the mission statement. They provided the vital definition link between purpose and performance:

1. Move the top line from 1 percent growth to high teens growth while maintaining the world-class gross margins.

2. Increase R&D from 8 percent to 11 percent.

3. Reduce sales and general administrative expenses (SGA) from 27 percent to 19 percent.

4. Reduce the tax rate 4 percentage points.

5. Lift return on assets (ROA) from 0 to 1 percent.

We went to the IPO market stipulating these goals as achievable. They were our short-term performance targets. We then sent Carly and her team out to do a rough-cut strategy that could provide a more textured set of strategic statements. We adopted a "roughly right" strategy by the end of 1996 and made our first modest organizational changes then. We refined the strategy all during 1997 and adopted a more robust strategy late in 1997 and reorganized the company around the same management cadre.

The results are history. The investment bankers told the board in 1996 to expect the $23 opening price to erode initially, then recover to a modest premium by year end, and that a range of $40-plus could be expected a few years out. The stock was at $320 (on the same basis) by late 1999, four years after the company was formed and three and one-half years after the IPO; it was among the top half-dozen largest firms in the world in terms of market capitalization. All five simultaneous equation goals were achieved.

Same people, same markets, same technology; the only thing that changed was our expectation of ourselves. There is no other explanation available.

Several points here: People will set higher targets and achieve them if they set them for themselves. Self-set goals based on credible evidence (benchmarking) always exceed imposed goals. People will rise to the occasion if given the opportunity.

As one of Lucent's "gang of sixteen" commented late in the process of mission setting, "We have been given the opportunity of a lifetime; we need to grasp this with an audacity of purpose and go for it."

Notice the elements that made a crucial difference in Lucent's emergence. First, the team began not with a statement of sweeping vision, but with a quantified idea of their aspirations. Next, they came together as a group to define what performance meant and establish some clear criteria. Further, they decided to be much more ambitious than their previous performance might have indicated was reasonable. It took time and teamwork for Lucent's eventual vision to emerge, and for the leadership behaviors that made it such a success story to manifest themselves. We will expand these topics in chapter 12. For now, the key message is to begin your efforts to spark an entrepreneurial mindset with a clear picture of what your target aspirations should be.

SETTING UP AN OPPORTUNITY REGISTER

The next step in creating an entrepreneurial frame is to decide on the format of your opportunity register—the place where you will inventory all the entrepreneurial ideas that emerge from applying the techniques we offer in the book and from other sources of insight.

As mentioned, one skill typical of successful entrepreneurs is the ability to hold onto their ideas over time, not necessarily moving on them right away, but not forgetting about them, either. A simple way to hold onto good ideas whose time may not be quite ripe is to create an opportunity register. The concept of the opportunity register was presented to us by a successful multiple-venture entrepreneur. His philosophy is that anyone who can access a full inventory of possible opportunities is unlikely to run out of good ideas for making the next competitive move or capturing the next prospect for growth. You want to store good ideas so that you can revisit them to see how new ideas might fit in, to determine whether the timing is right to implement older ones, or to figure out what to eliminate as your true strategic direction becomes more defined.[3] The originator of the concept registered his ideas on index cards that he would scan periodically.

We like to keep our register in the form of a database because it is easy to scan (and less likely to get lost). That doesn't mean it has to be complicated, though. A template for such a database is shown in figure 2-1, but we encourage you to discuss with your colleagues the type of register that best suits you and your business. Be it simple or sophisticated, the important thing is to decide how you will record and revisit the ideas that your team generates.

FIGURE 2-1

A SIMPLE OPPORTUNITY REGISTER

Field 1: Business concept. The business concept is a short description of the idea to be entered in the register. The initial business concept behind Amazon.com, for instance, was to offer an Internet-based service that allowed customers to search for and order discounted books for fast delivery. The company has since extended the concept to other products.

Field 2: Related trends. If you have come across important trends (in the marketplace, in technology, or elsewhere) that might have a bearing on the business concept, record this information here. Data on trends can help you anticipate whether and when a particular concept is feasible or potentially attractive. Conversely, trend data can help you identify when some ideas might become obsolete. For Amazon.com, trends to consider might be household penetration of PCs connected to the Internet and the willingness of consumers to buy over the Internet. The dark side of this trend is evident to local independent bookstores, whose business was already being threatened by big chain stores like Borders and Barnes & Noble—every book bought through Amazon.com (or a chain store) is a lost potential sale for the local independent bookstore.

FIGURE 2-1 (CONTINUED)

A Simple Opportunity Register

Field 3: Key data. In this field you should record more specifics on an opportunity by linking the concept to numbers. Specifically, identify the key customer segments you want to address. For Amazon.com, the key segment would be computer-literate frequent book purchasers with time constraints, and the relevant numbers might include total books sold and where, the margins on books, the growth rate of various kinds of books sold, the value to the customer of not having to go to a bookstore, and so on. The key thing here is not to deploy armies of researchers to capture information but to have a place to put any important information you run across.

Field 4: Obstacles and barriers. Here you note what is stopping you from grasping the opportunity. Some great ideas can't be developed unless certain barriers are broken down. These might be technological, market, regulatory, or even company-policy-related barriers. For instance, many experts believe that the Internet will not achieve its full potential as a mass medium unless several barriers are cracked simultaneously, including processor speed, bandwidth, and technology cost. It's important to note such barriers as you encounter them because it will generally require some investment to dislodge them. (Obstacles and barriers are further discussed in chapter 5.)

Field 5: Company position. Here, you note any particular competences, skills, or resources of your company that might make the business concept particularly attractive or defensible (see chapter 6).

Field 6: Competition. Here you note your likely relevant competitors and their likely response to your idea. Opportunities that are widely known to be attractive are often attractive to a great many firms, meaning that sometimes they are actually not such great arenas to enter (see chapters 8 and 10).

Field 7: Sources. In this field, note the sources for all of the information you have obtained; you may need to tap these sources again or use them to validate the information you are using. Such sources might be publications, Web sites, or personal communications.

Field 8: Type. Here you determine and record what type of opportunity you are pursuing. As we explain later in the book, there are generally two types of opportunity: *arena-building* (which takes you into a major new competitive environment) or *model-transforming* (which is designed to disrupt the business model in a current competitive environment).

continued

FIGURE 2-1 (CONTINUED)

A SIMPLE OPPORTUNITY REGISTER

Field 9: Timing. Here you consider the timing. Will you carry out an outright launch, or will you invest in a positioning option, a scouting option, or a stepping-stone option? Later in the book, we provide you with guidelines for determining which option is best.

Some advice on nomenclature: To the extent possible, be consistent in the names you choose for particular concepts, opportunities, and barriers across the entire database. This will make it easier to sift through the database to determine which opportunities you want to pursue. Consistent naming can also provide you with insights into related applications or products that you might otherwise overlook if they are treated as totally different simply because they meet the needs of different customer segments. This is particularly important for companies that are organized functionally or by major customer group. Unbeknownst to you, your idea may already have been put to work in other units of your company or for similar customer segments. For instance, making a breakthrough in the weight of a battery might be important to customers manufacturing mobile phones, but could also be extremely important to those making portable toys, radios, personal digital assistants and other battery-operated devices. When spread across multiple markets, the opportunity is more substantial than it would be were it to be applied only to a single market.

SUMMARY OF ACTION STEPS

At the end of each chapter, we summarize in a series of steps the chapter's implications for action. The idea is to start with some simple core ideas that you can tackle right away, and then move on to more complex challenges. Moving through the steps will naturally lead you to act increasingly like an entrepreneur. You will discover opportunities that others overlook and take advantage of insights that others don't have.

STEP 1: Identify the current key performance numbers of your business as it is.

STEP 2: Articulate a set of target numbers for your business in two to three years (or whatever time frame you select) that will represent a substantial enhancement in both profits and profitability. This set of target numbers becomes the goal for growth that you will achieve by thinking entrepreneurially.

STEP 3: Communicate your thoughts on these numbers with the others in your organization who might be important to help you achieve them. Revise upward or downward as the feedback and your own improved understanding of each individual's role suggests.

STEP 4: Monitor your own behavior to make sure that you yourself are modeling the entrepreneurial behavior you seek in others—specifically, make sure your growth goals are consistently on your agenda and in your conversation, and that you consistently express a sense of urgency with respect to these goals.

STEP 5: Create an opportunity register to record the ideas that you will use to meet the challenge you have framed.

CHAPTER 3

BUILDING

BLOCKBUSTER PRODUCTS

AND SERVICES

A KEY ASPECT OF ESTABLISHING AN ENTREPRENEURIAL MINDSET is creating the conditions under which everyone involved is energized to look for opportunities to change the current business model. These might include opportunities to redesign existing offerings, to differentiate products in novel and appealing ways, to reshape markets, and to transform the rules of the game by transforming the company's competences. This is the first of several chapters (3 through 6) in which we'll show you ways to change your business model.

The simplest way to change a business model is to redesign your offerings (products and services). What you should be aiming for is a blockbuster design—one that so appeals to your target customers that they feel almost compelled to buy from you. Identifying opportunities for redesign is what this chapter is all about. We will show you how to use the simple technique of attribute mapping to redesign your current offerings in ways that will be supremely appealing to your customers and highly profitable for your firm.

Don't worry about making the perfect product; it has never been invented. Instead, the idea is to look for opportunities to modify existing designs. The essence of the idea is to discover a bundle of features that your customers perceive to be worth a lot more than the price you are going to extract from them, as well as a lot more than the competitors are offering.

Let's start with the premise that your customers, essentially, could care less about what your company is capable of doing. Your company may be able to make wondrously sophisticated devices, but your customers won't care unless wondrous sophistication is what they need. Business-to-business customers, especially, are impatient with any product that they don't clearly see helps them to compete more effectively, no matter how elegant its design. As Peter Drucker said, the purpose of a business is not to create a product, "the purpose of a business is to create a customer."[1]

Any product or service utilizes some portion (but seldom all) of a firm's capabilities, that is, those skills, assets, and systems that allow a company to be an effective competitor. In designing their offerings, firms create various features, attributes, or characteristics—call them what you may—that in turn fill some (but never all) of a given customer segment's needs or desires. Trying to achieve perfection is a mistake because the translation from what your business has to offer to what the customer wants or needs can never be perfect. Although some features will attract and please customers, creating a positive reaction, others will be tolerated only because the benefits of the positive attributes exceed the inconveniences of the negatives.

Negative features are unavoidable. These may have to do with some risk or inconvenience associated with the product or service, or they may be a source of simple dislike. The most obvious negative attribute, of course, is price. Customers would love to be well served for no charge, but this is hardly practical for you. Since buying decisions are seldom made on the basis of one or two features but reflect a complex mix of trade-offs, your job is to grasp the essence of how customers make trade-offs and to use this knowledge to influence product and service designs.

USING AN ATTRIBUTE MAP TO ASSESS CUSTOMER ATTITUDES

A simple mapping process gives you a start on capturing how well your product or service is appealing to customers' needs at the

FIGURE 3-1

THE ATTRIBUTE MAP DEFINED

CUSTOMER ATTITUDE	ATTRIBUTE OF PRODUCT OR SERVICE, RELATIVE TO COMPETING OFFERINGS		
	Basic	**Discriminator**	**Energizer**
POSITIVE	NONNEGOTIABLE	DIFFERENTIATOR	EXCITER
	Performs at least as well as competition	Performs better than competition where it counts	Performs better than competitors
NEGATIVE	TOLERABLE	DISSATISFIER	ENRAGER
	Performs no worse than competitors	Performs below the level of competitors	Must be corrected at any cost (to capitalize on competitors' negatives)
NEUTRAL	SO WHAT?	PARALLEL	
	Does not affect the purchasing decision in a meaningful way	Influences segment attitudes but is not directly related to product or service performance	

moment. Such an *attribute map* is depicted in figure 3-1. The simplest way to get started is to identify an offering and an important customer segment for that offering. Then characterize the various attributes or features of your offering according to the cells in the map. Initially, prepare one map per segment per product.[2]

The first column of the attribute map lists the three basic attitudes that customers may hold about a feature of any product or service: negative, positive, or neutral. Positive attributes are those the customer likes. Negative attributes are those features that the targeted customer segment dislikes and would rather do without. An offering's neutral attributes are those that the customer simply doesn't care about at all—that is, the customer would feel the same way about the offering whether or not it included this particular attribute.

Along the top of the figure, we indicate the level of energy generated by the customer's reaction to the feature, *compared with competitors' offerings.* The customer might judge that this feature is basic—meaning that they take it for granted that any competitor could offer it. In the next column, we place discriminating features, attributes that cause customers to judge your firm to be superior or inferior to competitors. Finally we come to energizing features. These are attributes that customers consider overwhelmingly positive or negative and that dominate the purchasing decision.

The power of the attribute map lies in its simplicity. It is easy to use to initiate valuable, strategic conversations. These can be conversations within your business or with distributors, branches, brokers—in fact with anyone (including the customers themselves) who can provide insights into what the customer really will go for. We'll next consider how you can use the mapping process to generate useful insights, beginning with positive features.

Positive Features on the Attribute Map

Positive features are all good to have. Customers with positive attitudes toward your offerings will tend to buy more, remain more loyal, and sometimes even be prepared to pay price premiums. How you use a positive feature varies, though, depending on whether it is basic, discriminating, or energizing.

Nonnegotiables (Positive/Basic)   A basic positive feature is regarded by your segment as something you should provide as a matter of course. If you fail to offer it, the segment will abandon you, because to them, it is nonnegotiable. In most developed industries, the list of nonnegotiables can be incredibly long. Consider the automobile industry. We take for granted hundreds of features on our cars, from easy starting when the ignition key is turned, to air conditioning, built-in radio, and CD player, safety features, and many other characteristics that make the driving experience better.

The problem with basic features is that they don't generate great profits. Often, customers don't even notice these features unless they are missing or don't function properly. You fail to provide this feature at your peril, however. If it is a nonnegotiable, the failure to provide it might at best cost you significant customer support and at worst shut you out of a particular segment entirely. For example,

when Apple first introduced the iMac, the press generated by its positive features was almost nullified by loud complaints that there was
no built-in floppy disk drive. Although the iMac has become
extremely popular, many users still complain that the floppy drive has
to be purchased separately, and then that it consumes a rare port on
the machine when they try to use it. For some, the missing drive is a
serious enough problem that it deters them from buying.

Differentiators (Positive/Discriminating)   Differentiators are attributes
that distinguish your offering from your competitors' in a positive
way. In autos, for instance, Volvo has long differentiated its cars on
the basis of safety. Volvos are laden with safety-enhancing features,
extending to the heavy, reinforced car bodies for which Volvo historically was lampooned. For Volvo's traditional target segment, owning
a crash-resistant car was worth trading off the fuel economy and
sporty looks that other segments might prefer. Now, of course, Volvo
has introduced its own sportier-looking (but still safe) cars, and other
firms (such as Saab and Audi) have taken up the safety mantra.

Exciters (Positive/Energizing)   Attributes that so delight the customer
that they constitute the overwhelming reason for making a purchase
are called exciters. Be wary of a common misconception, however.
Businesspeople tend to believe that there is a correlation between the
expense and effort they put into a feature and the amount of excite-
ment with which customers will respond. There is often no such correlation. Exciters are often technically simple, relatively low-cost
advances that greatly add to the offering's convenience or ease of use.
This is why small entrepreneurial companies often come up with
exciters that their big, established competitors overlook. What else
can explain 3Com's enormous success with its personal digital assistant, the Palm series of handheld devices, when gifted and well-
established competitors like HP, Philips, and Apple were unable to
crack the market? The Palm made it simple to perform the most
desired functions without undue complexity.

Another example is insulin injection pens for diabetic patients,
which are relatively low-tech devices that make it easier for patients
to cope with treatment. Specializing in pens rather than insulin itself

has allowed the upstart challenger Novo Nordisk S.A. of Denmark to mount a credible challenge to incumbent Eli Lilly in the United States. Similarly, Nokia, the Finnish mobile-telephone manufacturer, found that customers get excited not about the complex technology inside the phones, but about how the phones look and what external features they have, like replaceable covers that match the customers' clothing, suit the season, or accommodate whatever other situation the customer fancies.

To understand how exciters work, consider the cup holder in automobiles. Honda, which introduced the cup holder as a standard feature in 1988, credits this feature and similar innovations with making its cars the best-selling in the United States for more than half a decade. Given little else to differentiate cars in its class, a person may think, why not buy the Honda with the cup holder? A cup holder makes it a lot easier to drink your morning coffee while driving to work—which more and more commuters began to do during the 1980s. What's more, its cost to the manufacturer is negligible. Thus entered one of automobile history's most surprisingly potent innovations.

This kind of consumer purchasing behavior can be the despair of engineers, designers, and scientific staff. They spend their lives worrying about things like fuel efficiency, advanced hydraulics, and wind resistance. To add insult to injury, the cost of putting a cup holder in a car is barely noticeable relative to the total cost of designing, manufacturing, and distributing the next-generation auto.

The story doesn't end there. Once drivers realized that they wanted cup holders, they wanted them with a vengeance. For many segments in the United States, cup holders rapidly migrated from being an exciter, a feature that dramatically and positively influenced customers' perception of value for Honda alone, to being a nonnegotiable basic feature of most cars on the road. For a surprising number of Americans today, no other attribute of the car—not its power, styling, design, or any other element—matters as much as the cup holder does. The trend suggests the more, the better. Witness General Motors' leading feature for its 1999 Suburban minivans, advertising not one, not two, but sixteen cup holders!

Be aware of this predictable dynamic of exciter features: As competitors realize how much customers want the feature, they will copy it. Although this is no big deal for a feature like a cup holder—as we noted, the cost of including it in cars is modest—the consequences can be serious when the feature is expensive, complex, or covered by intellectual property protections such as patents. What can happen after all the relevant competitors have adopted the feature is that no one is any better off in terms of competitive position, but the whole cost structure of the industry is increased as a result of having to offer the now nonnegotiable feature. Some people argue that automatic teller machines (ATMs) for retail banks had this effect. Although the banks that pioneered the concept of twenty-four-hour banking (such as Citibank) initially benefited in terms of customer satisfaction and market share, customers eventually came to expect ATM access from all retail banks. Consequently, the playing field was leveled, with no particular advantage remaining for the pioneers of ATM technology.[3]

Negative Features on the Attribute Map

Unfortunately, you don't have the option of avoiding negative attributes completely. Being conscious of them is crucial. A great source of opportunity for your business can be negatives that your competitors have failed to address. Fix it, and you'll have an edge over the competition. Let them beat you to it, though, and you'll be at a disadvantage.

All negatives are a potential source of entrepreneurial opportunity, particularly when your competitors focus on working the positive line. Adding value by creating more positive features and bulking up the product with enhancements are popular endeavors, whereas opportunities created by reducing negatives are often overlooked. Compaq captured such an opportunity with the introduction of its Presario series of home-oriented computers. The machines were among the first generation of ready-to-go computers. No fussing with cables beyond plugging them into a color-coded port, no irritating fiddling with disks to load software, no anxiety-producing and incomprehensible DOS prompts. Compaq found favor with a whole new group of novice computer users.

People who come in direct contact with customers or distributors have the most insights into the negatives as your customers see them. Staff in sales, service, complaint handling, returns processing, call centers, and accounts receivable are all likely to be exposed to customers who see your products in their worst possible light. Signals that things are not well include increased numbers of informal and formal complaints, returns, order cancellations, and increased difficulty in making sales.

Tolerables (Negative/Basic)   *Tolerables* are attributes that customers are willing to put up with, even though they don't like them. A great many entrepreneurs have made their money by eliminating negatives that were ignored by other providers. Charles Brewer, for instance, founded the high-quality Internet service provider (ISP) Mindspring in response to a negative experience he had trying to access the Internet. The company was founded in 1994, went public in 1996, and, as of this writing, has a market capitalization on the NASDAQ exchange in excess of $1.6 billion, with revenues that have grown from $18 million in 1996 to $114.7 million in 1998. Its management team credits this success to their commitment to operating without the infuriating lapses in services that other ISPs expect customers to tolerate.[4]

Eliminating tolerables is equally crucial in the business-to-business world. Firms in many industries, such as mining, energy, chemicals, forest products, agriculture, and transportation, create massive tolerables in the form of environmentally damaging by-products that increase costs and risks for customers and transaction partners. Figuring out how to eliminate these has led forward-thinking firms to seek less damaging technologies and to modify the impact of those technologies that they use. Other firms have explored recycling and electronic information processing as a way of limiting the negative spillovers from their business activity. The philosophy of all of these firms is that if they don't learn to eliminate the tolerables in their industries and if other firms do, they will be at a great disadvantage.[5]

Dissatisfiers (Negative/Discriminating)   It is important to be self-critical of one's own tolerables, because technological advances and competitors' creativity can quickly turn them into dissatisfiers. As soon as customers can be made to believe that they can avoid dealing with a negative attribute of your offering by buying a competitor's, that attribute is no longer a tolerable; it becomes a dissatisfier. *Dissatisfiers are features that differentiate you from your competitors, but in the wrong direction.*

In the 1970s Japanese auto manufacturers in the United States created new categories of dissatisfiers from the U.S. policy of planned obsolescence.[6] For decades, buyers of U.S. cars routinely put up with frequent repair and service visits—indeed, U.S. auto advertisers stressed the convenience of local suppliers to get spare parts and service as a reason to buy U.S.-made cars. High-quality Japanese cars, however, needed attention far less often and were much more reliable than their U.S. counterparts. With surprising rapidity, the service-intensive requirements of U.S. cars that had been tolerated for years became deeply dissatisfying.

Dissatisfiers act to segment your customers by causing some to reject your offering and seek those of competitors. By creating a perceived negative difference between your offering and a competitor's, dissatisfiers can erode the loyalty of long-term customers. As is well known in the literature on service quality, finding a new customer to replace a lost one is about five times more expensive than maintaining the loyalty of the existing customer in the first place.[7] Dissatisfiers can build up slowly then take hold fast. The customer doesn't realize a particular attribute is a dissatisfier until a competitor points it out. The resulting punishment can be swift, as Bank One Corporation found out.

In 1999, Bank One's First USA credit card unit began to implement an increasingly aggressive policy of charging late fees to cardholders. Previously, such actions had gone pretty much unnoticed by consumers. Indeed, First USA had typically achieved a 2.9 percent return on assets, much superior to the industry's 2.3 percent average. But as industry growth slowed and consumers became more savvy, the bank suddenly found itself facing a consumer backlash. Cardholders began dropping First USA in significant numbers, which resulted in a 23 percent drop in Bank One shares by August 25, 1999, a loss of nearly $15 billion in the company's market capitalization.[8]

With a plethora of cards to choose from and a saturated market, many customers decided they could do without the irritating charges imposed by First USA.

Enragers (Negative/Energizing)   Even more deadly to your competitive position is a class of attributes that are energizing, but negative. We call these attributes *enragers*, although they may inspire many other negative emotions, ranging from fear to disgust. Enragers can be the result of misfortune, such as the Tylenol cyanide poisoning in 1982, Valujet's (now AirTran) plane crash in the Everglades in 1996, and the contamination of Perrier water with benzene in 1990. In such cases, the customer reaction is relatively easy to anticipate, and we know a lot about what management is supposed to do. Johnson & Johnson's reaction to the Tylenol scare has become a textbook case of how to handle the sudden emergence of terrifying features in a previously trustworthy product. After someone—unidentified to this day—laced capsules with deadly cyanide in the Chicago area and seven deaths were linked to the ingestion of Tylenol, Johnson & Johnson announced a total recall of the product (involving 31 million capsules) and halted all shipping and manufacturing. The product was reintroduced only after considerable investment in tamper-proof packaging and rehabilitative advertising. This prompt, Herculean effort saved the brand. Today, it is still a best-seller.

Sometimes companies are simply not on the same wavelength as customers when it comes to an offering's enraging attributes. Consider the flaw in Intel's Pentium chip. Most customers believe that microprocessors calculate with perfect accuracy, although all industry experts and most sophisticated scientific users know that every one of them contains flaws. Still, for the most part, the flaws can't be detected by users and cause no real trouble. In one instance, however, the Pentium was different. A defect in all the chips released in 1984 resulted in occasional occurrences of imperfect division. This is nothing new for chips. The trouble is that this glitch, unlike many others, was brought to the attention of the public.

Even after the resulting public-relations firestorm, Intel executives failed to see why everybody was so excited. Reasoning that most users would never encounter the division problem and that the lightning-fast speed of the Pentium would still make it desirable, they decided not to take definitive action to solve the problem. It wasn't until negative public reaction led major customers—IBM among them—to cancel scheduled Pentium purchases that Intel's management realized that the public response was more than ordinary grumbling. What they had on their hands was an enrager. From the customer's point of view, the Pentium chip violated expectations in a significantly negative way: It represented a decline in accuracy relative to expectations. This illustrates the importance of looking at every product or service your company offers through the customers' eyes. Their expectations may be quite different from what you anticipate, and it is their expectations that matter.

If you are unfortunate enough to have to deal with an attribute that becomes an enrager (or a source of terror or disgust), it is critical to eliminate it, or you will lose the affected customer segment for good. The reputation of the once-popular Perrier, for instance, was so sullied by the highly publicized problem of benzene contamination that it has never recovered. Perrier, which enjoyed upward of 44 percent of the U.S. market for bottled water in 1990, is now struggling at half that share in the face of vicious competition. If you cannot eliminate an enrager, you may have to leave the enraged target market.

Neutral Features on the Attribute Map

Neutral responses to product or service offerings can be classified as *so whats?* or *parallels.* These attributes do not affect the purchasing decision of most customers or do so in a way not directly related to the offering.

"So Whats?" (Neutral/Basic)   Attributes that elicit a "so what?" response from customers are sometimes legacies from the past. Consider, for instance, the requirement from the energy-conscious 1970s that refrigerators have stickers showing their energy consumption. At the time, it was thought that this information would lead buyers to choose more energy-efficient appliances. Since then, however, energy prices in the United States have plummeted, and most customers barely glance at the information on energy efficiency. What

people want today are doors big enough to hold gallon-sized milk cartons. They want a refrigerator that minimizes the amount of bending, repacking, and searching they have to do, that is made of easy-to-care-for materials, and that operates quietly. Most couldn't care less about energy savings (however environmentally careless that attitude may be). At this writing, the rapid increases in energy prices may make this a more attractive attribute again.

Another reason why neutral attributes exist for one set of customers is that another set of customers wants them, and the company finds it less expensive to include them in a general offering rather than sell them as a separate package. Microsoft products are an example. Most of its programs include many functions that many customers don't use. Consider the extensive features available for Word-Perfect users in Microsoft's Word program. Designed to help WordPerfect users convert to Word, this whole set of features is a "so what?" for anyone who started off with Word.

Sometimes, incorporating a neutral attribute in a product can actually generate negative responses. For instance, in order to provide all the functionality that many user segments desire, Microsoft's programs also include negatives for virtually all customers. As authors, for instance, we are regularly exasperated by the length of time it takes a Windows-based computer to start up and shut down and by the voluminous amount of hard disk space that Windows soaks up, much of which is driven by the need to support functionality we probably will never use. And the problem gets even worse with Windows 2000, which will occupy a mind-blowing 250 megabytes of storage space.

When "so what?" attributes add cost without enhancing value, it's best to try to design them out unless a strong case can be made for retaining or including them. A useful side effect is that by getting rid of them, you may also lower costs.

More subtle and more dangerous than outright "so whats?" on the neutral line are "nice to have" attributes. These are features that may differentiate your offering from those of competitors but that most customers will not be prepared to pay for. If a small set of customers beguiles you into offering these attributes, you may find yourself adding significantly to costs without gaining in profits.

Consumer electronics firms deal with this dilemma constantly. Most consumer electronics, including camcorders, VCRs, and television sets, include built-in features that few customers ever need. This problem is also rife in service industries and, indeed, in the service components of ordinary businesses. Take overnight delivery. While most customers certainly prefer it, few are prepared to pay for it. Your challenge is to make a distinction between features that people want enough to pay for, and those that are desired, but not desired enough to make a difference to profits.[9]

Parallels (Neutral/Discriminating)   A final group of attributes bears mention here, because it is often overlooked. *Parallels* are features that are offered in parallel with the primary attributes of your product or service, but that seemingly have little to do with its function or purpose. The more commodity-like the offering, the more parallel attributes can create some kind of differentiation. For example, frequent-flier miles have nothing to do with the price of a ticket, the time of departure, the comfort and convenience of the flight, or the safety of the airline, but woe betide the airline today that does not offer miles in parallel with its flights.

CREATING BLOCKBUSTER DESIGNS

The point of attribute mapping is to provide a simple, powerful process for redesigning a given offering for a given customer segment. Over the years, we have found that the redesign process works best when it incorporates these elements: mapping attributes, checking assumptions about customer attitudes, prioritizing actions, capturing opportunities (see "Setting Up an Opportunity Register" in chapter 2), and keeping an eye on dynamics.

Mapping Attributes

The best and most recent information about customers and distributors is almost always in the possession of people in direct contact with customers and distributors. Ironically, because these people often hold jobs that aren't considered strategic, they are usually left out of the process of thinking through new designs. The service force, complaint department, application acceptance people, accounts payable staff, salespeople, technical support personnel, and their like often have great insight into customer thinking and behavior, yet they are more often systematically ignored than listened to.

Start with these employees in your search for redesign opportunities. Begin by filling in an attribute matrix with people who regularly interact with customers but who don't get much of a chance to interact with one another. The first time you try this, start with people in the same function—such as sales, service, customer relations, or credit. Later, expand to include people from mixes of all the functions in your organization. Ideally, you will want to capture the experiences of others' exposure to different aspects of the customer's experience with your offering or your organization.

Assign someone a specific product/service offering to evaluate, for an important customer segment or segments that you are already serving. Don't assign too many to one person, or he or she will become overwhelmed. For the time being, use whatever system you currently rely on for segmentation. Your people's task is to pool their collective experience with the segment to complete an attribute map. The idea is to have one map per product per segment. (A cautionary note: Although it may be tempting to bring in market research data, people tend to suppress interesting but "different" ideas when confronted with "expert" data.) The output of this first pass-through should be a roomful of attribute maps that can be viewed by everyone involved. This first step makes clear at a glance both your assumptions about how customers are responding to your offerings and your people's understanding of how these customers feel.

Sometimes there may be so many attributes to consider that people get overwhelmed with the details. If this happens, decrease the number of attributes that get evaluated. Use guidelines similar to those listed in figure 3-2.

Your goal is to identify specific places in which your company might create a blockbuster design for one of your target segments. An example of a company that did just that is Progressive Insurance of Ohio, which created a blockbuster service package for its portfolio of "nonstandard" auto drivers, who don't fit the profile of conventional

FIGURE 3-2

LIMITING WHAT GOES INTO THE MAPS ON THE WALL

Attribute Type	Focus Questions
Nonnegotiable	• Which three nonnegotiables are the most expensive to deliver? Can we do something creative to reduce their cost, particularly in ways that competitors can't imitate?
Differentiator	• Why does this segment buy from us and not the competition? • What do we offer that customers not only like but are prepared to pay a premium for? • What do distributors and customers say we do better than anyone else? • How close is the competition to matching us on these features?
Exciter	• If a genie in a bottle granted us one wish that would allow us to redesign our product or service and add or enhance an attribute in such a way that we could capture huge market share, what would we wish for? Is this within the realm of the possible for us?
Tolerable	• What features would our most important customer segments list if we asked them to complete the following sentence: "If only you could eliminate _____ from your offering, I would buy a lot more or a lot more often." • Can we get rid of a tolerable in ways that competitors can't? How? • Are we experiencing increasing complaints on this tolerable? • To what extent are target customers beginning to compare us unfavorably with the competition?
Dissatisfier	• On what subject do people who interact with customers hear the most grumbling? • Is it something all providers do, or something only we do? • To what extent is this attribute a key reason for recent customer defections? • To what extent is this attribute increasingly cited as a key reason for product returns? • To what extent are our competitors advertising their superiority with respect to this attribute?

continued

FIGURE 3-2 (CONTINUED)

LIMITING WHAT GOES INTO THE MAPS ON THE WALL

Attribute Type	Focus Questions
Enrager	• Are people who are in contact with customers observing reactions that go beyond minor irritation to enraging? • Have customers written letters of complaint or otherwise been proactively critical of this feature?
So what?	Look at every expensive attribute and ask what its elimination or reduction would do to sales: • Why do we offer these attributes? • Are there any cost/complexity-reduction opportunities associated with getting rid of them? • What are the three most expensive "nice to haves" we offer—that is, features that we believe to be necessary but that customers appear unwilling to pay for? • Is there a competitive reason to keep these features, or could we eliminate them?

policy holders.[10] Many of these nonstandard drivers are well-off, but short of time.

Conventionally, auto insurance providers have divided their customers into two segments: standard and nonstandard. Nonstandard drivers have traditionally been classified as higher risk. They include the young; the disabled; people having an occupation regarded as high risk, a poor claims history, points on their license, or a record of driving under the influence of alcohol or other substances; and in particular a highly affluent group that drives expensive luxury cars. Most traditional insurance companies disregard the special needs of the nonstandard segment of the market because they consider these types of drivers to be unprofitable. Figure 3-3 suggests how this might translate in attribute terms—including the enraging aspect of being turned down for insurance!

Progressive Insurance of Ohio, in contrast, decided to specialize in serving the time-sensitive and less price-sensitive part of this market and created a blockbuster offering for owners of expensive luxury

FIGURE 3-3

CONVENTIONAL INSURER ATTRIBUTE MAP FOR THE NONSTANDARD INSURANCE CUSTOMER SEGMENT

	Basic	Discriminator	Energizer
Positive	NONNEGOTIABLE	DIFFERENTIATOR	EXCITER
	Claims are paid	Scope of coverage	None
	Back office is efficient	Reputation for payment	
Negative	TOLERABLE	DISSATISFIER	ENRAGER
	Higher premiums	Interacting with claims staff is a hassle	Denied coverage!
	A hassle getting enrolled		
Neutral	SO WHAT?	PARALLEL	
	Number of branches	Availability of complementary products, such as homeowners' insurance	

cars; the offering is summed up in attribute terms in figure 3-4. Because drivers in this segment are time stressed and their repairs are expensive, the company reasoned, they need to be processed quickly by the company's claims operations, including the assessment, adjustment, repair, and claims-processing services. Progressive consequently focused on streamlining and improving the claims operations experience for such customers. Among the changes Progressive made were to institute a twenty-four-hour immediate-response accident hot line and highly responsive claims management.

One of this offering's most innovative features is its adjustment office on wheels. Using a van equipped with telephone, fax, and other office equipment, the mobile claims adjuster is authorized to go to the site of an accident and settle the claim on the spot. Contrast this with the usual tortuous process of having the damage assessed, waiting to see the bill, and arguing with various parties about who owes

FIGURE 3-4

PROGRESSIVE ATTRIBUTE MAP FOR THE EXPENSIVE LUXURY CAR SEGMENT

	Basic	Discriminator	Energizer
Positive	NONNEGOTIABLE	DIFFERENTIATOR	EXCITER
	Claims are paid	Rapid access to a large number of plan options	Quick and competent claims response
	Back office is efficient	High levels of service	
		Preferred repair service providers	Rentals arranged during repair
Negative	TOLERABLE	DISSATISFIER	ENRAGER
	Higher premiums	Complex time-consuming sales interactions	None
		Time-consuming claims processes	
Neutral	SO WHAT?	PARALLEL	
	Number of branches	Availability of complementary products, such as homeowners' insurance	

what to whom. Moreover, Progressive carries the process through to closure by providing recommendations on services such as repairs and towing.

Progressive's customer segment is made up of people who value convenience over price. They are actively looking for a provider and are often quite angry and upset with their traditional provider. This realization prompted Progressive to create a range of channels through which such customers could find the company—including aggressive TV advertising and direct-mail campaigns, an "express quote" service that provides insurance quotes over the telephone and on the Internet, and a set of rapid screening and pricing systems that allows Progressive to fine-tune its service offerings for individual customers. Once a customer shows interest, Progressive offers a large menu of options on liability limits and deductibles and has highly trained service representatives available to explain the pros and cons of various choices. Figure 3-4 shows how the offerings Progressive has created over time dovetail with the needs of its target segment.

Checking Assumptions

Your completed attribute maps represent your team's best assumptions about the customer's attitude toward your offerings and the extent to which the offerings satisfy customer needs. Unfortunately, assumptions are only as good as the data on which they are based. A vitally important part of redesigning an offering is testing the assumptions by involving the customer. You can do this with focus groups, face-to-face interviews, and even customer groups who complete attribute maps from their point of view. Any of the preceding will help you connect with your customer's perception of your offering.

Facing customers directly is particularly critical if you are not doing a good job of meeting their needs—even though the encounters can be far from pleasant. As Greg Brenneman, president and chief operating officer of Continental Airlines recently argued, customers need the opportunity to vent any irritations, to register that you have listened, and (it is hoped) to see that you have acted on what they have tried to say.[11] At Continental, this process was taken to an extreme: The company even featured television ads in which groups of enraged customers expressed their feelings to Continental's chairman, Gordon Bethune. Although a little unconventional, the ads helped to communicate to those who had totally given up on the airline that Continental's management was both aware of the dissatisfiers and enragers in their service and committed to doing something about it.

Be aware that it is all too easy to get feedback from your most demanding or most accommodating customers. The problem is that they may be totally unrepresentative of the vast majority of segments to which you wish to appeal. Personal computer (PC) makers have battled with this challenge for years—the early adopters of PCs tended to be very comfortable with computers and tolerant of their quirks. The mass market, however, consists of customers who want an easy-to-use, cheap machine that delivers on what they consider the most important functions—access to the Internet and the ability to manage basic applications and games, for instance. The high-end segment will give you a poor representation of the attributes likely to make a blockbuster offering for the mass market.

Prioritizing Actions

By this time, you should have a lot of ideas on how your product or service could be made more attractive or less undesirable. Easy-to-accomplish, inexpensive moves can be put in place right away. At Continental Airlines, for instance, employees came up with the idea of putting a priority tag on the luggage of high-margin or high-volume customers; as the plane is unloaded, these tagged bags get put on the first cart going back to the terminal and arrive at the luggage area first. This simple and inexpensive idea has found great favor with Continental's most desired customer set, the relatively price-insensitive but time-sensitive business traveler.

Once you've checked your assumptions on customer attitudes and determined what attributes require attention, you should give top priority to attributes that may represent lurking enragers. These must be eliminated, or you will lose critical competitive ground. Once you fix the problem, make sure that you have a communication strategy that widely disseminates this information so that those customers about to abandon the offering are retained and those who have already left might be encouraged to give you another try. There is, of course, the possibility that an enrager is a problem for only a few vocal customers (as described above). You need to decide whether keeping these customers happy is worth it. It isn't unusual for companies to move heaven and earth for the noisiest customers without stopping to consider if they are also the most profitable or desirable customers. If they aren't worth it, let the competition cope.

Your next priority is to tend to current and emerging dissatisfiers. These represent areas in which customers perceive your competitors to be doing a better job, not troublesome areas characteristic of your entire industry. Dissatisfiers may be product features, but they can also be operations- and service-related attributes, such as when your firm takes a substantially longer time than the competition to complete a particular transaction. The solution to such problems may have to be systemwide; tools such as competitive benchmarking and business process redesign may be indicated.

We recommend that you try to implement immediate and visible improvements (even if the way you do this is not particularly elegant) at the same time that you work on the longer-term redesigned solution. You should try, to the extent possible, to measure your payback, whether this occurs through more sales to the same customers, better referrals to new customers, or deeper penetration into an existing segment. If you can't measure the improvement, it will be hard to sustain your commitment to the process over the long haul.

Having dealt with the attributes that are likely to cause you to lose competitive ground, the next priority is to think about the "so what?" and the nonnegotiable attributes. As discussed, "so what?" attributes add cost or complexity to the offering even though most customers don't care about the attribute or see no reason to pay for it. Nonnegotiable attributes are those taken for granted by the customer. Whenever you identify a "so what?" attribute, you create an opportunity. The first thing to determine is whether the "so what?" reaction is universal (that is, no customer segment truly cares about it) or selective (a few customer sets actually do care about it). For those attributes that universally evoke a "so what?" reaction, you may have an opportunity to reduce costs and create efficiency by eliminating them altogether.

The (not always successful) proliferation of automated telephone answering systems represents the response to the fact that twenty-four-hour availability and speedy processing are usually desirable features, while interacting with a human being can sometimes be neutral. Rite-Aid pharmacy, for instance, first instituted an automated prescription renewal system that uses a Touch-Tone phone to register requests for refills. The system both eliminates the cost of tying up a pharmacist on such a routine matter and provides customers with a positive feature they never had before—the ability to call whenever they want to initiate a renewal. Note that nonnegotiables must still be provided: Customers still must be able to access their accounts and prescriptions must still be filled in a timely way; otherwise the new feature will also have negative effects.

Features that are selectively neutral (some customers care about them while others don't) can be more difficult to manage. If it is cheaper to simply include the feature for all customers (as is the case with built-in radios in automobiles) and it doesn't create negatives for other customer segments, then the attribute can remain in place. If, however, the feature is costly to your organization or if you believe that some customer segments would pay more for it, it may be time to offer it as part of a menu of options. This can lead to opportunities to profit from features that have never been priced separately. Telephone companies, for instance, are attempting to menu-price such services as call waiting and caller identification because some customers do not see them as neutral but as positive features for which they are willing to pay more.

With nonnegotiables, which, as mentioned above, no longer give you any competitive advantage, your challenge is to think through ways in which the expense of delivering the features can be reduced. It is often useful to carefully check out assumptions regarding the nonnegotiable nature of attributes. Companies can easily come to assume that something is a nonnegotiable when for many important segments it is actually neutral and could be eliminated with little damage to customer appeal.

Having dispensed with negatives and neutrals, you can move on to consider the next-generation differentiators and exciters. The goal is to identify areas in which your distinctive skills and competences can be systematically used or developed to offer new differentiators and exciters and to diminish current dissatisfiers.

Each function in the firm has a strategic role in achieving this goal. Market researchers should be looking for early signs of potential exciters and differentiators and communicating their findings to product and process design engineers. The marketing staff should estimate the size of various potential customer segments and develop promotional vehicles that will quickly advertise these exciters and differentiators, thereby capitalizing on first-mover effects. Early on, product or systems designers should be working on ways to reduce the cost of providing differentiators and exciters; they should not wait until after competitors have matched the offering. They should also be looking at the possibility of eliminating or

reducing tolerables that could catapult your offering into a differentiator position while at the same time pushing competitors into a
dissatisfier position.

If your products and services are not sold directly to end users
or customers, the above process should be aimed at the intermedi-
aries you need to reach these end users or customers. Insurance,
wholesale and retail distribution, component sales, integrated systems solutions, and a host of other enterprises have this flavor to
them. You need to make a distinctive effort to reach your channel
partners because they often couldn't care less about the attributes
that your customers care about. They are typically more interested in
attributes that make a competitive difference to them, such as revenues per square foot of shelf space, margins, reliability of supply, and
assistance with promotions. If you want your product to get shelf
space and sales attention, your blockbuster offering should be compelling to distributors as well.

The same applies to other critical stakeholders. If you are highly
dependent on certain suppliers and need their attention, you need to
know what they want so that you can become a blockbuster customer
for them. If your organization is highly dependent on critical
employee skills, then you need to think through what would make
you a blockbuster employer.

Keeping an Eye on Dynamics

The final activity in redesign involves bringing the future into current decision making. Research suggests that people in successful
growth companies consider the future even as they deal with today's
challenges.[12]

Some trends are easily predictable. Inevitably, yesterday's exciting features will become nonnegotiables as competitors adopt them.
Inevitably, some of today's tolerable features will become dissatisfying. Furthermore, once customers have become completely satisfied
with a major purchasing criterion, they inevitably look for something
new. Research on product evolution suggests a consistent pattern.[13]

Early in a product life cycle, customers go for new features. As
customers learn, competitors imitate, and as the competences
improve, customers get used to the features that first excited them

and start to look for new attributes. Early calculators pleased customers by doing calculations. Later versions featured built-in memory, improved power supply, and more sophisticated calculations. Today, calculators come in many shapes and sizes and cost so little that simple ones are often given away as promotions. The movement of attributes from new features to reliability to bundled offerings to quality/price competition is a common pattern.

Other important trends are those that might completely overhaul the way attribute maps look to key customers. This can include changes in lifestyle, demographics, technology, and competitive context. Take the sad case of Kellogg's Corn Flakes as a cautionary tale of missed trends and tired attribute sets. From 1990 to 1998, the percentage of all breakfasts consumed in the United States that included cereal dropped from nearly 38 percent to just under 34 percent, even as the company's share of overall cereal sales in the nation declined from 36 percent to 32 percent. Trends producing this effect are many, including an increase in dual-career households, longer commutes (resulting in people's wanting breakfast food they can eat in the car), and a plethora of alternative breakfast foods. To the delight of bagel makers, drive-through restaurants, and purveyors of handheld food, corn flakes have faded in popularity, and the formerly differentiating properties of cereals (that they are good for you and easy to prepare, for instance) are no longer appealing. Further, technological advances have enabled competitors to produce corn flakes at cut-rate prices. Clearly, the energized and positive reactions that characterized consumer response and that had been the foundation of the company's success over its long history have lost their potency.[14]

It's especially important to stay abreast of high-impact trends—those likely to have the greatest impact on your business, even if they have a low probability of actually coming to pass. Also look at major competitive changes that could occur in your industry. A good framework to employ is Michael Porter's five-forces approach: What are the major factors that could have an impact on buyer power, supplier power, potential substitution, potential entry and exit, and competitive rivalry?[15]

When several important but unpredictable changes take place at the same time, we have found it useful to put together several major scenarios should various combinations of outcomes come to pass.[16]

For instance, competitors in mobile telephony are right now faced with several different approaches to competing in the United States, but as of this writing, no technical standard for mobile phones has yet emerged. What many businesses are doing is thinking through how well they will be positioned under each potential standard in order to understand what features they will need to offer if one or another comes to pass.[17]

Summary of Action Steps

The action steps that follow are meant to get you started on the concepts and processes discussed in the chapter. Feel free to elaborate in a way that works for your company.

STEP 1: Put together a working group of people who come into contact with your most important existing or desired customer segments for a particular product or service offering that you wish to redesign. Describe these segments.

STEP 2: Using the group to brainstorm, develop a preliminary attribute map for each of these major customer segments. Sometimes it pays to start with small groups of people from a particular function that involves regular interaction with customers (or distributors)— people in sales, service, or customer relations; telephone operators; order clerks; credit clerks; and so on. If you can't get a group together, send individuals a blank attribute map and do the work over a series of telephone calls. Once you have gone through the mapping procedure with these functional groups, put together a consolidated map for discussion with a group of people that represent all of the functions in your organization.

STEP 3: Validate the assumptions in the working version of the attribute map by taking a reality check with customers and/or customers' companies (and distributors, if appropriate). Revise the map.

STEP 4: Prioritize the actions suggested by this early analysis. Identify opportunities to do the following:

- Eliminate emerging enragers, if any.

- Implement immediate and visible improvements in dissatis-fiers.

- Carry out cost reduction of nonnegotiables (beginning with the most expensive).

- Identify and introduce next-generation exciters and differen-tiators.

- Eliminate neutrals that add no value for any customer set.

STEP 5: Record those opportunities you have unearthed in your opportunity register.

STEP 6: Identify major trends in customer segments that may present opportunities to redesign an offering. Examples include changes in customer needs or a customer's no longer having the need, which translates into obsolescence for a particular attribute; emerging new needs; and changes in the size and growth rate of a major market segment. Capture in your opportunity register ideas for future block-buster designs that these trends suggest.

STEP 7: Identify major external trends that might pose opportunities or threats. These would include changes in the marketplace, technology, demographics, the regulatory environment, and competitors. Add to the opportunity register any opportunities that arise.

CHAPTER 4

REDIFFERENTIATING

PRODUCTS AND

SERVICES

IN THE LAST CHAPTER, WE FOCUSED ON FILLING THE OPPOR-
tunity register with ideas based on redesigning the mix of attributes
you currently offer your customers in existing products and services.
Next, we consider finding new opportunities for *differentiation*, meaning ways that you set yourself apart from the competition and that
customers perceive as positive. We start with a method we call
quizzing, which you can use for developing insight into customer
behavior. Quizzing can eventually form the basis for new opportunities to differentiate. Then, we show you how to identify specific
opportunities for differentiation by carrying out what we call *consumption chain analysis*.

We should probably lay our biases on the table here and now.
We believe that no market is so mature that you cannot further differentiate your offerings, although we hear this lament all the time,
particularly from managers in embattled business-to-business industries. Shelly Weinig, one of the first Americans to open a manufacturing plant in Japan and a habitual entrepreneur himself, didn't
believe it either: "Show me a manager who claims he's in a mature

business," Weinig said, "and I'll show you a manager who's asleep at the wheel."

Sure, some managers seem naturally adept at creating opportunities from what seems to be nothing. Years of teaching and working with many different organizations have convinced us, however, that this is a skill that can be learned.

QUIZZING FOR CONTEXT

It's surprisingly easy to forget that customers don't really care about your offerings. What customers care about is their own needs and how to meet them. A way of reminding yourself of this is to recall that your customers are always embedded in a context. The context is full of influences that will affect how the customer behaves at any given point in time. What they are doing, worried about, looking forward to, and trying to avoid are all usually far more important to them than your product is. In addition, they can be influenced by whom they are with, their physical location, where they are going, and where they would prefer to be. Given these competing claims on a customer's attention, it is the unusual product that captures their full attention.

Understanding the customer's experiential context is your key to bringing about great differentiation.[1] You can get at it by means of quizzing, a process of asking and getting answers to questions in much the same way that a reporter tracks down a story. In Journalism 101, students are taught that every story should, to the extent possible, provide an answer to these questions: who, what, when, where, and, the trickiest, how? For each of your offerings, you want to consider the what, who, when, where, and/or how proposition from as many angles as possible. In some cases you'll be able to ask and answer all of the questions; in others, only a few. You can also elaborate on these basic questions, asking, for example, "what else?" once you have your first "what" scoped out. The idea is to use this process to deeply understand what is motivating the customer at that particular moment. Ideally, it will help you to differentiate in ways that are overlooked by companies taking a more conventional view. Examples of the kinds of questions you'll want to ask are listed in figure 4-1.

FIGURE 4-1

QUIZZING: SAMPLE QUESTIONS

WHO?

- Who is with customers while they [use][a] the offering?
- How much influence do these others have on the customer?
- If we could arrange it, who would we want the customer to be with?
- If we could arrange it, how might we want these people to influence the decision to purchase?
- Who does not [use] our product, but the competitors' products? Why do they not [use] our product?
- Who is experiencing problems similar to those our customers are experiencing? Current competitors' customers? An expanded customer set—for instance, a similar kind of customer who is in a different location or part of a different demographic group? Indirect customers who might benefit from our offering?
- What is stopping us from servicing these other potential customers?

WHAT?

- What do our customers experience as they [use] the offering?
- What need provokes the [use] of our offering?
- What change in conditions takes place for customers?
- What problem does it solve for them?
- What problems does it not solve for customers? What stops us from solving these problems for them?
- While customers are [using] the offering, what else are they doing? Identify all the major activities a customer may be engaged in while [using] the offering.
- What new activity might they engage in if it were possible? (This gets at possibilities for new offering enhancements.)
- What concerns do they have as they [use] the offering? Can we find ways of alleviating those concerns?
- What other related problems are our customers experiencing that we could solve? What is stopping us?

WHAT ELSE?

- What else might customers have on their minds as they are [using] the product?
- What else would they prefer to be doing rather than [using] the product?

continued

FIGURE 4-1 (CONTINUED)

QUIZZING: SAMPLE QUESTIONS

WHEN?

- When do our customers [use] the offering?
- If we could arrange it, at what other times might they [use] it?

WHERE?

- Where are our customers while they [use] the offering?
- If we could arrange it, where else might they be?

HOW?

- How do customers learn to [use] the product?
- How do they make trade-offs between [using] this product and deploying some other solution to their problem?
- How did early customers start [using] the product? How did later adopters start [using] it?
- How do customers know when to start and stop [using] the product?

---

[a] The term *use* is bracketed because it represents only one aspect of the customer's experience of your offering. Others include *purchase, search for, select, install,* and *repair.* Use the same quizzing process to stake out opportunities for differentiation in these areas.

To demonstrate how quizzing works, let's walk through an example of how one very successful entrepreneur differentiated a product that most people would regard as a slow-growth commodity. Our example involves a company called Blyth Industries. Blyth's chief executive officer, Bob Goergen, has met with incredible success in manufacturing and marketing—of all things—candles. Goergen is the sort of person we like to study—someone who has perceived and grasped opportunities that were seemingly invisible to others. How did he come up with a way of differentiating a product that is not only utterly common but easy to manufacture as well? Let's see how the quizzing process influenced what his company did.

Let us first ask what the candle is being used for and where it is being used. Candles can be used for many reasons in different places, for instance, to celebrate or provide light in the home, to provide light and atmosphere in restaurants, to provide light outdoors, to express reverence in places of worship, and to pay homage at vigils.

For each major reason and location, we can probe deeper and ask specifically where at each location candles are used. For example, where in the home are candles used? Some obvious examples included the following locations: dining room, bedroom, basement (near the fuse box), patio, and bathroom.

Each of these locations in the home presents a different experiential context. Except during an electrical power outage, the emotional context of candle use at home is vitally important if you intend to sell lots of them. Candles might be wanted to create a festive mood, a romantic mood, a cozy mood, and so on.

Consider the dining room. To get at the context, you might start with who might be with the customer in the dining room when candles are used. Depending on who these other people are, you might sell very different kinds of candles. For instance, one could be entertaining family, having a neighborhood party, enjoying a romantic evening with a date, or entertaining business associates.

Let us now focus in on home, dining room, and family and ask when the candles are used? Again there are a number of possible occasions, each with its own connotations. There are, for example, birthdays, anniversaries, holidays, graduations, Valentine's Days, and job promotions.

This process can be repeated over and over again for different types of companions gathering in different rooms. By thinking through the context and emotional tenor of each situation, you might add value to the candle offering by providing ancillary products. So, we might ask, what else can be offered with the candle? Candles of different designs, colors, and scents thus might be sold on their own or provided with accessories such as potpourris, special-occasion wrappings and decals, fragrance dispensers, aromatherapy kits, festive place-setting packages, party kits, and cake decorating kits. Figure 4-2 depicts just three of the many differentiated lines of candles that Bob Goergen's company has brought to market.

The potential for differentiation is limited only by the imagination. As Goergen will tell you, "This industry has been in decline for the past three hundred years!" Yet that didn't stop Blyth Industries from differentiating and then redifferentiating its products. Goergen launched one new product after another, tailored to the specific

FIGURE 4-2

USING QUIZZING TO DIFFERENTIATE MARKETS FOR CANDLES

Where can candles be
used? Examples include
- At home
- Outdoors
- On vacation
- At restaurants
- At places of worship
- At vigils

Let us select *At home*	Let us again select *At home*	Let us select *Outdoors*

Where in the home can candles be used? Examples include • Dining room • Living room • Bedroom • Patio	*Where* in the home can candles be used? Examples include • Dining room • Living room • Bedroom	*Where* can candles be used outdoors? Examples include • Camp site • Picnic site

Let us select *Dining room*	Let us again select *Dining room*	Let us select *Picnic site*

Who might people be with when they use the candles in the dining room? Possibilities include • Family • Friends • Business associates • Date	*Who* might people be with when they use the candles in the dining room? Possibilities include • Family • Friends • Business associates • Date	*Who* might people be with when using candles on a picnic? Possibilities include • Family • Friends • Business associates • Members of a club • Charitable event

Let us select *Family*	Let us select *Date*	Let us select *Business associates*

When do people use candles with family in the dining room? Possibilities include • Birthdays • Anniversaries • Holidays • Graduations	*When* would someone use candles in the dining room when with a date? Possibilities include • First dinner • Subsequent dinner • Valentine's Day • Welcome back	*What* might people be concerned about while using candles at a picnic with business associates? • Candles blow out • Candles attract insects

FIGURE 4-2 (CONTINUED)

USING QUIZZING TO DIFFERENTIATE MARKETS FOR CANDLES

What else might someone want while using candles on a date?
* Romantic atmosphere

What else might these people need while using the candles?
* Relaxed atmosphere

Let us select *Holidays*

What else might these people need while using the candles on holidays?
* Festive atmosphere

Using its unique skills in shaping, scenting, and coloring candles, the firm created an array of differentiated products and accessories.

FESTIVE CANDLES	ROMANTIC CANDLES	OUTDOOR CANDLES
• Candles in autumnal browns and oranges with scents like cranberry and cinnamon for Thanksgiving • Striped red and white or green and white candles with scents like cinnamon and mint for Christmas	• Tall, fluted candles in exotic colors for formal first meals • As relationship develops, floating candles scented with aromatics to establish mood • Red spiraled candles with rose or carnation scents for Valentine's Day	• Large, long-lasting candles infused with insect repellant, such as citronella • Candles in windproof hanging containers, similar to Chinese lanterns

locations (where), companions (who), and occasions (when) for which the candles were to be used. He then extended the reach of the company beyond the U.S. market to other markets where candles were likely to be valued. There are, of course, places where the company still has not made much headway—in Japan, for instance, the development of the domestic candle market is likely to be slow because many residences are built with considerable amounts of wood and paper. The company (which Goergen acquired in the late 1980s as a "hobby" for $200,000) grew from $3 million in sales in 1982 as a producer of religious candles to nearly $500 million in sales in 1996 as a global candle and accessory business. Its market value in 1997 was $1.2 billion. If Goergen can do it with candles, we believe you can do it with whatever products and services you are selling.

The best opportunities allow you to create differentiation on the basis of skills and capabilities that your business has and that your competitors do not. This makes it difficult for the competitors to match quickly. For Blyth Industries, Goergen used a combination of outstanding market research capabilities coupled with the company's technical skills at being able to deploy highly sophisticated production techniques to blend candle waxes, colors, and fragrances into shapes and styles that other companies couldn't match at the same price.

Goergen put two principles of entrepreneurial thinking to work. He developed a detailed understanding of the contexts in which his product was (and could be) used and then found ways of developing and deploying the firm's capabilities to deliver differentiated offerings that his competitors had trouble matching. You can do the same.

When we present this example to managers of industrial businesses, they often grumble that this is well and good for the consumer market but it doesn't work for the industrial market. We hope to convince you otherwise. There are many ways in which industrial firms have changed the rules of the game by differentiating—not only on the basis of products but also on the basis of the services provided with that product. For many years, for instance, IBM commanded price premiums for its services, even with plenty of competition. Indeed, the sourcing consultants Mitchell-Madison Group (MMG) (now part of USWeb/CKS) found that competitors would have to offer a total cost savings of 15 percent before their bids would even be entertained by IBM clients.[2]

If your customers are industrial, the single most important thing you need to do is to understand how they are trying to compete. To the extent that you understand how they are competing and can help them compete, you have a key differentiator. For instance, a senior executive at LSI Logic pointed out that if you are selling semiconductor arrays to Sony, for which the goal is primarily to be the leading innovator, the appeal is unique features and functionality. Matsushita, on the other hand, is a determined "fast follower," so it is primarily interested in speed to market and reliability.

CONSUMPTION CHAIN ANALYSIS

If looking at usage doesn't lead to a lot of great ideas, do not despair—there are many more places that you can do this! Enter a second tool that can be used for strategic differentiation: consumption chain analysis.[3] This works on the premise that opportunities for differentiation lurk at every step of the way your customers take, from the time they first become aware of their need for your product or service to the time they finally dispose of the remnants of the used-up product. We call these steps the customer's consumption chain.

Identifying the Links in the Chain

Any link in the consumption chain has differentiation potential—your job is to find out which links are the most promising for your organization, and why. The first step in doing this is to understand how the chain works. Figure 4-3 illustrates the typical links in the chain for a manufactured product.

FIGURE 4-3

A TYPICAL CONSUMPTION CHAIN

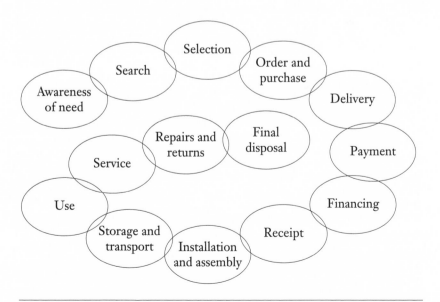

Awareness of Need   How do customers become aware of their need for something you can provide, a problem you can solve? If you are a toothbrush manufacturer, your challenge is to persuade massive numbers of consumers not only that brushing their teeth is important but that your particular kind of brush is the one they have to have.

Managers at the Oral B division of Gillette were particularly entrepreneurial with respect to awareness. They took advantage of the fact that for most customers, buying a toothbrush is a low-priority event. Most people are not aware that a toothbrush's ability to stimulate the gums (which reduces gum disease) deteriorates with age. Customers can't tell when it's time to change brushes by just looking at the brush. In fact, even though dentists have recommended for years that people replace their brushes every three to four months, the average consumer hangs onto a brush for nine months or more.[4] This is a situation in which a customer has a need for a product (in this case, a new toothbrush) but is not aware of it.

Oral B's managers developed a line of toothbrushes that they called the Indicator line in 1992. The toothbrushes incorporate a patented method of dyeing the center bristles of the brush blue. When the blue dye has been leached away, it's time to change the toothbrush. In effect, the product tells the consumer when it needs to be replaced. This turned out to be a major win. Customers benefit by taking better care of their teeth. The company benefited by being able to charge premium prices—the Indicator toothbrush sells for about 15 percent more than Oral B's other brushes, which themselves cost double the price of standard store brushes. Partly because of more frequent replacement, even with the higher price, Oral B's growth has been impressive, exceeding 12 percent annual sales growth from 1988 to 1998; and profit growth in excess of 21 percent (1988–1993) and 17 percent (1993–1998). Remember, these results are for a product category that many would write off as mature.

The time for this kind of cheap, pervasive "intelligence" on the part of products has certainly come. Oral B pioneered with toothbrushes that tell you when they need to be replaced. The idea of building smart functionality into ordinary products, however, is everywhere.

Take batteries, a product category in which demand for portable devices has created booming demand. In 1996, Energizer pioneered the first on-battery tester, a technology that allows consumers to test battery power on the spot, creating an information benefit that people never had before. Indeed, this innovation so impressed the editors of *Popular Science* magazine that they selected it as one of the best home technological innovations of the year.[5]

Duracell International (now part of the Gillette Company) responded with its own tester, embedded in the PowerCheck battery. Hewlett-Packard and other manufacturers of copiers, fax machines, and printers, have long incorporated usage information in their products, so that customer can purchase replacements before the ink supply is exhausted.

With industrial products now beginning to "communicate" their status to the people who use them, it can't be long before enterprises for servicing these products crop up, ready to step in when components and parts exhaust themselves. For instance, logging trucks in Alaska and Northern British Columbia are linked through satellite to onboard computers that optimize various aspects of the truck to the information and weather systems. For instance, the tire pressure in the truck's tires can be adjusted to fit the ambient conditions, which saves not only the cost of premature wear, but the cost and expense of downtime when a tire blows unexpectedly. Each truck is a big investment—downtime is expensive. Servicing those trucks is faster and less expensive now that the right parts can be anticipated and made ready in advance.[6]

Search How do customers identify alternative solutions? The key objective here is to increase product visibility. Making the customer's search easy, positioning your offerings where he or she is likely to find them (whether in cyberspace or more earthly realms), finding occasions for purchase when customers simply don't want to be bothered doing a lot of comparison shopping—these are all ways to capitalize on differentiation in the search process. At this search link, the Internet is having enormous impact. Companies such as Priceline.com have turned the traditional shopping equation on its head. Rather than offering a product or service and setting the price, this company has the customer set the price and looks for vendors willing to sell for that amount. Time will tell if this concept will work in the long run, but in the meantime, Priceline.com has made a unique impression on the minds of many consumers.

Selection Why does a customer pick one solution over another? Consider the purchase of a used car, an experience fraught with bad publicity and, often, bad previous experiences. It carries a lot of negatives, including not only the possibility of buying a lemon that someone else has dumped but also having to negotiate the price and deal with pushy salespeople. As *Washington Post* correspondent Brock Yates observed in 1987, "I am about to engage in that 20th-Century flog known as buying a car. To most of us, that generates about as much pleasure as root canal work."[7]

These sentiments were not lost on entrepreneurial managers. Companies like CarMax and AutoNation offer customers the opportunity to use computers to scroll through detailed descriptions of cars for sale on the lot. A nonnegotiable price is listed. When customers have winnowed the list down to the most attractive set of choices, they can then request a salesperson to show them the autos of interest. Many customers have responded to this way of shopping to free themselves of one of life's many sources of stress and discomfort. A second revolution in used-car buying is under way, made possible, of course, by the Internet. It is now entirely possible for a customer to specify what car he or she is looking for, what price range, and what geographic location, and subsequently find a ready seller, for virtually no investment of time or energy.

Order and Purchase What must a customer do to buy from you? Surprising though it might seem, many companies are successful at interesting the customer and persuading them to select their product, only to lose the game at the point of sale. Many sites on the Internet are guilty of making the most difficult part of the process the actual purchase of a good or service, by requiring time-consuming entry of customer information, and often multiple, slow-to-load validation and verification screens. The result? Would-be buyers never complete the transaction, and the sale is lost. Other firms have tackled this link with more imagination. Amazon.com, for instance, created a one-click system in which repeat customers can simply press a single button on the screen and order from prestored information with no further effort. Of course, stores in the bricks-and-mortar realm are also guilty of making purchasing difficult, as anyone who has ever waited in an endless checkout line at a major discount store can affirm.

Delivery How does an offering get from you to the customer? An entire cottage industry in the music and prerecorded content business is focusing on the location and delivery of music to the customer. Firms such as CD-NOW promise to revolutionize the consumption of music from recorded media by making it possible for customers to create their own CD-ROM disks, in batches of one. Rather than having to go to a music store or purchase music from a catalog, the customer creates his or her own collection. Another take on this idea is being developed by Audible.com, a firm that provides an Internet site with downloadable content, and a special, Walkman-like device on which this can be played back. For many firms, of course, delivery is their business, and we have all consequently benefited from enormous advances in logistics and packaging, prompted by the innovations of firms such as Federal Express. For many other kinds of firms, such as commodity shippers, construction companies, and food and newspaper companies, delivery has significant competitive implications as well.

Payment How does the customer pay? How do you receive payment? Optimizing the payment link can improve business in multiple ways. Obviously, if payment is more convenient, that helps to differentiate your product. Second is the substantial benefit your organization should enjoy in terms of reduced costs to process payments, more rapid positive cash flows, or both. Consider Mobil's Speedpass. Customers enrolled in the Mobil Speedpass system use a miniature radio transmitter attached to a key chain or to their car's rear window. The transponders transmit a special code that is recognized by a receiver in the pump. The two devices then simply charge the customers' fuel purchase to a designated credit or checking card. This eliminates the hassle of waiting while a credit card is charged, or conversely having to handle cash. The automatic payment system was introduced in 1997. By 1999, over 3,800 Mobil stations were participating in the program and the company had signed up over three million users. Company studies show that customers using the Speedpass technology purchase gasoline at Mobil an average of one time more per month than those not using the Speedpass. Think about the considerable advantage this is giving Mobil in terms of market share—all because the company recognized that customers wanted more speed and convenience at the pump.[8]

Receipt Once customers have it, what do they do with it? Questions to consider with respect to receipt, especially with service offerings, are whether the process can be made more convenient, more efficient, or more enjoyable. One of our favorite examples is Progressive Insurance, which we mentioned in chapter 2. It's hard to imagine a more responsive or rapid way to receive claims adjustment services than to have an adjuster in a mobile van settle the claim right at the scene of the accident. Not only that, but think of the reassurance Progressive provides by helping clients locate all the parties needed to get the car repaired, get a rental car, and tend to any insurance concerns raised by medical issues. Serving customers in this way has also had an unexpected benefit. Progressive suffers some of the lowest levels of nuisance lawsuits in the country. It appears that service is received so quickly that there is simply no time for fraud mongers to get involved.

Installation and Assembly How does your customer put the product to work? An example of capitalizing on installation difficulties is how Otis Elevator used wireless technology to expand the market for its remote elevator-monitoring systems. Otis Elevator formed an alliance with Novatel Wireless and Bell Atlantic Mobile to tackle installation problems with Otis's remote elevator-monitoring systems. Customers previously used land-line modems to relay information about elevator performance to OTISLINE, the company's twenty-four-hour maintenance dispatching center. This required the installation of phone lines in the elevator machine room. If for whatever reason it was infeasible to install phone lines, the customer could not use the service. The three companies developed a solution in which a wireless Novatel modem could be used to communicate information directly to Otis, eliminating the need for phone lines. Novatel executives estimate that this technology would allow Otis to reach a market of over 60,000 elevators that might otherwise not have been suitable for the service.[9]

Storage and Transport   What bothers or worries the customer about storing the product? In the industrial gas business, for example, focus on storage and transportation of the product by leading producers has transformed the way business is done in the industry. In the traditional business model, products come out of centralized plants and are transported by truck to user sites, where customers put them to work in their own manufacturing process. The expense and complexity of shipping, storing, and distributing large volumes of industrial gases have been overcome by plants in which the focus is on on-site generation of needed materials. This represents savings for customers, because most gases require either high-pressure storage or low temperatures in special tankers, increasing carriage costs. BOC Gases is known as a leader in the business of on-site generation of nitrogen, oxygen, and hydrogen and has also developed an attractive business marketing its technology and know-how to promote the use of these gases in new industrial processes.[10]

Use   What is going on while the customer is using the product? What help does the customer need in using the product? BOC Gases again provides a good example in this area. The company created significant value by assisting its customers to reduce the total systems cost of using gases in the biotechnology industry. In January 1998, the company announced that it had become the sole, preferred supplier of gases and related services to the Massachusetts Biotechnology Council, a trade association representing over 190 biotechnology companies. BOC's approach was to focus on the total cost of using gases in the laboratory and in bulk, through implementing such practices as Internet ordering, cylinder tracking, and gas management services. In addition to these services designed to make their products easier or less expensive to use, BOC also offers a special technical hot line, a support service that provides customers with information and support for handling its products.

Service   What happens when the offering needs service? How is it provided? A good example of a company that differentiates on the basis of service is Otis Elevator, with its remote diagnostics systems. In high-traffic office buildings, Otis can predict possible service interruptions and send maintenance staff to carry out evening preventative maintenance before the elevator actually fails.

Repairs and Returns   What happens when the offering needs repair or is returned or canceled? Retailers are finding that differentiating on the basis of ease of repairs and returns is one way to combat the incursions of Internet-based businesses in their markets. Most online merchants require that customers wishing to return products ship them back to their warehouses. Dayton Hudson's Target stores, however, are betting that they can differentiate their offering by allowing consumers to return items purchased on-line at any one of their 881 bricks-and-mortar stores. They are seeking to take advantage of unexpectedly hostile customer reactions to hassles in returning items purchased on-line.

Previously, many thought that customers would treat the experience of returning a product purchased from an Internet site just as they had traditionally done when purchasing from catalogs. On-line returns can present some startling differences from the catalog model, however. For instance, some Internet vendors' systems are programmed to send gift purchase refunds automatically sent to the giver, not the recipient, because the ordering information is linked to the giver's account. Other customers are irritated by their inability to return the product to the physical affiliate of a store's Internet site. Still others find the process of having to deal with a return when they expected a painless shopping experience particularly vexing. Inflated expectations on the part of customers only make matters worse.

To some extent, these difficulties in returns relate to the fact that shopping over the Internet is becoming a mass market, mainstream experience. Firms without experience in this arena are often ill equipped to meet the intense service challenges of a mass medium. Forrester Research, for instance, estimates that more than $4 billion was spent on Internet purchases during the 1999 holiday season. Difficulties in arranging returns and getting service are a budding enrager in this increasingly rich market.[11]

Final Disposal   What does the customer do with the offering once it's no longer of any use? All good things come to an end, which raises the question of whether there is a way to differentiate by increasing the convenience of disposing of the exhausted product. Canon, for instance, has developed a system that allows customers to return used-up copier cartridges, which are then rehabilitated. This creates a positive feeling of being environmentally responsible for the customer, while at the same time enhancing the image of Canon as environmentally friendly. It also reduces costs for Canon, since it is much less expensive to rehabilitate a used cartridge than to manufacture a new one.

The disposal link can be particularly profitable if you can structure disposal in such a way that the customer is naturally led to replace the exhausted or obsolete product with your next-generation offering. Computer retailers, for instance, appeal to fears of rapid obsolescence through various forms of creative computer rental. One recent example is a company that takes a monthly lease fee from customers for the use of a computer and also upgrades it as soon as it becomes out of date. This frees the customer from worries about product obsolescence and from the need to come up with several thousand dollars each time he or she wants or needs a new computer.

Improving the Links in a Consumption Chain

The purpose of consumption chain analysis is to help you identify opportunities to differentiate—opportunities with the potential to go beyond what your firm and others are doing today. Let's illustrate how this works with four links from a typical chain: search, storage and transport, use, and purchase.

Search   How do people search for a family car? Consider some of the numerous ways people might search for their next family automobile:

- Go to the same dealer with the purpose of buying the latest model of current auto.[12]

- Go to different dealers with the purpose of buying the latest model of current auto.

- Go to different dealers to find a newer, used model of current auto.

- Go to different dealers and compare new and/or used models of different autos.

- Watch TV ads and go to the advertised dealers.

- Read all the ads in automobile section of newspaper.

- Search on-line.

- Discuss the purchase in detail with friends and relatives.

- Consult *Consumer Reports* in print.

- Consult *Consumer Reports* on-line.

- Visit several dealers to see comparable autos.

- Do multiple test drives of many autos.

- Read dozens of industry magazines, do detailed analyses, and then do multiple test drives.

To a certain extent, the procedure that a potential car buyer uses to search for a car will determine the kind of advertising he or she is most likely to see and be most receptive to. The same is true for your customers—that is, you may find ways to add value for potential customers searching for your sort of product or service by improving the ways in which they search. For instance, if you wanted to target people who usually buy the latest model of the car they currently own, you might target advertising to them when models change if you are the current provider, or offer a target discount and a point-by-point comparison of why your car is superior at the time models change.

Storage and Transport   How do people stock (and carry) headache pills? Here are some ways in which customers might behave with respect to the storage and transport link in the consumption chain:

- Wait until the pills have run out and then buy replacement pills.

- Keep single replacements available in the medicine closet at home.

- Keep backup replacements in the medicine closet.

- Carry the pills in a briefcase or purse.

- Carry the pills in a briefcase or purse and keep a backup at home.

- Carry the pills in a briefcase or purse and keep a backup at home and in the office.

- Buy new pills when they have a headache and leave half-empty packs lying around at home, eventually to be discarded.

Here we could speculate that customers with different storage and transport habits might find different kinds of packaging or promotion enticing. For instance, if some customers buy pills only as needed, why would they want to buy a large box? A little box or an envelope will do. Those customers who carry pills with them routinely, however, may want a box because sturdy packaging keeps their pills from being pulverized while carried from one place to another.

Use How do people handle difficulties with product use? For example, what might different customer segments do with respect to an expensive sweatshirt that has shrunk in the wash?

- Throw it out with a philosophical attitude—this is the kind of thing that just happens sometimes and there's no need to get upset about it.

- Throw it out and complain to family.

- Throw it out and complain to family, friends, and co-workers.

- Throw it out and vow never to purchase that brand again.

- Throw it out and vow never again to purchase that brand or anything from the store where it was bought.

- Call the store and complain over the phone.

- Visit the store and complain in person.

- Visit the store in person and demand a refund.

Here again, different customer segments will respond differently to the way in which your organization handles this kind of problem. If they fall into the "throw it out and never buy that brand again," you'll never know how you lost them. Because these may be some of your most profitable customers, you need to find a way to encourage them to take some action when they are dissatisfied with a purchase. For instance, many firms offer full refunds if an unsatisfactory product is returned. This allows you to analyze what the problem was and try to recapture that customer's confidence.

Totally different actions may be called for with the noisier segments of customers—some of whom may have a legitimate beef about the sweatshirt but who may also be unrepresentative of the kinds of customers you want. For instance, they may chronically ignore the use and care instructions for clothing and create the problem themselves. By getting the shirt back to be analyzed, you can tell first of all whether you have a genuine problem with customer carelessness and, second, whether you might want to position differently with respect to how the shirt is sold.

Purchase How might quizzing be used to differentiate customer behavior in, say, the purchase of consumer gasoline? Differentiating consumer gasoline sales is tough. But let's say it is your problem to do so. There are many questions you might ask.

What are consumers doing when purchasing gasoline? They may be commuting to work, going on a leisure trip, going on a business trip, going shopping, going on vacation, or just filling a spare gas container in order to operate home equipment (such as a lawnmower).

The next step in the quizzing process is to select one of these contexts for further inquiry. Let us select "Going on a business trip." Who are these customers with when purchasing gasoline for the purposes of a business trip? They could be alone, traveling with one or more business acquaintances, traveling with a group of people, or traveling with a spouse.

Let us say that a potential customer is going on a business trip alone. The logical next question might be to consider where the customer might buy the gasoline. He or she might buy it at the local gas station the person usually uses, at convenient locations between cities en route, or at a gas station that is preapproved by the person's company, even if it isn't the one he or she personally uses.

Suppose we are interested in capturing customers who are buying along the route to a destination other than their home or workplace. We might then think about when they would be likely to make their purchase. They could by gasoline mainly during daylight hours, sometimes at night, mainly during the week, or sometimes during the weekend.

Let's say now that we want to focus on those who sometimes have to buy gas en route at night. What might concern these customers who are making an uncustomary purchase? They might worry about getting lost, having enough money to pay, having to stop again, or running out of gas, or their personal safety while making the purchase.

Now let us further define the "who" we are dealing with by deciding to focus on women, driving alone, on a long business trip that might require them to stop during odd hours during the night in unknown places for gas. Several ideas for differentiation present themselves. One would be to reconfigure the gas stations along highways that are principal driving (as opposed to flying) business routes to appeal to the concerns of this segment. This might include providing the customer with the following amenities:

- Well-lit stations

- Gas station attendants to pump gas

- A local travel adviser at each gas station with detailed knowledge of the area—for instance, which roads are safe, which exits should be avoided, which restaurant stops are pleasant and safe, and which hotels might be appropriate

- A loaner mobile phone that will be given to them at the first station on their trip and taken back at the last station

Going a step further, you might specially cater to this segment by setting up a travel chain that would extend from gas station to gas station. Each time your customer buys gas, the station calls ahead to the next station on her route to alert attendants there of her expected plans and destination. If she doesn't arrive within a specified time, this service might send a car out to look for her.

This example raises a few points that are worth noting. First, once your gas stations have a reputation for being safer, you can capture spillover effects: People will be inclined to stop there irrespective of whether it is night or day, whether they are alone or not. Second, not all of these ideas will be profitable. Before making a big investment in restructuring stations or adding services, you would have to consider whether there would be enough customers in the target group and enough spillover to make your efforts worthwhile. A third point is that there is no reason you have to provide all the material for differentiation yourself. For instance, a mobile phone company might be happy to provide services based at the gas station, creating differentiation for you (relative to other gas stations) without any expense or investment on your part. Now that's entrepreneurial thinking.

Mapping the Attributes of the Consumption Chain

Every link in the consumption chain is laden with attributes that can be mapped to further differentiate a product or service for a particular customer segment. The tools of attribute mapping and consumption chain analysis are made more powerful when used together. Let's return to the example of Progressive Insurance and look at the receipt link in the chain for an automobile insurance claim.

Suppose a Progressive enrollee has just had an automobile collision and her car requires moderate body work. She is a very busy person who has little time to devote to such problems. The attribute map for the receipt of insurance services for such a person might look like the one in figure 4-4.

Busy people will be highly gratified to receive on-the-spot claim assessments and a loaner auto to drive while repairs are being made. A smaller group of such people—with luck, enough for Progressive's needs—will also be relatively price-insensitive. They will, in other

FIGURE 4-4

RECEIPT LINK FOR AUTOMOBILE INSURANCE SERVICES FOR TIME-CONSTRAINED CUSTOMER SEGMENT

	Basic	Discriminator	Energizer
Positive	NONNEGOTIABLE	DIFFERENTIATOR	EXCITER
	Damage reimbursement	Provision of automobile loaner	On-the-spot assessment
Negative	TOLERABLE	DISSATISFIER	ENRAGER
	$600 deductible	Cumbersome forms and reporting	Discontinued coverage
Neutral	SO WHAT?	PARALLEL	
	Company infomercial literature	Detailed quotation from recommended body shop	

words, tolerate higher deductibles and more substantial premiums because saving time, not money, is a key driver of value for them. These might well be the most desired target segment for Progressive. Providing these customers with fast, efficient service not only is likely to increase their propensity to repurchase but is also likely to spur them to spread the word, giving Progressive positive word-of-mouth references. On the other hand, having to set aside time to complete lengthy, cumbersome forms is likely to be a source of great dissatisfaction for these customers, and being dropped for coverage (especially if the collision was not their fault) is likely to be enraging. This matters even more to the extent that people's feelings about the product have a spillover effect—an enraged customer might, for instance, withdraw from other insurance policies held with Progressive, or sever ties with other providers associated with the same parent.

Breaking the customer's experience into the component consumption chain links makes even more detailed attribute mapping possible. You can start to systematically identify opportunities for differentiation by building an attribute map for each segment at each link in the consumption chain. The goal is to make sure that you are aware of what attributes fall into which categories for key customer segments at each link in the chain. You can then begin to ask questions like this:

- How can we deliver the positive attributes faster, more cheaply, and otherwise better than we do now?

- How might we reduce or remove negative and neutral attributes?

- How can we meet new needs that customers may be developing?

- What might customers find useful if only we could give it to them?

The answers to each of these questions will show you the opportunities to move from the attribute maps in place today to the blockbuster offerings that can drive profitability tomorrow.

As you begin to flesh out ideas about what future blockbuster offerings might look like, try to be diligent about capturing opportunities in your opportunity register. Since it is hard to anticipate what will eventually prove to be valuable, the more ideas you can identify now, the more you will be to be positioned to act on when an opportunity materializes.

Identifying the Triggers That Precipitate Customer Action

Customers move from one link to another in the chain on the basis of trigger events. These are events that cause a new need to emerge, that change the customer's perspective on a need, or that signal the end of a consumption event. You must know what these triggers are and be able to act on them before the competition does. For instance, the search for a new product is often triggered when the customer's current product breaks down or becomes obsolete. Anyone who has been caught in a cycle of continual computer upgrades knows what this is like. Triggers will differ by customer segment. People who like to drive late-model cars, for instance, will be triggered to look for a new car simply by the passage of time. On the other hand, someone who likes to tinker may happily go on driving a vehicle that requires frequent attention.

The same goes for many other kinds of products. Consider washing machines and other household appliances. Some customers will replace their appliances whenever they move, fashions change, or new features are offered. Others will use them until they are worn completely out. All too often, companies lump these very different segments together in a useless, generic category, like "upper-income suburban families."

Companies often fail to check their assumptions about what triggers a move along the consumption chain for a particular segment. This often results in missed opportunities. Consider, for example, the unhappy experience of one of us (McGrath) with her washing machine (box 4-1).

It is not stupidity that leads companies to lose such opportunities. Rather, it is a consequence of assumptions made about how customers behave at each link in the chain—assumptions that may be entirely correct for one segment and dead wrong for others. For your more important segments, it is worth spending the time to identify the key events that lead them to transition between links—awareness of need, search, selection, purchase, and so on. You must then decide who within your firm is in the best position to spot these events, so that when they occur you will be informed and poised to react. For instance, your complaint line and technical support people may be the most likely to have the information before anyone else does.

Differentiating within Customer Segments

If you have a number of different customer segments, each will have its own consumption chain. In that case, your first task is to pin down the entire consumption chain for your product or service, segment by segment. If possible, call or personally interview distributors, customers, and customer service representatives to articulate the path taken by each segment and the needs it has as it moves along each link in the chain. The result of this process should be a consumption chain that looks something like figure 4-3 for each strategically important customer segment. Remember—you don't need comprehensive coverage of all segments to start. It is enough to identify one or two segments that you think are of most interest and work through these, returning to other segments later.

BOX 4-1

**A MINOR WASHING MACHINE TRAGEDY
(OR HOW ONE COMPANY'S LOSS IS ANOTHER'S GAIN)**

My trusty Whirlpool washing machine (which came with the house when I bought it from the original owners) broke for a second time. I called the Whirlpool help line. Here's what happened:

I gave a customer service representative my phone number and address (from which she should have been able to pinpoint the socioeconomic region I'm in). I explained the reason for my call: My existing washer had stopped working. I indicated that I had owned this Whirlpool washer for five years and that I did not buy it myself, but that my experience with it had generally been positive.

The customer service representative's next question was whether I wanted to try to repair the machine myself. No, I indicated, I have no interest in repairing it myself. Nevertheless, she (very nicely) switched me over to the repair hot line. The gentleman at the repair hot line tried to get me to describe what noises and behavior the machine exhibited before it died, in order to locate the correct repair parts for me. At this point, I hung up. This is an exemplary case of a trigger event in the making—a current customer, ripe for a solution, and looking to your company to provide it. The company didn't respond appropriately.

So I went off to the local appliance store, where a knowledgeable salesperson walked me through the pros and cons of all the machines. Unfortunately for Whirlpool, I ended up buying a Maytag. I'd had good experience with other Maytag products, their sales display was more convincing (they had a display with a part-by-part comparison emphasizing the durability of their washing machines), and I liked the feel of the knobs better (so much for sophisticated assessment of all the new appliance technology). The store offered not only to deliver the new machine but also to take away the old one within forty-eight hours. I didn't even mind paying a little more for the Maytag than the comparable Whirlpool. Half an hour and $600 later, the decision was settled, and with any luck, I won't be in the market for another washing machine for ten years or more. Whirlpool thus suffered a long-term loss.

Had the company been focused on trigger events such as this one, the outcome might have been different. Rather than sending me off to the repair people and losing the replacement sale, they could have switched to a different sales pitch, for instance, offering a special replacement machine deal. Further, in removing the old machine, the company could have gone over it to detect any areas that could benefit from product development. They might have found, for instance, which bits broke, how the machine had been used, and whether there is a systematic problem that requires attention in the manufacturing or design process.

Not only that, but by having their own delivery people come to my home, the company could have learned what other appliances appeared to need replacing, what I don't have that I might need, how I do my wash, and so on. All this data could have been used to help the company tailor its offerings and more finely segment its customers. I would have been happier, and they would have gotten the sale.

Of course, the one question Whirlpool should ask before going to all this trouble to serve my customer segment is whether the segment is big enough and price-insensitive enough to make it worth the company's while. If not, then they shouldn't bother.

Mobilizing the Organization

Mapping the consumption chains for your most important segments represents an area in which getting multiple people involved can really pay off, particularly people who are directly engaged with the customers. Bob Crandall, the former chief executive officer of American Airlines, for example, made a point of expecting his managers, including himself, to spend one day each month talking directly to the people who interact with prime target customers on a daily basis. The reservation clerks, the gate attendants, and the baggage handlers were all regularly asked, "What are you hearing from the business-class passengers? What will make them more likely to want to fly with us?"

Among other things, this led to the continuous redifferentiation of the frequent-flyer offering for business-class passengers. American began by borrowing from Scandinavian Airlines System the idea of developing a different service offering for business-class travelers than for coach-class travelers. Business class separated out the highly desirable business segment from either first class (which many companies regarded as excessively extravagant) or coach class (which many business travelers experienced as excessively taxing). Breaking out the business-class segment from others was a concept that was then extended into other service offerings. Thus, frequent business travelers were offered what was essentially a special discount in the form of frequent-flyer miles, which allowed them to take personal travel inexpensively after accumulating enough corporate travel. Business customers were encouraged to stay loyal to American by having their mileage program linked to car rentals, and then hotel stays. American Airlines flyers then were permitted to benefit from flying on partner airlines, spending on affiliated credit cards (such as Citibank's Advantage card), and membership in American's Admiral's Clubs at important airport hubs. Companies were also approached with offerings such as consolidated travel and expense reports to keep track of their travel and entertainment expenses.

No advantage lasts forever. Other airlines aggressively entered the competition for the business-class passenger. For years, however, American was considered the airline of choice for the business-class passenger, easily the most profitable segment of customers for airline services. Crandall was relentless in his focus on finding new links in the frequent-flyer consumption chain to use for differentiation. For years he made the American Airlines frequent-flyer program the easiest for customers to work with—from recording miles to cashing them in, making reservations, and receiving tickets. The major benefit was his emphasis on saving time and hassle for that most important business segment.

There is nothing to prevent you from doing what Goergen and Crandall did. To the extent that you can mobilize others in the company to genuinely understand what is going on for key customer segments as they move through the consumption chain, you have the opportunity to free up enormous entrepreneurial energy in your organization.

SUMMARY OF ACTION STEPS

The following action steps are meant to get you started on the concepts and processes discussed in the chapter. Feel free to elaborate in a way that works for your company.

STEP 1: For each significant customer segment (and perhaps each key distributor and key supplier), sketch out the consumption chain. Do so by interviewing—or including—as many people as possible who are in direct contact with the customer at any link.

STEP 2: Identify the trigger events that precipitate customer movement from link to link in their chain (awareness, search, selection, etc.). Articulate how your organization could get the information to know when a customer is moving from one link to another.

STEP 3: Put in place procedures to alert you when the trigger is pulled, and plan your responses when it does. Get the people responsible for executing the response on board—knowing what the trigger is and what to do when it is pulled.

STEP 4: Starting with the order/purchase and use links, start quizzing to get at needs that may not be met appropriately as products and services are currently configured. If one of the questions (what, who, when, where, or how) leads to a dead end, go on to another.

STEP 5: Create an attribute map for each major link in the consumption chain, for each important segment that you serve or seek to serve, again beginning with ordering/purchasing and use. Later move on to other links in the chain.

STEP 6: Use your insight into the customer's experiential context at each link to identify opportunities to forge a blockbuster offering for each segment you intend to serve.

STEP 7: Put the ideas that you generate into your opportunity register.

STEP 8: Revisit the process above with each of the other links in your customer's consumption chain.

STEP 9: Repeat the process for other key stakeholders (like brokers, distributors, suppliers).

CHAPTER 5

DISRUPTING

THE RULES OF

THE GAME

WE HAVE SO FAR LOOKED AT TWO WAYS TO DEVELOP NEW BUSI-
ness opportunities: redesigning and redifferentiating your products
and services. In this chapter, we focus on a third approach to capturing opportunities by developing new business models: reshaping your
competitive markets. We begin with methods that can be used to
resegment existing markets. By *resegmenting*, we mean honing in on,
or better serving, subsegments of existing markets. We move on to
explore how you can initiate increasingly challenging moves that
actually reconfigure the competitive arena. *Reconfiguring* an arena
means completely changing the existing basis for segmentation by
altering existing value chains or introducing entirely new types of
solutions.

Scoping Out New Market Segments

The idea that clusters of customers can be targeted based on certain
similarities is nothing new. Typically, firms segment customers on the
basis of demographics: age, gender, geographic location, and so forth.

The problem with this is that demography is not destiny; people who share a demographic profile often don't behave in the same way, don't have the same needs, and won't share the same perceptions of value.

Observe Behavior to Uncover Need, Uncover Need to Discover New Markets

The upshot is that an entrepreneurial mindset calls for insight into the people in the target segment's *behavior* rather than settling for the same old segments everyone else uses. Ideally, you not only discover a new segment, but can actually carve this segment out of conventional ones by resegmenting.

A client of ours, an entrepreneur, put this idea to work in the insurance industry. He was having dinner with a business acquaintance, who was recounting the trouble he had been having switching his property and casualty insurance, after having decided that a new company would better meet his needs. The experience had been awful. Before the man could even get a quote from the new company, it put all kinds of obstacles in his way. He had to provide copies of his existing policy, track down his wife's drivers' license information, and get written appraisals for some valuable items he wanted to add. This was hassle enough, but after having collected all this data, he was then told that he'd have to carve out the time to meet face to face with a broker from the new company. Things came to a crashing halt at the time. Imagine the irony—here was a highly desirable customer trying to give his business to a company, and yet the company couldn't have made the experience of closing the sale more difficult.

The entrepreneur decided that his friend's irritation was an opportunity waiting to be captured. Within the insurance firm he worked for, he mobilized an initiative that focused on busy, high-income people like his friend. He created a service that eliminated the paperwork and permitted applications to be submitted on-line or over the phone, twenty-four hours a day. Our client covered his costs and risk by charging higher premiums for a blanket coverage at a level that the customer selected, using actuarial estimates to assess the risk at the selected level. In two years, he has achieved considerable success in carving a high-margin niche out of the conventional insurance segment by focusing on the time-pressured, economically comfortable customer segment. He overcame the predictable resistance within his own firm by giving the venture a different name and operating it out of an office separate from the regular business in order to focus entirely on this particular customer segment.

So, here's the challenge. Can you identify a significant subset of customers whose behavior and motivations are not well served by companies using conventional segmentation approaches? Finding them involves discovering two things: First, what is different about the needs of this subsegment that is reflected in behavioral differences, and second, how can you respond in such a way that your offering is more compelling than those of competitors? Let's look at how this worked in a project we did for a telecommunications equipment company a few years ago.

Traditionally, business-to-business customers for telecommunications equipment have been segmented by size, geographic reach, and industry. We started quizzing, as usual, this time focusing on the use link in the consumption chain. When we started to ask the "what" questions (what was the customer doing when using telecommunications, what else was going on at the time, and so forth), we identified and zeroed in on the occasions when our client's customers were using telecommunications to sell (as opposed to order, schedule, coordinate, etc.). We noticed an intriguing set of subpatterns. While nearly all the companies used telecommunications to support their sales efforts, the way in which they employed telecommunications for selling cut across the way the industry was segmented at the time—by industry, sector, and geography. We began to look at whether these different selling behaviors might provide a meaningful basis for resegmentation.

We named the first potential new segment *order capturers*. These firms marketed heavily in the media to attract interest in their offerings, then used incoming telecommunications to take orders. Their key needs involved capturing and processing incoming orders as fast and efficiently as possible. This was doubly important in the consumer-oriented businesses within this segment, in which many customers make calls on impulse.

The second category, which we called *customer seekers* (to be polite), consisted of a group of companies that make telemarketing calls en masse. Their key needs were for extremely efficient dialing and redialing, for extensive linkages to databases of information on target customers, and for ease of use—since much of their workforce is high-turnover and transitory, these companies don't have time to train their telemarketers.

The third segment, *sales force leveragers*, were companies that use the phone to coordinate the activities of their sales force across many points of sale. PepsiCo was a pioneer in this approach, aggressively using communications between a large, mobile sales force and the firm's distribution warehouses to offer high-speed, high-quality service to its retailer customers. Companies like PepsiCo needed integrated sales communications with other operational systems and highly efficient two-way communication.

Interestingly, even when they were of similar size, geographic reach, or target industry, the firms in different behavioral segments had different priorities. The result was that each segment needed a different kind of sales telecommunication configuration, as shown in figure 5-1.

Design a Blockbuster Attribute Map for Each Segment

After we used quizzing to resegment the telecommunications customer groups, we then started thinking about ideal attribute maps for each of these key segments. A telecommunications package designed

FIGURE 5-1

BEHAVIORAL SEGMENTATION ON THE BASIS OF DIFFERENT
TELECOMMUNICATION NEEDS

	Order Capturers	Customer Seekers	Sales Force Leveragers
Incoming message efficiency and effectiveness	Very high	Low	Moderate
Outgoing message efficiency and effectiveness	Low	Very high	Moderate
Two-way remote connectivity	Minimal	Minimal	Very high

to serve one segment would not meet the requirements of the other two. At the same time, a package designed to meet the essential needs of all three segments would have to incorporate many potentially expensive, neutral attributes (from the point of view of the segments that don't care about them). The remote connectivity prized by sales force leveragers is a matter of indifference to the order capturers and customer seekers. They certainly aren't going to pay premium prices for services they don't care about. The goal was to envision what characteristics in an attribute map might make it a blockbuster success for a given target segment. Remember, the blockbuster concept means creating a bundle of attributes that are so perfectly aligned with the needs of a target segment that the customer is almost compelled to buy from you.

Let's first take the order capturer segment and determine what its blockbuster attribute map might look like. A simplified version is shown in figure 5-2.

The nonnegotiable attribute, caller self-routing, allows a caller to enter Touch-Tone numbers to quickly work his or her way down a decision tree to the correct telephone operator. Doing this quickly

FIGURE 5-2

SALIENT ATTRIBUTES FOR ORDER CAPTURERS

	Basic	Discriminator	Energizer
Positive	NONNEGOTIABLE	DIFFERENTIATOR	EXCITER
	Caller self-routing	Programmed call prioritizer	Self-programming call prioritizer
		Frequent user function	
Negative	TOLERABLE	DISSATISFIER	ENRAGER
	Limited line capacity	Caller waiting time	System failure, downtime
Neutral	SO WHAT?	PARALLEL	
	Remote connectivity	Speed dialing	

and efficiently is essential in an impulse-buy situation because delays or misdirection irritate customers and give them time to rethink the purchase and decide against it altogether.

Programmed call prioritizers might be differentiators. These allow the firm to program the system to categorize and then prioritize incoming calls. When there are inevitable periods of system overload, priority is given to calls with area codes that represent the locations of customers most likely to purchase. In a more sophisticated system, certain key customer numbers with solid records of purchase histories could be given priority. Even more valuable would be a software package that could analyze past telephone calls and use sales and profit data regarding these calls to *self-program* incoming calls, continuously updating and resetting parameters within the telecommunications system.

On the negative side, limited line capacity would be tolerable, provided that competitors were not able to offer more lines for the same price. If competitors should develop hardware that provides greater line capacity per unit price, then the tolerable will become a dissatisfier. If systems switching inefficiencies impose longer waiting times on callers than the equivalent competitive system, this would be a significant dissatisfier, increasing the chances that the order capturers could lose sales. Finally, if the order capturer's system fails, it loses business for every second the system is down, which qualifies this attribute as an enrager.

This segment would be totally indifferent to all the remote connectivity features one might offer a sales force leverager, so these attributes would be "so whats?" Likewise, the speed-dialing features that one might offer an order seeker could be considered "parallel" since the order capturer is hardly going to base its purchase decision on this attribute.

A potentially attractive parallel feature for order capturers would be a form of loyalty reward, such as a frequent-callers discount, as might tools to help the operator encourage these callers to buy more (perhaps by directing them to ask about complementary products or ancillary services).

Our client went back to representative companies from the target segments with revised attribute maps (for selling and for other telecommunications activities). The reaction was favorable—so much so that our client was able to ask for more aggressive pricing than it had previously dared to try, leveraging the claim that it was designing systems tailored to the way their clients did business. What's more, because this way of segmenting on the basis of behavior was not initially obvious, our client gained a significant edge on the competition by developing software packages custom-designed for each segment.

Seek Resegmentation Opportunities Systematically

The same process can work for you. As you spend time thinking about and discussing major differences in the what, who, where, when, and how of your offerings, new insights will emerge. One sign that you may have an opportunity for resegmentation is when a significant subset of customers undergoes a similar experience at a link in the consumption chain that is quite different from other subsets of customers. For instance, if all firms that seek customers have the same needs at the usage link, even though they operate in different industries, are of different sizes, and serve different customer sets, they may represent a viable new segment even if they would not be picked up by conventional methods. Again, you can apply this approach at any link in the consumption chain—you can segment on the basis of how the people behave when they search, when they order, when they purchase, when they use the offering, and so on.

Sometimes resegmentation can be created on the basis of the most mundane of activities. Take payment, for instance. Our client was a distributor of electrical supplies that was experiencing problems with many late payments. On investigation, we found that a number of delinquents were paying late because they were contractors who were only paid after their contracting job was finished. They had to wait until their client paid them before they in turn could pay our client. The resegmentation opportunity this represented was adding features to allow the contractors to better manage their own cash flow in exchange for more aggressive payment terms, thus carving this segment out of the mainstream customer base for electric supplies.

Any time you spot a difference in behavior, you may be looking at an opportunity to resegment, just as in the telecommunications and electrical distribution cases. We don't mean to imply that you have to throw out all your existing segmentation work, by the way. The idea is to make sure that you segment on the basis of insights with respect to customers' behavior throughout their consumption chain.

When we can, we like to be systematic about discovering segmentation opportunities by using a grid similar to that in figure 5-3. After applying consumption chain analysis and quizzing at a particular link, list your potential behavioral segments across the top of the chart and the major attributes you believe to be important for the segments down the side. Feel free to include the current industry segments in the analysis, since this may highlight places where adding or removing attributes will create major opportunities to disrupt the current segments. Then, in the cells, enter your best judgment as to how each potential segment would categorize the attribute (non-negotiable, tolerable, etc.).

If you have done a good job of segmenting, attributes will be regarded differently by each segment. In particular, there should be several attributes that separate the segments in terms of their reactions, evoking different negative, positive, or neutral reactions in the different segments. Using a grid like that in figure 5-3 helps to simplify the question of which customer segments can be created or reshaped or collapsed by changing the attributes of your offering. It can highlight four kinds of opportunities:

1. Opportunities to resegment by adding attributes that competitors don't offer

2. Opportunities to get rid of attributes that some segments find dissatisfying, tolerable, or neutral

3. Opportunities to change the way positive attributes are offered or to reduce the hassle or undesirability of negative attributes

4. Opportunities to collapse segments together by adding or removing attributes

For instance, if attribute 5 in Figure 5-3 is not currently being offered by competitors, segment 4 in the grid represents an opportunity for

FIGURE 5-3

SEGMENT COMPARISON GRID

	Segment 1	Segment 2	Segment 3	Segment 4	Segment 5
Attribute 1	So what?	Tolerable	So what?	Non-negotiable	Tolerable
Attribute 2	So what?	So what?	Dissatisfier	So what?	Tolerable
Attribute 3	Non-negotiable	Tolerable	Non-negotiable	So what?	So what?
Attribute 4	Differen-tiator	Differen-tiator	Differen-tiator	So what?	Differen-tiator
Attribute 5	So what?	So what?	So what?	Differen-tiator	So what?

resegmentation. The segment differs from all others in that it insists on attribute 1 (which is a nonnegotiable for this segment) and is the only segment that finds attribute 5 to be differentiating. If competitors are not currently offering attribute 5, you may be able to create and dominate a niche in segment 4 by coming up with a design that incorporates attributes 1 and 5 and downplays (or even removes) the other attributes, thereby reducing costs. Many software packages (such as the statistical analysis packages SAS and SPSS) have this quality—they provide software that delivers solutions to specialized problems that may not be particularly appealing to many users but are essential to some—and they often require time-consuming programming, a tolerable which requires training of users. By being the first to offer a graphic interface that eliminated the need for programming, SPSS captured many customers that had been loyal to SAS.

You can also begin to consider what attributes you might want to modify in your current offerings, perhaps to the point of removing some. Consider segments 2 and 5, both of which find attribute 1 tolerable. If you could remove attribute 1, you might collapse and capture both segments by pushing competitors into a situation where their product is now dissatisfying and yours isn't. This is what Progressive Insurance did when it introduced its mobile assessment office. People who lose income by having to spend time to go to conventional assessors (the equivalent of segment 2 in the grid) and people who need their vehicle to earn income (segment 5) are a natural target market for Progressive.

Another kind of opportunity is opened up by more or less universal negative attributes. For instance, look at attribute 2. For every segment, this attribute is either a "so what?" a tolerable, or dissatisfying. In eliminating this attribute, you would improve your attribute map relative to others and perhaps even reduce your costs. If you get there first, this could become a differentiating selling point. The introduction of electronic ticketing at airports is an example: It appeals greatly to electronically savvy credit card carriers who are either highly unwilling to wait in line or those who would normally be forced to wait in line because of last-minute changes in travel arrangements. At the same time, the new ticketing procedure reduces the number of people who need tickets issued by conventional means, reducing the lines overall for all segments.

You can also use this map to see whether there are opportunities to collapse one or more segments together, which should gain the potential scale advantages of a larger market. If you could remove or reduce the impact of attributes 1 and 2, you could reconfigure the entire market into three segments, the largest of which you could dominate. The three segments would consist of the old segment 4 that wants attribute 1 (you would lose this customer segment), the old segment 1 that remains indifferent to attributes 1 and 2 (and where you would still have competition), and a large new segment comprising old segments 2, 3, and 5 (where your new offering has removed a dissatisfier or tolerable for each of these old segments). Amazon.com's book sales is an example. For one segment, the behavioral segment of people who are fond of browsing books, the ability to visit the store is a nonnegotiable. For many other segments, however, having to physically visit a store to make a purchase is a tolerable that became a dissatisfier when Amazon.com made online ordering easy and secure. For instance, anyone who needs a book but is pressed for time would enjoy the convenience. People who need to access more material than what a conventional bookstore would regularly stock would also be drawn to Amazon's offerings. But, of course, anyone who needs the book immediately and doesn't want to wait for delivery would not be satisfied with the Amazon.com offering.[1]

A caveat is in order at this point: you cannot rest on your laurels. In the telecommunications case, and for the illustrations we have discussed in relation to figure 5-3, your success will oblige your competition to follow sooner or later (with luck, later), as happened to Amazon.com. Enter all the resegmentation ideas in your register. Once you have entered all the opportunities to resegment in your register, you can begin to look at opportunities to reconfigure your markets.

UNCOVERING OPPORTUNITIES FOR RECONFIGURATION

If this is your first pass through the book, you may want to skip the next chapter. What often prevents theoretically great business ideas from getting off the ground is a technological, regulatory, or organizational barrier that gets in the way of implementation.[2] We define *barriers* as the forces that set limits on the attributes you can offer or on the way in which consumption chains can be configured. This brings us to our second recommended approach to transforming your competitive arena: breaking down the barriers that cause the current market to be structured as it is—we call this market reconfiguration.

To develop an understanding of what barriers you most need to eliminate, you first need to go back to the major attribute maps that you developed for the use and purchase links in your consumption chain analyses. Your reconfiguration challenge will be different, depending on the nature of the barriers: how much impact their removal will have on the market and how much of a challenge their removal will present. There are three types of reconfiguration. *Evolutionary reconfigurations* break through current barriers to create an enhancement of your current offering. *Radical reconfigurations* break through barriers in a way that allows you to significantly change the structure of your current markets. *Revolutionary reconfigurations* bring new products to markets that do not currently buy your products.

Evolutionary Reconfigurations

To consider whether you have the chance to spark an evolutionary reconfiguration, go back to the attribute maps you developed for the major links in the consumption chain of your current business. Then start asking yourself these questions:

- What is stopping us from delivering positive attributes faster, better, and more cheaply than we do now?

- What is stopping us from reducing or removing negative and neutral attributes?

- What is stopping us from adding attributes for which customers have expressed a desire?

- Why can't we do something that would make a positive attribute more universally appealing?

Having identified an initial list of barriers, you now dig deeper by working the powerful so-called *five whys* popularized during the Japanese quality movement of the 1970s and 1980s. This requires you to ask at least five levels of *why* questions for each barrier. Citibank's experience with the development of its credit card business is a good example of how the five *whys* work.

Consider Citibank's unenviable situation with its credit cards in the inflationary 1970s. New York State's usury laws capped interest rates, and Citibank was thereby forced to charge consumers less than its cost of capital for credit card debt. The New York State Legislature, despite numerous appeals, failed to act to raise the limits. Had Citibank carried out a five-*whys* exercise, the questions might have looked like this:

1. Why can't we charge higher interest rates? *Because New York state law (where the credit card operation was located) caps interest rates at 14 percent.*

2. Why can't we get the law changed? *We have been lobbying and are in negotiations with the legislature, but they are currently unwilling to act.*

3. Why are they unwilling to act? *Because the cardholders in New York will blame the legislators for high interest charges; it is seen as politically unpopular.*

4. Why do we have to stay in New York and be subject to New York state law? *We've traditionally been located in New York.*

5. Why couldn't we move the credit card operation to a location where the unpopularity of interest rate ceilings would be of less concern to regulators? *This would be a big adjustment for our company and our people.*

6. But is there any substantive reason why we couldn't move somewhere else? *Not really.*

This line of reasoning ultimately led Citibank to move its credit card operation to South Dakota, where the state government, in exchange for the investment and employment that the credit card business represented, was willing to be more flexible about interest rate ceilings. The move generated billions of dollars in profits.

As you consider specific barriers, think about whether removing them might reconfigure the market or create new market spaces, or whether shifting their configuration could help you carve out a new and desirable segment or, conversely, collapse several subsegments into a larger group. You may see that certain barriers recur across several opportunities for reconfiguration. The removal of such barriers is an opportunity in and of itself, so add them to the opportunity register. In this situation, the opportunity that you list simply becomes the removal or reduction of the barrier.

When you find a barrier that is the result of your company's policies, you may have come across a great opportunity to change the way your company competes. Moreover, this opportunity lies mostly within your firm's control. Your firm may have decided that a certain segment or technology is not of interest, or that certain kinds of businesses are not desirable. Often these choices are not made consciously but represent holdovers from earlier times or reflect realities that no longer apply. Citibank, for instance, turned the credit card business on its head and created a multibillion-dollar opportunity by changing an internal barrier related to the definition of a creditworthy customer.

In traditional banking, a creditworthy customer is a person with lots of assets, stable employment, and a good credit repayment record, until one of our interviewees at Citibank had the imagination to ask themselves why this mattered. "After all," said the senior executive, "as long as the bill gets paid, why do we care what the customer's credit record is?" Instead of viewing any bad debt loss as something to be avoided in traditional banking's risk-averse culture, the team at Citibank began to refer to such losses as the financial services equivalent of "cost of goods sold." This breakthrough transformed the credit card business as it is today. Literally millions of people who would have a difficult time obtaining a conventional bank loan can borrow thousands on their cards (at premium interest rates, too).

For instance, this created a major advantage for Citibank in the college student market. Under traditional criteria, college students are a terrible credit risk—they have no job, own no home or other major asset that can be repossessed, are transient, and have no history of reliable repayment. But once you focus on whether the bill will be paid, it turns out that most students are a pretty good risk for a credit card, because Mom or Dad will usually come through in the event that the student overspends. Citibank gained a hugely profitable, dominant franchise with the college student segment by removing this internal barrier years before the competition caught up.

Radical Reconfigurations

Entrepreneurially minded entrants to existing markets often take advantage of incumbents by creating a compelling new business model.[3] Incumbent players then find themselves locked behind barriers stemming from their long-established ways of doing things or their investments in sunk assets. When the need for change finally becomes undeniable, incumbents may find that they have few or no customers left—the attributes they offer have been rendered inadequate by firms that created a new minimum level of acceptable performance with a breakthrough business model.

Radical shifts like this are becoming a fact of everyday life. As this chapter is being written, rapid technological improvement in digital imaging is challenging traditional photography, a variety of electricity-based power sources is challenging traditional ways of powering automobiles, telecommunication through the Internet is putting conventional telephone network operators on edge, and new forms of residential lighting are threatening manufacturers of traditional lamps and fixtures.

Of particular interest are two types of reconfiguration that radically change currently successful attribute sets. These are the radical reconfiguration of functionality, and the radical reconfiguration of consumption and value chains.

Radical Reconfiguration of Functionality   Functionality is radically reconfigured when a new entrant allows customers to meet needs, in a revolutionary way, that could never be met before. The rapid replacement of impact-based printing by laser-driven printing is a case in point. The rapid invasion of digital cameras into markets formerly dominated by 35-millimeter point-and-shoot cameras is a current example. With the advent of high-quality, low-priced color printers, capturing simple images is now possible at relatively low cost. Meanwhile, digital cameras allow people to do things such as upload images to the Internet, send them by e-mail, and capture them in overheads and written materials, which can't be done using a conventional camera.

Radical Reconfiguration of Consumption and Value Chains   Michael Porter, in his 1985 book *Competitive Advantage*, laid out the idea of the value chain as the set of linked activities that occur to create a product or service, beginning with the acquisition of raw materials through delivery of final service after sale. Value chains intersect with consumption chains. Typically, each consumption chain link has its own associated value chains. For instance, in doing the wash, a consumer's "usage" link might involve the value chains of the washing machine manufacturer, the detergent provider, the designer and manufacturer of the clothing being washed, and the electricity and water utility providers. This intersection of value chains and consumption chains opens the opportunity for a second type of disruption. This happens when you reconfigure the value chain so as to become better, faster, or less costly, while still delivering the same basic need at the given link in the consumption chain. Shifts that thereby dismember existing value chains are often difficult to comprehend at first because the differences from the previous way of doing business may not be obvious.[4]

A recent example of a firm that has radically reconfigured the value chain for sales of electronic equipment is PC/Mac Connection, which allows customers to search for, select, order, pay for, and assemble their home or office computer system, including all software and peripherals, in a single phone call. An experienced representative works through the customer's needs on the phone and then recommends the most appropriate configuration. If the customer then provides a credit card number, the entire system—with software loaded and upgrades installed—is delivered the next day.

As of this writing, the Internet has already demonstrated its potential to revolutionize value chains. Consider the emergence of Internet-based business-to-business virtual communities. These are Web-based services that offer business customers and vendors access to goods and services, often specializing in a given industry. An example is e-STEEL, a site developed specifically for the $700 billion global steel industry. The site allows buyers and sellers to connect; professional buyers and sellers to exchange information; purchasers to put up orders for bid; and suppliers to post information such as production availability or inventory levels in stock. The gains in efficiency such sites make possible completely transform the way procurement and purchasing are handled. This changes the economics of the business rapidly, making obsolete any incumbents that rely on "business as usual."[5]

When the logic that previously held together value chains (often based on the business's constraints of time, location, or information flow) evaporates, the business model associated with them does as well. Countering such shifts can be almost impossible to do within the framework of the existing business. For instance, when the brokerage firm Merrill Lynch announced that it would offer on-line stock trading to compete with new Internet-based entrants, its stock dropped by 10 percent, as analysts judged that the new business would cannibalize the firm's highly profitable broker-based business.[6] It takes real entrepreneurial leadership to resist the pressures to cling desperately to the old model.

A radical reconfiguration of either type can pose either a significant threat or an opportunity. It can yield a phenomenal new basis for competing, or it can effectively make obsolete and replace your current business model. In either case, your task is to try to anticipate such potential disruptions.

A way to start on this is to return to the consumption chain analyses that you prepared (from chapter 3) for your major customer segments. Now map the value chains that intersect each link of your consumption chain. You now have a model of the points at which your business activities touch on the experience of your major customers. With this analysis before you, look at the questions in figure 5-4. They will help you tease out the potential for radical reconfiguration of your current business model.

If you are facing a clear and present danger to your current model, you have no option but to give a lot of thought to what actions may be required to rework your current attribute maps. If you have some good ideas, enter them as opportunities in your register. They constitute defensive as opposed to offensive opportunities—you need them to weather the impact of the pending reconfiguration, but you

FIGURE 5-4

IS THERE POTENTIAL FOR RADICAL RECONFIGURATION OF THE CURRENT BUSINESS MODEL?

To what extent do you see the following patterns emerging in your markets? Enter next to each item below the number that corresponds with your conclusion: 1 = not at all, 2 = to some extent, 3 = a great deal.

____ One or more steps in our value chain could be completely eliminated by new developments in the near future.

____ We are facing enormous pressure to reduce prices or to offer more value for the same prices.

____ For one or more links in the consumption chains for our most important segments, the customers' needs could be met in completely new ways.

____ For one or more links in the consumption chains for our most important segments, the customers' needs are being met by competitors from an industry other than the one we primarily associate ourselves with.

____ Many new entrants have come into our markets, but are serving customer segments that we don't care about.

____ Solutions developed for market segments that we currently find unattractive are improving rapidly in terms of price, functionality, or other attributes.

____ The factors that kept our customers loyal seem to be losing their potency.

____ We seem to be facing a wave of consolidations and acquisitions in our industry.

____ We are experiencing completely new sources of competition compared with those we have historically faced.

____ Customers increasingly view our offerings as commodities.

Scoring: Add the numbers. If you score less than 12, the current potential for disruption is low. If you score between 12 and 20, you have a moderate potential for disruption. Scores higher than 20 suggest that you should actively be considering your actions in anticipation of disruptive change.

may elect not to pursue them at all after analyzing your full portfolio of opportunities, which you will do in chapter 7.

Also try to identify opportunities to proactively reconfigure the game yourself, by identifying projects that you could use to radically disrupt the current industry model. In this case, you would consider whether the questions in figure 5-4 might apply to your competition. If your competition gets high scores, that is a good sign. Enter your ideas for configuring your business into your opportunity register.

Let's say that you do spot an opportunity to develop a business model that has radical disruption potential, or you think you may be facing a disruption and want to be proactive in defending against a reconfiguration. Since such projects are generally high-risk, very uncertain, and likely to require substantial investments of time, if not of other resources, we are not advocating the blind pursuit of such projects without circumspection.[7] However, if you do identify a radical idea with high potential, enter it into your opportunity register and review it periodically to determine when its time is ripe.

Revolutionary Reconfigurations

This last type of reconfiguration completely reshapes current business models and delivers an offering with completely new and different attributes. If this is your first pass through the book, you may wish to revisit this section in a later pass. The academic community's views on technological change and industry reconfiguration is presented in box 5-2 (near the end of the chapter).

We suggest you approach revolutionary reconfigurations with a focus completely different from any you have considered so far—a focus on which customers or markets are not being attracted to your offering. Start by working through the series of questions we list below. As you explore these questions, you can garner ideas for revolutionary new offerings that are out of the box as far as thinking about the current markets is concerned.

Who Are Not Our Customers?   Take the example of laptop computers, which was the focus of a team we recently worked with. There are millions of people who own laptop computers, but there are tens of millions who do not. The issue is, which groups of people who could afford a laptop do not own one, and why? It is useful to begin by focusing on negative attributes. By doing some brainstorming, using attribute mapping and consumption chain analysis on laptop computers, our team decided that laptop computers have many such negative attributes. The machines are heavy (even the lightest weighs several pounds once the user has installed the battery and peripheral devices). The batteries not only are heavy but have a limited life. Laptops take forever to boot up. They are prone to theft and are a security risk. Connecting one to a network is a hassle. There may be huge, completely unrecognized groups of potential customers who are currently not in the laptop market, because, as configured, laptops are too difficult or inconvenient for these people to use.

What Are Some Major Behavioral Segments of Nonusers?   The next challenge is to identify several (perhaps three, for starters) different segments of nonusers that behave differently at different steps in the consumption chain. Again, we start with the usage and purchasing links.

Our laptop team was charged with finding major behavioral segments of nonusers. They came back with three segments. The first consists of *senior executives*. Most use a cell phone, some use a personal digital assistant (PDA) but not laptop computers. When asked why they don't use a laptop, their responses reflected many negatives, such as weight, complexity, and lack of need. This segment uses e-mail extensively but usually has an assistant who handles the bulk of it and gives them the rest as paper printouts. They tended, as a group, to be particularly averse to typing and didn't use even a desktop computer much. On their wish list was an easy-to-use method of getting important information from corporate and Internet-based resources on demand and a means of checking on updated schedule and calendar information without having to contact the office.

A second segment was *professional laptop novices*, people who use a desktop computer but have not yet felt the need to invest in a laptop. They have experimented with or own such devices as mobile phones and personal digital assistants. Complexity, cost, and keyboard-only access are huge negatives for this group. The team felt that big potential positives would be the ability to access e-mail and Internet-based information sources and to use the device for multiple purposes (storing images, getting addresses, reading electronic documents, receiving messages, making payments, etc.). Right now, these people depend on their desktops for these functions.

A third segment was named *cybervisuals*. These are people whose formerly paper-based work environment either has gone or is likely to go completely digital. This group includes architects, engineers, graphic designers, systems integrators, systems technicians, and the like. Simultaneously, their communication patterns are moving from being predominantly local to an Internet- or intranet-based shared environment. At the moment, laptops are highly dissatisfying because image resolution is inadequate, the processing power for manipulating the images they must work with is inadequate, and sharing is cumbersome. A portable device that would facilitate their collaborative work and enhance productivity while traveling would be welcome.

What Attributes of a New Offering Might Attract the Nonusers?   As you look at the problems that these major groups of nonusers have with the existing offering, you can begin to brainstorm about offerings with attributes that would solve these problems. For the time being, you should set aside the technical feasibility issue. Simply list the attributes for the solution of each and how each major segment might react.

As before, we suggest that you keep it simple and try to focus on the most important attributes. Figure 5-5 shows a possible early attribute map for each of the three segments of laptop nonusers.

As the laptop team worked on the disparate problems of these three groups of nonusers, they came up with a potentially revolutionary idea. Their concept was to do away with many of the downsides of using a laptop and creating something very different—a "superproduct" that would appeal to customers who don't currently use laptops but that would provide at least as much of the laptop's functionality in a less expensive, more user-friendly, and more portable package. They called the innovation a *mobile intelligence device*.

FIGURE 5-5

SEGMENT COMPARISON MAP FOR LAPTOP NONUSERS

Attributes	Segment 1: Senior Executives	Segment 2: Professional Laptop Novices	Segment 3: Cybervisuals
Portability (low weight)	Non-negotiable	Differentiator	Differentiator
Long-life power supply	Non-negotiable	Non-negotiable	So what?
Big, high-resolution images	So what?	So what?	Exciter
Standard office software support	So what?	Differentiator	So what?
Remote access to Internet-based e-services (including e-mail)	Exciter	Exciter	So what?
Remote access to stored digital documents	So what?	Differentiator	Non-negotiable
Price half that of existing laptops	So what?	Differentiator	Differentiator
Seamless interaction with other devices (laptop, calendar, other)	Differentiator	Non-negotiable	Differentiator
Voice and handwriting recognition (no typing)	Exciter	Differentiator	So what?

What Would a Superproduct That Solves All Problems Look Like? We have found that the most exciting place to start is to see what it would take to develop a perfect product. In the laptop example, you want to develop a description of a superproduct that meets the requirements of all three segments. Aim high—you can always lower your aim later.

As you will see in chapter 12, framing is crucial at this point. You need to articulate clearly what this superproduct is supposed to deliver. A cautionary note: Do not let the engineers or systems engineers dominate at this point; you could then end up with an incredibly cool product that nobody will buy. Engineers are trained to focus more on technical excellence and elegant solutions than on meeting nonuser needs at minimum cost.

The output of this process is a brief description, or image, of what the ultimate end product might look like, as described in box 5-1. Such a device doesn't exist and may never be feasible, but it suggests what a never-before-conceived offering might look like. Now—back to reality.

BOX 5-1

THE ULTIMATE MOBILE INTELLIGENCE DEVICE

The mobile intelligence device (MID) is a shirt-pocket-sized digital assistant with accessories that allow it to function as a laptop computer, tape recorder, personal digital assistant, and mobile phone. It weighs a maximum of 12 ounces with batteries and all accessories. It runs for seven days or more on two rechargeable AA-size batteries. The device has two displays: one on the pocket device and one that hooks into a visor that can be worn like a cap and shows a full thirteen inches of display space. An optional display device looks like a pair of glasses. The device can also power a conventional computer display. It can receive input by means of voice recognition, an incredibly light standard-sized keyboard that folds up, or handwriting on the flip side of the foldout surface. Earphones provide auditory output. It connects to the Internet and other networks, such as the Global Positioning System (GPS), through the built-in mobile phone or through other connections that can be tapped into without a hard-wired cable connection (via infrared or other device). It can support existing applications (such as word processing) and provide access to new ones (such as translation). And it will be available at half the price of existing laptops.

What Barriers Have Prevented Such an Offering? Figure 5-6 illustrates the case for the ultimate MID product. This analysis makes the nature of the technical and marketing challenges crystal clear. An MID would require several simultaneous breakthroughs to become a reality for any new segment.

What Barriers Should We Look to Remove First? Another way to state the question is, Which breakthroughs have the most potential to capture brand new segments while we work on the others? Start pragmatically by figuring out what breakthroughs are needed to satisfy the nonnegotiables for each segment. Figure 5-5 clearly shows that the team has the opportunity to go after the market for senior executives if it can deliver a highly portable, long-life-battery product. The opportunity exists to pursue professional laptop novices if the team can develop a light, long-life battery MID with seamless interaction. The cybervisual MID must be able to provide remote access to stored documents. Finally, to produce the superproduct MID, the team would need to overcome barriers to portability, battery life, interactivity, and remote document access.

Simultaneously, look at what would be needed to create exciters. Recall that exciter features are so powerful that they can fundamentally shape the purchasing process and thereby overcome nonnegotiables.[8] In this case of the MID, the opportunity to deliver exciter features to the senior executives involves breakthroughs in remote access/bandwidth and voice or handwriting recognition. The opportunity to develop exciter features for the professional laptop novices requires breakthroughs in remote access/bandwidth. For the cybervisuals, exciter features require breakthroughs in image resolution.

The superproduct opportunity would offer remote access/bandwidth, voice and handwriting input, and high-resolution display capability.[9] Should these features genuinely prove exciting to these segments, the potential superproduct could allow you to access all the segments with a single design—creating significant opportunities to capture scale and scope advantages. These opportunities should also be entered into the opportunity register.

Recognize that you need not go it alone. Entrepreneurial firms today are brilliant at leveraging the capabilities of others. In other

FIGURE 5-6

BARRIER ANALYSIS FOR MOBILE INTELLIGENCE DEVICE

Attributes	Potential Technical Solution	Barrier(s)	Comments
Portability—no heavier or clunkier than a personal digital assistant	Nanoelectronics	Technological manufacturing	This much functionality in this small a package is beyond current component and manufacturing limits.
Long-life, dirt-cheap power supply	Super energy efficiency of product	Energy consumption of chip	Current chip designs and processing power won't allow all this to be run on a standard supermarket battery.
High-resolution image	New technology in a new form (for instance, a visor)	Technological market	Currently, this technology exists in the laboratory. We don't know whether it is robust enough for the uses envisioned. We don't know whether customers will accept the proposed form factor.
Standard office software support	**ALTERNATIVE 1:** Miniature super-storage and superchip	Technology not yet developed	We can do it, but not within the weight guidelines. Consumer acceptance of stripped-down functionality also an issue. For instance, many customers have not been happy with the limited functionality of Microsoft's Windows CE, a limited-function version designed for personal digital assistants.
	ALTERNATIVE 2: Remote storage of mass data, local processing only of current work	Adequate bandwidth and connectivity not yet available	Until it's possible to access files from any location at high speed, a local hard drive or other storage device will always be preferable. Consider also concerns about security, privacy.

continued

FIGURE 5-6 (CONTINUED)

BARRIER ANALYSIS FOR MOBILE INTELLIGENCE DEVICE

Attributes	Potential Technical Solution	Barrier(s)	Comments
Remote access to Internet-based e-services (including e-mail)	BANDWIDTH: Geographic reach of mobile communications	Same as above	Same as above
Remote access to stored digital documents	Next-generation infrared or other cable-free connections; backup with conventional storage media	Technology not yet developed; bandwidth not in place	Once heavy-duty graphics or complex images come into play, bandwidth and connectivity problems become acute.
Half the price of existing laptops	Position it below computers, above PDAs	Technology still too expensive, unknown economies in mass manufacture	Could be a major plus— would speed adoption tremendously, especially among current laptop nonusers.
Seamless interaction with other devices (laptop, calendar, other)	Standard interface for data exchange	No standards yet in place— concern about power and compatibility	We would have to meet the existing standard or help create a new one for the sharing of information. Ideally, interaction would not require a physical connection.
Voice and handwriting recognition (no typing)	Speech/voice recognition technology, handwriting recognition technology	Early versions of technology exist, but they're still clunky	Need to consider appropriateness of voice in noisy travel environments (airplanes, railcars). Accuracy still too low for most prospective customers.

words, it is not only appropriate, but desirable, to aggressively use joint ventures with other firms that have the capabilities that you do not have.[10] Review the list of breakthroughs you need to make, and identify opportunities to develop new capabilities alone or in conjunction with others that will allow you to deliver either nonnegotiables or exciters. Enter them into your register.

Finally, revisit the attribute maps for your existing business and assess the extent to which the new attributes you have identified will enhance your offering(s) for existing market segments. The more such new attributes have the potential to excite or differentiate the existing segments, the more revolutionary potential the breakthrough project has.

The above process should help you to identify opportunities to generate next-generation offerings and markets that are simply not on your current radar screen. Note that we have not yet decided whether these reconfiguration opportunities are worthwhile from an economic point of view. This is considered later in the book.

BOX 5-2

ACADEMIC PERSPECTIVES ON RADICAL CHANGE IN TECHNOLOGY

In considering how academics have tended to view technological revolution, one can trace three different lenses through which change has been viewed. Interestingly, these lenses operate at three different levels of analysis and sometimes seem to look past one another.[a]

The first perspective can be thought of as technology driven. A firm achieves competitive advantage by capitalizing on a proprietary position with respect to a dominant design or standard. Huge profits can accrue to such firms if they can preserve their proprietary position. Technological change, though, is driven by more or less random developments in the technologies themselves that lead to substantial market shifts. The process is commonly viewed as moving through a technology cycle of discontinuous change, ferment, closure on a dominant design, and incremental improvement until the next discontinuity.[b]

A second point of view is based on the idea of firm-level resources as significant drivers of technological process.[c] In this point of view, competitive advantages derive from the path-dependent accumulation of idiosyncratic, firm-specific knowledge, resources, and routines that yield technologies. Because it takes a long time to build up significant technological competence, it's not easy for competitors to follow swiftly. The goal of managers in this case is to shape the evolution of technological progress in ways that suit a firm's particular competences.[d] An important distinction between the two perspectives is that in the competence-driven viewpoint firms are the key drivers for the evolution of technologies, while the technology-driven perspective sees change in technologies as the key driver.

A third perspective looks instead to the demand-pull aspects of technological evolution. This "demand-driven" perspective emphasizes linkages between technologies and needs. Advantage emerges when a firm deploys technology to solve problems for customers and, in so doing, generates numerous need-satisfying transactions.[e] The existence of needs or problems motivates both basic and applied research, which is followed by development, commercialization, diffusion, adoption of the innovation, and a set of consequences, sometimes far-reaching, that set the stage for subsequent rounds of technological progress. Although this approach has been found to work well empirically with technologies that are familiar to customers, customers find it very difficult to articulate needs that they have never considered having met.

a. McGrath (1997).

b. Tushman and Anderson (1986); Tushman and O'Reilly (1997); Utterback and Abernathy (1975); Utterback (1994); Birnbaum-More, Weiss, and Wright (1994); Gersick (1991); Birnbaum-More and Weiss (1990).

c. Dierickx and Cool (1989).

d. Winter (1995); Nelson and Winter (1982); Barney (1991); Garud and Kumaraswamy (1995).

e. Kamien and Schwartz (1975); Scherer (1979); Myers and Marquis (1969); Mowery and Rosenberg (1982); Schmookler (1966); Adler (1989).

SUMMARY OF ACTION STEPS

Once again, the action steps that we propose below are meant to get you started on the concepts and processes discussed in the chapter. Feel free to elaborate in a way that works for your company.

STEP 1: Analyze the current market for significant subgroups of customers who behave in ways that distinguish them from the rest of the market. Use quizzing to tease out the differences, starting with the purchase link and the usage link in the consumption chain. List all the current and potential new segments that you have identified.

STEP 2: Develop attribute maps for all the segments, new and existing, that you consider to be target segments.

STEP 3: Complete a segment comparison grid similar to that in figure 5-3.

STEP 4: Work through the grid to find opportunities to resegment by developing alternative blockbuster designs. Enter the opportunities in your opportunity register.

STEP 5: Revisit your major attribute maps. Use the *five-whys* process to determine why you can't improve on the attribute maps that you have identified, and uncover the key barriers to making improvements that will enhance positive attributes or remove key negative attributes (or make them less objectionable).

STEP 6: For each barrier, assess whether its removal could lead to significant gains. If the answer is yes, add these projects to the opportunity register aimed at reconfiguring by removing these barriers.

STEP 7: Use the questions provided in the chapter to identify potential alternative solutions that could radically reconfigure the functionality, the value chain, or the consumption chain for your industry. If such alternative solutions pose a threat to you, identify defensive opportunities and enter them in your opportunity register. If you can identify opportunities to introduce radical reconfigurations yourself, enter them into your register as well.

STEP 8: Identify three to five behavioral segments of nonusers of a current offering.

STEP 9: Develop a segmentation map for these nonuser segments, identifying attributes that you think will excite, differentiate, or be nonnegotiable for each segment.

STEP 10: Develop a superproduct concept—a description of the product that will capture all the nonuser segments.

STEP 11: Identify all the major barriers—technological, market, regulatory, and so on—that prevent you from delivering the attributes of the superproduct.

STEP 12: Identify the barriers that, if removed, would allow you to deliver nonnegotiables for each segment and for the aggregation of these segments, using, if necessary, the capabilities of other firms. Enter these opportunities into your register. Repeat the process for exciter features.

STEP 13: Identify which opportunities to push back exciter and nonnegotiable barriers will also have a positive impact on the attribute maps of your existing major segments. Flag these as particularly attractive opportunities.

CHAPTER 6

BUILDING

BREAKTHROUGH

COMPETENCES

SO FAR, WE HAVE DISCUSSED SEVERAL WAYS IN WHICH YOU CAN build a robust stock of potential opportunities in your opportunity register. We have shown how you can use product and service redesign, redifferentiation by honing in on customers' behavioral context by quizzing, resegmenting customers using attribute mapping, and reconfiguring whole markets by breaking barriers. This chapter is the last that focuses on identifying new opportunities.

We will focus on entrepreneurial opportunities you can create by deliberately reconfiguring your company's *competences*—the combination of skills, assets, and systems you use to compete—to change the business model for your existing business or to create a business model for an entirely new venture. We present some ways to assess where you are with respect to target competitors and to identify new ways to beat competitors on criteria that increase your profits and profitability.

There are two realities that no organization can avoid. The first is the reality that competitors simply cannot allow you to go unchallenged and must try to erode your position. Understanding where to create a competitive position that cannot easily be overcome is thus essential. The second reality is that you are not only competing with other organizations in customer markets. You are also competing with them in the capital markets for the critical funds you need to build future competitive position.[1] The people who provide you with funds are not fools. Venture capitalists, investment and commercial banks, market analysts, co-investors, and other resource providers (such as alliance partners) are a hard-nosed, analytical lot. They are going to scrutinize the portfolio of profit-growth initiatives that you select from your opportunity register with a single fundamental question in mind: Will investing in this opportunity provide a better return than I can get by investing in something else?

To cope with these two realities, you must demonstrate that your organization has what it takes to beat the competition in one simple way: creating superior ability to deliver on one or more key ratios that drive profitability in your business. Key ratios are measurable components of your business model that allow your business to be compared to others and that give you an early indication of where your opportunities are taking your profit growth. You can use your insight into these ratios to build new competences.

The key ratio concept invokes a core discipline you'll need to develop an entrepreneurial mindset. This is to make things as simple as possible, and to stay focused. Understanding your ratios and developing new ones will allow you to know when you are performing well (or badly) and how to target the few critical areas that will make a true, competitive difference.

DELIVERING ON KEY RATIOS

Let's begin with a conclusion supported by considerable research. For the vast majority of businesses, profitability and profit growth can be anticipated on the basis of the organization's performance on no more than seven to ten critical numbers.[2] When we say this to managers awash in numbers, performance indicators, and MIS (management information system) reports that purport to provide critical information, they are usually surprised. Given the amount of data that a typical company generates, one can be forgiven for thinking that understanding what drives profitability is complex, time-consuming, and detailed at the fundamental level. It's not. All you need is seven to ten key ratios. The trick, of course, is figuring out which ones they are.[3]

Identifying Key Ratios

In established industries, time and experience eventually create a consensus on key ratios. In the airline industry, for instance, profitability has to do with the operation's overall efficiency, because a huge cost component for airlines lies in the relatively fixed costs of purchasing and operating planes, reservation systems, and staff. How good the airline is at filling its planes also makes a difference. Unused seat capacity on a flight represents potential revenues (hence profits) that can never be recaptured. As a consequence, two of the key ratios commonly used by airlines analysts are cost per passenger-mile flown and passenger yield (meaning the overall percentage of the seats on the planes that are filled).

The insurance industry operates with a different business model and hence different key ratios. In insurance, revenues come in long before the bulk of claim expenses go out the door. The fewer the losses claimed relative to the revenue received, the greater the company's profits: hence the loss ratio is important. If the firm keeps a good handle on the ratio of administrative expenses to revenues, it will be more profitable. As with airlines, the administrative cost burden is not variable. In the insurance industry, therefore, managers and analysts look at the loss ratio (the proportion of losses claimed to premium revenue received), the expense ratio (the proportion of sales and general administrative expenses to premium revenue received), and the combined ratio (a mix of the two). Interestingly, many companies in the insurance industry today earn the bulk of their profits not on their underwriting, but on the investment yield that they earn after premiums are received and before losses are claimed.

Retailers face a different challenge. Conventional bricks-and-mortar stores have only so much floor space for the display and sale of items. This space limitation has for years led analysts of retail stores to use ratios such as same-store sales (in which sales for one period at one store are compared with a similar previous period) and sales per square foot (either compared to the store's previous record, or compared to the performance of different stores). Higher stock turnover means that more stock is moved, less money is tied up in working capital and the company can enjoy greater velocity of sales, all of which have a positive impact on profitability. Another key ratio in traditional retail businesses is thus *inventory turns*, on an annual basis, meaning the number of times inventory must be restocked per year.

In the United States, such numbers are readily available and easy to obtain. Each industry can rely on different sources. For U.S. retail stores, for instance, a variety of vendors supply information on-line. Examples include the International Council of Shopping Centers, which publish data on aggregate sales by store type and mall sales per square foot by store type (http://www.icsc.organization/srch); the magazine *Chain Store Age*, which also provides on-line resources for retail executives (http://www.chainstoreage.com); and government publications that list monthly retail inventories and inventories/sales ratios (http://www.census.gov/mrts/www/data/html/inv99.html).

In new industries, or industries whose value chain is undergoing rapid change, it's harder to determine which key ratios to use. Sometimes, this is because the critical relationships between numbers have not yet been established. For instance, nobody yet knows what the critical ratios are for e-businesses (Should the model be transaction based? Should it be an advertising model? Will customers prefer fixed prices or dynamic pricing?). Indeed, one of the great ironies of the Internet revolution is that many entrepreneurs who thought they could avoid making investments in fixed assets and inventory are finding that this is unrealistic—they can't deliver quality service without controlling many of their key operational parameters. As a result, many of the business models originally developed to support Internet-based businesses are less attractive than originally expected. Although this lack of clarity with respect to which models to use can be frustrating and confusing, it also creates a lot of latitude for entrepreneurial thinkers to envision new business models whose success will be measured by key ratios that are different from the traditional ratios of the established industry.

Creating and managing new key ratios is particularly important for corporate entrepreneurs in established businesses who want to revitalize their organizations. New ratios also signal that the business model has changed, which can be critical both within the firm and for its outside constituencies. For instance, when the Finnish telecommunications service company Sonera went public in November 1998, it used new key ratios to communicate its intentions to become a player in the emerging global telecommunications services markets to analysts and investors. In both its land-line business and its enormously successful Finnish mobile telephony business, the company made the bulk of its profit by selling time on its network. As the 1990s drew to a close, however, globalization and deregulation in the telecommunications industry led the CFO to realize that this business model would no longer be profitable. Excess network capacity meant that prices for such services as local and long-distance voice telephony would be driven relentlessly downward. Fifty-eight out of every hundred Finns now possess a mobile phone subscription, among the highest rate in the world. This means, unfortunately, that organic domestic growth would be unlikely to generate growth in profits. To boot, although Sonera is a large company relative to most in Finland, it is one of the smallest telecommunications firms on a global basis, a disadvantage in any business in which scale of operations gives advantage.

Among the company's communications to analysts, investors, employees, and their government stakeholders is a phrase intended to signal the firm's movement to services, and away from minutes-based businesses: "Make things click." This phrase signals management's commitment to pursuing businesses fundamentally different from its traditional line of business by focusing on two new revenue model ratios: revenue per click and revenue per transaction. The company has, for instance, developed an entire line of products that allow secure transactions to be made on a mobile phone, under the name SmartTrust. It is also a pioneer in the development of a mobile Internet portal (Zed) that is providing access to a wide-ranging set of services based on Internet access to mobile handsets. Sonera's performance since going public has been strong, with its mobile communications business experiencing 32 percent growth in revenues from 1997 to 1998.

The reason key ratios are such a powerful device for directing entrepreneurial thinking is that they help align the efforts of everyone in the company around a common set of measures. Describing and consistently using these ratios makes abstract statements about strategy more concrete for people and helps focus their energies. Kept simple and meaningful, key ratios can be crucial.

One habitual entrepreneur we study uses the key ratio idea aggressively. He starts businesses and hires managers to run them, in effect operating at the center of web of somewhat related, but independent businesses. Before handing over a business, he'll ask a new manager to create a simple numerical model of the particular operation and to present these models to other managers. His guiding principle is that the model should be used to help the manager achieve a *ten-× target*, meaning, a contribution of 10 percent growth in profits and 10 percent better profitability for the manager's business compared with last year (if an ongoing business). If it is a new business, the ten-× target would be a 10 percent performance improvement over the manager's average business. Asking managers to boil down the business challenge to a few key ratios makes their challenges in achieving the ten-× goal more realistic. Setting key ratios in this concrete, realistic way allows our entrepreneur to operate many businesses (at last count, he had more than thirty in his portfolio) with a high level of assurance that the critical issues will be addressed without his having to micromanage people.

We saw a similar focus on a few key ratios in the team working to create Lucent (chapter 2). By doing insightful benchmarking and deeply understanding what excellent performance would be, the team defined and executed credible plans to transform the company into a high-performance player in the global telecommunications equipment market. The basic idea is that once you as a manager have thought through the essential elements that will drive the performance of your business model, you can handle enormous complexity without getting sidetracked. You can also communicate more effectively to others.

After you have articulated some potentially attractive opportunities by using the techniques presented in chapters 3 through 5, your challenge now is identifying the new ratios that will drive your competitiveness. The new ratios are not accomplished without creating new competences to build their competitiveness. We turn now to the topic of creating such new competences.

Applying Key Ratio Analysis to Remodel a Business

Let's illustrate how a manager transformed his business by first determining what the most important key ratios were, then creating the organizational competences to do better on these ratios than the competition did. The example is of one of our more prosaic engagements—not a high-flying Internet start-up or a glitzy technology-based venture, but an industrial distribution business. The company's primary business was distributing industrial equipment parts and supplies (such as switch boxes) for contractors and small manufacturers. The manager of this business shared our belief (see chapter 4) that with an entrepreneurial mindset, even businesses that others might dismiss as a gritty, low-margin loser could become formidable, and profitable, competitors. He asked us in to take a look at the operation and offer some thoughts on how it could be improved.

We began by trying to get a sense of where the company stood. Distribution businesses in general have a well-known set of key ratios, so we started with these. (There is absolutely nothing wrong with using current key ratios to begin your analysis. For starters, you can get analysts' reports on your company or industry and look at the numbers they use to evaluate and project future performance.) We then elaborated on these basic numbers by adding two ratios that we believed might reflect the outcome of a successful strategy for change. These were the percentage of customers who made the firm their first choice and the employee satisfaction index, which we thought would reflect how well employees were being managed and which would in turn influence customer satisfaction and loyalty.

Next, using the firm's records and publicly available information (such as annual reports; public bid documents, including trade records; and information we gleaned from customers he had in common with his competitors), we collected data on how the business was doing relative to the two competitors we believed to represent the most significant opposition. We looked at our client's numbers for the year immediately preceding the start of the project. Where appropriate, we averaged by month. The results of this analysis are presented in table 6-1.

Although this might seem like an exercise in the obvious, the company had never before looked at its operations in this way. The competitive comparison revealed some chilling gaps in our client's performance, relative to the capabilities of its key competitors. Our client's competitive position, in other words, showed some major weaknesses.

If this seems familiar, don't despair. Competitive weaknesses can lead you to discover new opportunities, which emerge as you learn to overcome weaknesses through the creation of new combinations of skills, assets, and systems—or competences. New competences can generate entrepreneurial profits in two ways. First, if you can deliver what customers already want and expect (basic attributes) but do so at a lower cost than your competitors do, you can generate better margins than the competition's, even without price premiums. Second, if you deliver more positive and/or fewer negative attributes than your competitors do, you can get premium prices or better payment terms.

The first conclusion we drew from our analysis was that the company had some serious catching up to do with respect to customers' perceptions. This was signaled by our client's poor performance on the preferred-choice customer indicator, or the percentage of customers that regarded the relevant firm as their vendor of first choice (table 6-1).

Further analysis showed that our client did very well with those customer segments who simultaneously had a high need for on-time deliveries and staffed a large inventory-management operation. Years of focus by our client on on-time delivery had resulted in relatively good performance in this area.

For another segment, however, the firm's relatively higher error rates were enraging, so much so that customers in this segment bought from the firm only when they had exhausted all other options. For this segment, packing errors created enormous problems at the receipt link in their consumption chain. They tended to be contractors without the budget to keep a lot of inventory around and without the staff to handle incorrect shipments. For them, the process of

TABLE 6-1

KEY RATIO ANALYSIS FOR AN INDUSTRIAL DISTRIBUTION BUSINESS

Ratio	Client's Performance	Competitors' Performance
Annual sales growth	6%	6%
Margins	8%	9%
Percent "preferred choice" customers	70%	90%
Inventory turns	8×	9×
Fixed-asset turns	3×	3×
Days receivables	85 days	70 days
Deliveries within expected time frame	95%	90%
Error rates	3.5%	1.5%
Employee satisfaction index	75	Unknown
Debt-to-equity ratio	1.25	1.20

identifying errors, correcting the paperwork, and returning incorrect items was enormously costly—to the point that some would keep the incorrect items rather than go through the hassle of returning them. But, having been through this deeply dissatisfying experience, they tended to use our client only as a last resort.[4]

Similar performance gaps existed in the ratios that tapped operating effectiveness. We found that the top competitors were turning inventory faster, getting paid more quickly, using less debt to finance operations, and capturing slightly higher margins than our clients were. These gaps suggested a need to think through what new competences might be needed (1) to bring our client's competitive profile up to industry standard and (2) to create new areas of distinctiveness.

The manager started by setting up an internal task force to identify what could be done about the customer preferred choice percentage. He organized a mix of sales, delivery, marketing, and telephone service people to complete a consumption chain analysis for key customer segments. His reasoning was that if the company could improve repeat sales, it could maximize the returns it would receive as a result of addressing the newly identified operational problems and make the most of the investments made to create those customer relationships in the first place. Simultaneously, a different task group, consisting of inventory management, MIS, and back-office people, was assigned to work on ways to improve performance on other ratios that reflected asset utilization and operating effectiveness.

The manager charged his groups with, at minimum, coming up with ways to meet industry benchmarks. Ideally, he suggested, they should be looking for major opportunities to capture profits by reconfiguring the competences of the firm. If, for instance, they could come up with a way to do much better than the industry with respect to the time needed to collect receivables, the competences put in place to achieve this could be a significant source of profit growth. By collecting more, faster, without increasing costs, the firm could increase profits without increasing investment. The result is a productivity enhancement, which could contribute to superior competitive performance.

Most of the problems the groups identified derived from the way the firm had historically organized its functions. As we suggested in chapter 5, when the primary barrier between your competitive position today and an attractive direction tomorrow has to do with an internal barrier, you are in control of the most important limitations to your future success. Among other things, the groups deployed the five-*whys* exercise discussed in chapter 5. This analysis yielded a wealth of detail about where the company was going wrong. By the time (a few weeks later) that the task forces turned in their final reports, we had learned a lot about how deficient the company's competences were.

Our client's company was using an unwieldy twenty-year-old system to manage inventory and deliveries. The programs were old and hard to maintain. To feed the system, someone had developed a set of arcane commodity codes for items. The codes were nonintuitive and lengthy. The process of getting customer orders in and generating picking and packing instructions was largely paper-based and depended on special printers that pumped out multiple carbon copies of orders. By the time the last copy had been printed (the one used by the stock pickers), it was smudged and difficult to read. Not only that, but the organization of the warehouse had changed little since the computer was installed. It had not kept pace with changing customer demand patterns, which made it difficult for stock pickers to locate new items. Even worse, the whole invoicing and payment system depended on paper copies and manual reconciliation, as this operation had never been integrated with the stocking system.

The result of all this was that customers found it hard to order what they needed and often ordered incorrectly. The pickers in the warehouse found it hard to get the right stuff off the shelves. The packers, similarly, found it difficult to match up the items picked with original orders and delivery instructions. Finally, the whole invoicing system was so complicated that customers were perennially late in paying the company because (among other problems) they couldn't figure out why they owed what they owed!

All the preceding situations translated into a barrage of negative attributes throughout the consumption chain. A substantial percentage of orders and invoices were contested. Customers received deliveries that reflected incorrect orders on their part or orders that were packed incorrectly. In these cases, unwanted items had to be repacked and shipped back, items had to be reordered and resent, and everybody's nerves became frayed in the process. This put the company at a competitive disadvantage, even relative to slower-delivering competitors. As one customer observed with respect to the competition, "Well, they miss more delivery dates than you do, but if they are going to be late they call and tell me so that I can reorder from somewhere else, and when it finally does come in, it's right."

What we discovered in our analysis is not unusual at all, particularly for operations that are not deemed to be strategically important. Want to see if your company has similar problems? See if you can get three employees, selected at random, to explain what each item on a typical invoice means. The results can be shocking.

At first, the task force groups recommended tackling the problems piecemeal, by adding staff in quality control and inspection, for instance.[5] This didn't satisfy our client, who didn't believe that treating only a part of the problem would deliver the kinds of financial returns he was looking for. He elected instead to begin a process of reconfiguring the competences of the firm. As we will show, this can generate opportunities every bit as attractive as those emerging from the reconfiguration of markets and segments (discussed in chapters 4 and 5).

Using the two new key ratios, the customer first-choice percentage and the employee satisfaction index, to explain his reasoning to his people, he showed how the numbers were interrelated. If operations could be improved to lower error rates, returns should drop. This in turn would reduce receivables and allow better control—and therefore, faster turnover—of inventories, which would in turn improve asset utilization. Better performance on packing should help the repeat purchasing process, which in turn should allow greater volumes and better margins on the same asset base.

Through his task forces, the manager gained a deeper understanding of how the customers did business and how his company could better support them. What gradually emerged was a vision of his company as a supplier not only of goods but of information that his customers could use to better manage their operations. They could compare the likely need for parts in the future, based on how different kinds of parts moved through the system, for instance. Thus, a new building development that might generate demand for insulating material and piping early in construction would predictably generate demand for switch boxes and fixtures later on. This allowed customers to get a better handle on their work-in-process expenses and better anticipate storage and stocking needs. The company would become essential business partners rather than suppliers and would be part of the system through which these customers competed.

Borrowing a page from the just-in-time movement, in which companies cut down on inventory costs by obtaining materials close in time to when they will be used, our client found that he could generate considerable economies for customers by promising to deliver goods on an as-needed basis in the amounts needed for a particular job. This was a major advance over prevailing practice, in which customers ordered lots of extra supplies and let them sit around until needed to avoid being caught short. By capturing data on customer use, the company could be more proactive—reminding customers when they had forgotten something they usually ordered, for instance.

To make this vision concrete, the firm began to build what (at the time) was a highly innovative electronic data interchange ordering system based on the Internet. The system replaced cumbersome inventory codes with simple descriptions and pictures. Customers could order on-line without filling out a single form on paper. Moreover, customers could call up past orders, sorted in a number of ways (by similar items, by time of year, by nature of project), so that all they had to do was make minor adjustments and submit the order as new. In the warehouse, a reorganized stocking system utilized electronic identification tags to help employees find items, pack them, and ship them, significantly reducing the error rate.

Obviously, such a massive reconfiguration of competences wasn't easy or inexpensive. There was a price in terms of heavy investment in systems development and information technology (IT) equipment and in personnel retraining. Initially, this investment was expected to reduce fixed-asset turns and require a higher debt-to-equity ratio. Being realistic about the investments that will be required to upgrade competences is as much a part of the entrepreneurial discipline as any other part of the process.

To clarify the desired performance targets for the new system, the groups began to develop the performance profile depicted in table 6-2. As you can see, they planned to do much better than the competition in some areas but were realistic about the investment required to do so, as shown in the increased leverage of the company.

ASSESSING AND DEVELOPING COMPETENCES

The work done at the industrial distribution firm just discussed illustrates what a disciplined approach to managing competences can do for a company. If a company's competences don't clearly influence performance on one or more key ratios, we ask why the company is spending money to sustain them. In addressing this question, a firm

TABLE 6-2

REVITALIZING AN INDUSTRIAL DISTRIBUTION BUSINESS

Ratio	Current Performance	Competitors' Performance	Target Performance
Annual sales growth	6%	6%	6%
Margin	8%	9%	9%
Percent "preferred choice" customers	70%	90%	95%
Inventory turns	8×	9×	9×
Fixed-asset turns	3×	3×	2.8×
Days receivables	85 days	70 days	65 days
Deliveries within expected time frame	95%	90%	99%
Error rates	3.5%	1.5%	0.50%
Employee satisfaction index	75	Unknown	90
Debt-to-equity ratio	1.25	1.20	1.30

can sharply curtail the number of activities people may claim to be core competences and focus their attention on the competences that really count. To determine the relative value of various competences to the firm, it is useful to divide them into three categories: mandatory, distinctive, and latent.

Mandatory competences give you competitive parity. Creating or acquiring the competences that allow your company to meet industry (or major competitor) performance on key ratios is not optional if you are to sustain your competitive position. Activities that allow you to deliver nonnegotiable attributes and avoid dissatisfying ones seldom convey a significant advantage. Not having them, however, can put you at a major disadvantage.

Distinctive competences give you comparative advantage. These are the activities that lead to differentiating attributes. They allow a firm to deliver performance that positively differentiates it from competitors on a key ratio. This difference may be in value to the customer, in which case the company can generate better margins over alternative offerings by getting premium prices, or in efficiency, in which case the company can generate better margins by operating more productively.[6]

Latent competences are possible activities through which your company could offer future differentiating or nonnegotiable attributes. Major sources of future competitive advantage typically emerge from the mobilization of latent competences.[7] DuPont's ability to produce Gore-Tex, for instance, grew out of its existing ability to manufacture Teflon. In consumer applications, Gore-Tex eventually became wildly successful in ways that were unforeseen at the time of its invention, including by DuPont, who licensed it to W. L. Gore!

If you cannot at least match competitive benchmarks, you will not be able to match competitors' prices or other positive attributes for very long and success in the marketplace will not be attainable, or at least sustainable. Furthermore, if you can't outperform competitors on at least one industry benchmark, you probably cannot deliver the kind of profits needed to attract prime investors in your competition for capital.

Let's get into the issue of how competence development created distinctiveness by considering the evolution of GE Financial Services, introduced earlier.

The Building Blocks of Distinctive Competences

GEFS (GE Financial Services), today a financial powerhouse, had humble beginnings as the credit department of GE (General Electric) Appliances, managing installment loans for customers who bought GE appliances on credit. The main drivers of profitability in this business are the ability to evaluate potential customers' creditworthiness, to handle huge numbers of transaction records efficiently and flawlessly, to manage cash flows with skill, and, of course, to collect on defaulted payments. Among the many competences the company developed, the most fascinating to us was its competence in handling delinquent accounts. At one stage, the GEFS bad-debts-to-book ratio—a critical benchmark for industry profitability—had dropped as much as 30 percent below industry norms.

In its early days, the financial services industry handled delinquent accounts by means of very simple processing systems that consisted largely of a roomful of people shuffling piles of delinquent bills and making telephone calls. Staff were recruited on very broad criteria and were trained by being given a routine set of questions to read to delinquent customers over the phone. The effectiveness of the process, as might be anticipated, was limited. At this time GEFS met the industry benchmarks for collection efficiency.

Consider the difference once GEFS began to focus on creating significant competences in the handling of delinquent accounts.[8] It began by the company's attempting to understand a different sort of consumption chain, namely, what might influence a potential delinquent to pay his or her debt rather than go into default. The company initiated some serious research into the behavior of delinquents and developed an interesting profile. The research showed that for a short time after a payment has been missed for the first time (about ten days), the propensity to repay is much greater; delinquents feel guilty and uncomfortable about their unpaid bill. As time goes on, however, these feelings of guilt diminish rapidly and so, too, does the ease with which collection can be made. This insight provided GEFS with a focal point for competence development.

Today, potential delinquent payments are identified by an electronic tracking system. Once a potential delinquent is identified, an automatic dialing system is activated and places a call to the customer every twenty minutes. When a real voice answers the phone, the call is immediately switched to a carefully selected and highly trained GEFS representative. Taking cues from a comprehensive on-line record of all the information GEFS has about the customer, the representative uses her training to compose a highly personalized conversation with the delinquent. (Most representatives are women, who generally tend to be less confrontational than men are in this uncomfortable situation.). In particular, she has been carefully selected for her skill at very nicely and politely but equally firmly persuading delinquents to pay their bills.[9] In addition, GEFS has developed automatic systems to eliminate paper handling and to keep her from wasting her time on anything other than using this skill. Thus, the system brings up records as appropriate and saves the information in a central file without requiring the representative to handle the forms manually. Should her approach not succeed, the debt can be referred to the collections department for further action. GEFS thus developed a distinctive competence—a combination of delinquency-handling skills, assets, and systems that for many years allowed it to incur a cost of bad debt on installment loans that was far below the industry average for durable goods loans.

The two examples we have discussed so far in this chapter illustrate the building blocks of distinctive competence. The first building block is an entrepreneurial insight that is not widely shared. In the case of GEFS, it was early insight into the behavior of delinquent customers. For the industrial distribution company, it was insight into how the company could help its customers compete.

The second building block is determining the linkage between the entrepreneurial insight and the key ratios that fuel performance. For GEFS, the critical linkage was time—if potential delinquents could be reached during the time at which they felt most uncomfortable with their failure to pay, the company would have to spend less money and would likely collect more than if it allowed these customers to become hard-core delinquents. The critical linkage of the distribution company had to do with a different kind of time. The company developed ways for its customers to get on with their businesses without spending time on obtaining routine supplies. By helping the customers compete, the business improved customers' propensity to repurchase.

The third building block is the creation of a combination of skills, assets, and systems that allow the company to achieve a distinctive level of performance with respect to the identified linkage. Thus, GEFS's investment in building the persuasion skills of its delinquency handlers by careful selection and training can be connected directly to its achievement of better collection results, and its investment in assets and systems to leverage the persuasive skills of its staff

achieved maximum leverage. For the industrial distributor, the information intensity and responsiveness of the new system directly
affected customer satisfaction and propensity to repurchase. Further,
in dismantling its old system, the distributor was able to leverage
employee skills that had been underutilized—their ability to relate to
and creatively serve their customers.

The Insight behind the Competence

We have spent a lot of time emphasizing entrepreneurial insight as
the foundation for building distinctive competences. The reason is
that in order to capture above-average returns, the company needs to
create a competitive position that competitors will find difficult to
attack. Keeping your entrepreneurial insights to yourself is key here.
Most reasonably competent competitors can match whatever you do
in terms of benchmark processes or technologies, but without the
entrepreneurial insight behind the competence and without the deep
familiarity that comes from experience, competitors can only grope
their way toward your competitive position.[10]

A dilemma, however, is that to capture a legitimate position in
the capital markets, you must explain your strategy to analysts and
investors in a way that is compelling and believable. This forces you
to share critical elements of how you plan to compete. Understanding the key ratio idea can help you to tell a convincing story without
necessarily giving up critical insight.

Take GEFS as an example. It would be easy for GEFS to show
potential investors how superior performance in handling delinquent
accounts can generate better returns without also showing them
exactly how GEFS does this. Indeed, what would competitors have
seen if they had spied on GEFS? They would certainly have seen
things that differed from industry practice—selection and training
programs, use of automatic and preprogrammed telephone systems,
extensive automation, and the like. What they would not have seen is
the entrepreneurial insight into how emotions affect the customer's
propensity to pay. Even if they put the same training program and
computer systems in place, these competitors would not be privy to
one crucial element—the insight that makes it all meaningful.[11]

SETTING THE STAGE FOR COMPETENCE CREATION

With the preceding examples as references, you can now think about applying the concepts of key ratio analysis and competence creation to your business. The first task is to identify the seven to ten benchmark ratios that you believe to be behind profit growth in a business like yours. Begin your research by reading reports evaluating your industry. Investment bankers, commercial bankers, and industry analysts and associations can provide a wealth of ideas. An incredible array of new industry and competitive information is also being loaded on the World Wide Web. Industry-specific sites, such as e-Steel, investment sites such as those run by E*Trade, and information-oriented sites such as Hoovers.com all offer inexpensive sources of rich information. Another inexpensive source of information can be your firm's investment adviser or financial officer. Even if this person doesn't have the information you need, she can often point you in the direction of useful resources.

You can also get some good ideas by scanning the business sections of libraries and bookstores. Several well-regarded business books can provide a starting point for thinking through how to increase profitability.[12] If your business is diversified, you will want to identify key ratios for each major product line.

While you are gathering information on your industry (or your segment of it), you will start to learn about your standing in relation to competitors on each of the benchmark measures. The next step is putting these numbers together in a comparison table similar to table 6-1. Comparisons can often be found with a little persistence. Data has often been collected by commercial bankers and investment analysts to assess the relative performance of competitors. The profits of the bankers and the very survival of investment analysts depend on their ability to do at least as well as their competitors in identifying and interpreting this information. Why not take advantage of the wisdom of an entire industry focused on understanding the basic drivers of competitive effectiveness? Data may also be also available in publications like *Value Line*, in on-line data services like Compustat, and through industry associations.[13]

In countries where information sources are less well developed than those in the United States, key industry parameters are still used by investment bankers and particularly by commercial bankers who specialize in loans to the particular industry, because loan officers use such data to make loan and financing decisions. Benchmarking against private companies can provide a bit more of a challenge, as they are not required to report large amounts of data. You may need more extensive intelligence gathering to make estimates of these competitors' performance.[14] For instance, you might rely on inferences based on responses to bids, or on information from key customers or knowledgeable industry experts.

Once your benchmarks are in hand, your next step is to understand how each group within your company influences performance on the key ratios, which in turn affects the profitability of your business model. People can compete much more effectively if they see enough of the big picture to understand their role in profit growth. Linking functional activities to competitive benchmarks is crucial. Unless all the members of the firm know what connects their day-to-day actions with the firm's performance factors, how can they possibly know how best to contribute to profitability?[15]

More often than you might expect, the linkages are only vaguely understood. Consider telling inside salespeople that you want to increase market share. They may agree, even enthusiastically, but if they don't know how what they do influences market share, they cannot help improve it. On the other hand, if they know that when a customer calls, they can increase market share by getting the customer to add two lines of items to the original order, they will now know what to do to increase share. This is why the server at McDonald's asks, "Would you also like fries? A soda?" and why the telephone salesperson at Lands' End might suggest that the belt on page 23 of the catalog would look great with the shorts you just ordered.

You are now ready to begin addressing the gaps (whether positive or negative) between your performance and that of your competitors. Adverse gaps represent opportunities for competence development. The critical question becomes one of generating some kind of insight around which you could build a distinctive competitive position.

You may already have these insights in your opportunity register. Scan it for indicators that would suggest you have a significant opportunity to do better on a particular benchmark. Has a competitor carved out a customer segment whose specific needs are being much better served than they would be by your firm? Has some trend that you have not acted on materialized in such a way that it puts you at a disadvantage? Are you pushing up against some sort of barrier, like those described in chapter 5, that might get in the way of meeting benchmarks? Has a change in the marketplace created new needs? If your opportunity register doesn't yield insights that you believe to be actionable, you may need to revisit the attribute mapping and consumption chain analyses discussed in earlier chapters, this time focusing on how your interactions with customers at each link in the chain help or hinder your performance on ratios you consider to be critical.

With your new insight, you can take specific steps to create new competences. The more specific you can be about the outcome and the linkages, the easier it will be for your people to execute your ideas.

SUMMARY OF ACTION STEPS

The action steps that follow are meant to get you started on the concepts and processes discussed in the chapter. Feel free to elaborate in a way that works for your company.

STEP 1: Create a short list of the seven to ten key ratios associated with growth and profitability for your business model. If you have multiple businesses with different business models, you will need a different set of ratios for each of them.

STEP 2: Collect data on your performance on each of these key ratios as well as on competitors' performance and put together a table similar to table 6-1. Identify gaps, both positive and negative.

STEP 3: Whenever you are below competitive parity on one or more key ratios, repeat the five-*whys* exercise in chapter 5 to begin to understand why. Involve people with exposure to the diverse functions of your firm, so that they can help you make the necessary linkages among different operations. Document your findings.

STEP 4: If none of your key ratios shows that you have a distinctive competence, you at least have an opportunity to build new competences. Scan the opportunity register, repeat the consumption chain and attribute mapping activities described in chapters 2 and 3, or do both, with the objective of uncovering insights that might form the basis of a new, distinctive competence.

STEP 5: Building on these insights, start first to consider what you can do to attain competitive parity on most of the important ratios and second to create distinctiveness relative to competitors on at least one ratio.

STEP 6: The best ideas should be entered into the opportunity register, especially if they offer the potential for major improvements in productivity.

CHAPTER 7

SELECTING YOUR

COMPETITIVE

TERRAIN

UP TO THIS CHAPTER, WE HAVE DISCUSSED HOW TO IDENTIFY new opportunities: opportunities for redesigning products and services, redifferentiating for customers, resegmenting existing markets, restructuring markets, and creating world-class new competences. By now, with luck, you have a well-stocked opportunity register. That's the good news. The bad news is that no matter how attractive the ideas look now, the chances are that you can't successfully pursue every opportunity that you have come up with. In fact, you will probably fail if you try to pursue too many. Your team will become bogged down. Furthermore, if you try to do too many new things, you risk not capitalizing on the benefits of all the competences you already have in place.[1]

At this point, another major component of an entrepreneurial mindset kicks in—unrelenting focus. Entrepreneurs focus in two ways. First, they select only arenas from the competitive terrain that are attractive; then, they pursue only opportunities in the selected arenas that allow them to strengthen their position. Focus means making trade-offs, including tough choices to abandon or at least defer many possibilities, sometimes even to the point of dropping things that have historically been important to you. Thus, you will look at the challenge of achieving focus from two perspectives. First, you'll target attractive arenas in the competitive terrain, selecting those business arenas to compete in that represent your best chances for profitable growth.[2] Then you will decide on the priority of the opportunities in each of your selected arenas. Start by charting the current terrain; then use that as a basis for selecting your future arenas.

CHARTING YOUR COMPETITIVE TERRAIN

In chapter 6, we suggested that achieving an unbiased, comparative understanding of your competitive position through the use of key ratios can help frame your challenge to develop new competences and get people to focus on common goals. We're now going to take this line of thought a level deeper. When looking at opportunities, we will consider both opportunities to do new things and opportunities to stop doing old things.

As your company undergoes an entrepreneurial transformation, not all the customers you serve today, the products or services you sell today, the distribution channels you use today, or the geographical areas in which you operate today are going to fit with the new business domains you are creating. Identifying opportunities to stop pouring resources into a particular activity is every bit as important as coming up with ideas for growth, though firms often pay less attention to such pruning. Every budget line, skilled person, good technologist, or expert sales or service person dedicated to the pursuit of a business arena without a good chance at profitable growth is a resource going to waste.

The best place to start is to develop simple stratification maps, which highlight the contributions of your business activities to your current performance. Stratification maps analyze in a straightforward yet powerful way the contribution that each component of your business is making to current performance. The most attractive of these components will be selected as your springboard to the future; the least attractive are the candidates for pruning.

Stratifying Your Current Position

First stratify, or rank order, your current sources of revenue. We will illustrate stratification mapping by stratifying revenues from the perspective of a manager in charge of a portfolio of businesses. Bear in mind, however, that the relevant arena for you might not be a business—it might be products, customer segments, geographical areas, branches, distributors or brokers (in a distribution-intensive business), or services. Start with whatever category you deem most important; you can always go back and do another.

Like the example below, collect data on how much revenue each business arena generated last year. You can then create a revenue stratification map, which involves completing the following steps:

1. Rank each business arena according to its revenues, in descending order (column 2).

2. Calculate the cumulative revenues (column 3).

3. Calculate the cumulative percentage revenue (column 4).

4. Assign the businesses that deliver the first 65 percent of cumulative revenues to the category *aces*.

5. Assign the businesses that deliver between 65 and 85 percent of cumulative revenues to the category *jacks*.

6. Assign the businesses that deliver between 85 and 100 percent of cumulative revenues to the category *deuces*.

You should end up with a table that looks something like table 7-1, which maps the annual revenues for a hypothetical company. The names of the categories are derived from the logic of card games. In virtually all card games, the ace is the most valuable card and allows the player holding it the greatest leeway to gain points. The jack is also valuable, a high-value card but at the top of the medium-value range. Players holding jacks have high potential to gain points, but only under the right circumstances. Low plain number cards, such as a deuce, are of marginal value in a card game, except under unusual circumstances.

TABLE 7-1

SIMPLE EXAMPLE OF REVENUE STRATIFICATION

Business	Revenue ($000s)	Cumulative Revenue ($000s)	Cumulative Percentage of Revenue	Category
1	100	100	50	Ace
2	55	155	78	Jack
3	30	185	92	Deuce
4	10	195	98	Deuce
5	5	200	100	Deuce

In selecting names to represent the value of the business arenas, we therefore used the ace, jack, and deuce analogy to make it easy to remember. Businesses that are aces give you high potential and leeway for action. Jacks are good businesses, but need to be carefully managed to have their potential brought out. Deuces can be useful, but often more for maneuvering and trading than being played on their own account.

The pattern shown in this simplified example is quite typical—most revenue comes from just a few products. Often, unfortunately, big revenue generators are not necessarily the biggest contributors to profits.[3] To get a sense of how profitable each product line is, do a second analysis, stratifying this time by profit, or (in the case of high-fixed-cost businesses) amount of contribution to profit. To take into account the fact that profits can be negative you may need to make adjustments, as we show below. The following steps are necessary to create a contribution stratification map (as shown in table 7-2):

1. Rank each business according to its contribution to profit, in descending order (column 2). If you have losses, add the largest loss to each contribution number to obtain the "adjusted contribution." Loss-making businesses should be ranked below all the profitable businesses, with the largest loss coming last.

TABLE 7-2

SIMPLE EXAMPLE OF CONTRIBUTION STRATIFICATION

1 Business	2 Contribution ($000s) to Profit	3 Adjusted Contribution ($000s)	4 Cumulative Adjusted Contribution ($000s)	5 Cumulative Percentage of Contribution	6 Category
2	25	25 + 8 = 33	33	33 ÷ 79 = 42%	Lucrative contributor
1	18	18 + 8 = 26	33 + 26 = 59	59 ÷ 79 = 75%	Productive contributor
4	5	5 + 8 = 13	59 + 13 = 72	72 ÷ 79 = 91%	Marginal contributor
5*	–1*	–1 + 8 = 7*	72 + 7 = 79	79 ÷ 79 = 100%	Marginal* contributor
3*	–8*	–8 + 8 = 0*	79 + 0 = 79	79 ÷ 79 = 100%	Marginal* contributor

*Businesses registering losses.

2. Flag with an asterisk all businesses that are making losses so that you remember that these businesses generate losses.

    Calculate the adjusted contribution (column 3). Adjust each contribution in column 2 by adding the largest loss. In the example, the largest loss is 8, so we add 8 to all the profits in column 3.

3. Calculate the cumulative adjusted profit contribution (column 4).

4. Calculate the cumulative adjusted percentage profit contribution (column 5).

5. Assign the businesses that deliver the first 65 percent of cumulative contribution to the category "lucrative contributor."

6. Assign the businesses that deliver between 65 and 85 percent of cumulative contribution to the category "productive contributor."

7. Assign the businesses that deliver between 85 and 100 percent of cumulative contribution to the category "marginal contributor."

If you do not have contribution figures, you can either make some educated guesses (making sure to note that the numbers are based on assumptions) or proceed with the second best alternative, which is to use only your revenue stratification map.

Finally, cross-map the revenue and contribution categories to produce a chart similar to figure 7-1. You can see at a glance that although business 2 generates a lot less revenue than business 1, it is actually making more of a contribution to the company than business 1, which contributes proportionately less profit from a larger revenue base. Obvious questions this situation suggests are whether something should be done to business 1 to enhance its profitability or whether resources ought to be put into growing business 2.

Businesses 3 and 5, on the other hand, are both low-revenue money losers. A lot depends on how long these businesses have been in this category—if they are start-ups, then they may need time to get rolling. If they have been around for a while, however, it may be time to take a good, hard look at why the firm is still supporting them.

If you can get the information, create similar maps for your businesses dating from two or three years ago. Then, in addition to knowing where you are now, you'll be able to see how you got there and to make some guesses at future trends. Let's say, for instance, that business 1 was formerly in a lucrative position but has slipped to

FIGURE 7-1

STRATIFICATION MAP: REVENUE VERSUS CONTRIBUTION

	Lucrative Contributor to Profits	Productive Contributor to Profits	Marginal Contributor to Profits
Ace		Business 1	
Jack	Business 2		
Deuce			Business 3* Business 4 Business 5*

*Businesses registering losses.

being only productive. For such a product, you need to consider whether this represents a short-term problem that might be corrected by your identifying new opportunities, or a long-term trend indicating that it may be time to phase the business out or even sell it off.

Interpreting Winners and Losers

A stratification map gives you a concise, relatively unambiguous portrayal of your business's high points and low points. Let's consider each of the cells in the map, using the categories in figure 7-2 to structure the discussion. We repeat that you may want to break out your data differently. You might be better off breaking it out by customer sets, by products, by geographic regions, or even by branch or by distributor, depending on what operation you are managing.

Lucrative Aces   Your company's lucrative aces are the cornerstone businesses of today. They are the force behind most of your profitability, but are likely to be highly attractive to your competition, and therefore vulnerable to all the ills of competitive rivalry, such as price erosion. It is also highly likely that such arenas of your business are building up what we call *slack*—excess resources that may be used to fund growth.[4]

Some slack is essential; it represents resources that people can draw on to experiment and try new things. Too much, however—especially if it is an indication of inefficient processes or carelessness with respect to expenses—and the business may be wasting precious resources that could be used to fund the pursuit of new opportunities.

FIGURE 7-2

CATEGORIES IN THE STRATIFICATION MAP

	Lucrative	Productive	Marginal
Aces	Lucrative aces	Productive aces	Marginal aces
Jacks	Lucrative jacks	Productive jacks	Marginal jacks
Deuces	Lucrative deuces	Productive deuces	Marginal deuces

If those managing the businesses in this category get too complacent, they can end up in a high-cost position when competition catches up. The root cause is the tendency to continue investing in assets at the same rate you did when the business was growing rapidly, even when underlying business conditions have led to slower growth. A quick check on this is to look at the ratio of sales and general administrative expenses (SGA) to sales or to profits over time. If SGA is growing more rapidly than revenues or profits, then clearly you may have a problem emerging.

Productive Aces   Productive aces deliver a lot of revenue, but don't do as much for profits. It is often a dangerous category for an established firm, because the managers of productive aces typically command influence in the company disproportionately to the profits they deliver. By continuing to support productive aces, you can starve smaller, more profitable enterprises that need the resources for growth.

Take a look at trends. If this product category was formerly a substantial profit generator, what's going on now? Has it come under margin pressure? Suffered at the hands of a new technology or substitute product? Gotten sloppy about asset utilization? Whatever the cause, there is an urgent need to make some decisions with respect to this category. This might be the time to scale back and raise prices or reconsider objectives for growth. Selling it off while it still looks attractive is an option as well.

The cases in which productive aces may not be bad news is in network-oriented industries. Value in such industries (such as software, communications systems, network systems, and systems built from common components) is largely a function of how many other people have adopted the product or system. Thus, the value that I place on my fax machine or word processing package increases to the extent that many other people are using the same fax technology or the same (compatible) word processing software. In such cases, a company's strategic objective is to at least share the standard and, at best, to dominate it, as Intel does in the market for microprocessors. Often, a company will give up early profitability to capture and sustain a standard or to control the development of a network.[5] In this case, the goals should be to supplant current products with far more profitable next-generation products and attain high market share positions.

Marginal Aces This category may represent once-great arenas with an eroded competitive position or, in the case of a network, may represent a bid by an early mover to capture a standard or gain the dominant position. For non-network businesses, serious strategic pruning may be warranted. Marginal aces can easily become large-scale distractions, sucking up time, resources, and talent in a futile defense of volume. If someone can't come up with a compelling reason to continue the pursuit of this line, the best course of action may be to kill it, restructure it, sell it, or harvest it by raising prices. However, because revenues from such businesses are often substantial, eliminating the business or restructuring may require a wrenching strategic decision. The problems that established organizations have in pursuing such dramatic changes have been well documented in the academic literature. Box 7-1 presents the main conclusions from the research on organizational inertia and change.

In rapidly changing competitive environments, such decisions need to be made all the time. Consider the difficult decision by Texas Instruments (TI) to sell what had been its core business: products and services for the military defense market. This business had driven much of TI's success over the years and had been home to many of its most senior executives, including former chief executive officer, Jerry Junkins. Upon Junkins's sudden and untimely death in 1996, his successor, Thomas Engibous, completely refocused the company on businesses related to digital signal processing (DSP). In 1997, TI sold its notebook computer business to Acer, its defense electronics business to Raytheon, and its enterprise applications business to Sterling. In 1998, the company sold the memory chip business to Micron technology and began to make acquisitions in DSP-oriented companies such as Amati Communications. The resulting focused portfolio of businesses was seen by stock market analysts and other observers as having high potential, and TI's market capitalization has climbed steadily upward ever since.

BOX 7·1

THE PROBLEM OF ORGANIZATIONAL INERTIA: THEORETICAL PERSPECTIVES

The observation that established organizations find it hard to change the combinations of people, assets, and offerings they support has spawned voluminous academic (and practical) research. A critical question this literature seeks to address is, Why is it so hard to let go of the old in order to focus on the new?

One factor is routinization. People tend to repeat actions that have led to success. Actions associated with failure, on the other hand, tend to be eliminated. Because discovering bright future prospects requires experimentation, and thus entails possible failure, many people will be too risk-averse to try. A second factor that causes inertia in organizations relates to the tacit knowledge embedded in an organization's routine behaviors. Over time, operating procedures become embedded in a complex set of beliefs, values, and reinforcing processes, making them both hard to detect and difficult to disentangle. Moreover, it is difficult, at a strategic level, to analyze the inner workings of routines carried out at a local level.[a] Effective local learning, ironically, may make the problems invisible at a decision-making level.[b] The implications of all this are that adaptive processes tend to lag behind environmental challenges unless these processes are proactively managed. Further, adaptive processes tend to influence local conditions (for instance, incremental changes to a product or service) more readily than they provoke systemwide change, unless the organization goes into a crisis resulting from external shocks. Apple Computer, for instance, was propelled to make major strategic shifts in the late 1990s only because the company was struggling for its very survival. With luck and preparation, you can avoid having to change under the pressure of a major external jolt.[c]

Whether an organization is capable of changing at all is a question raised in a school of thought known as *population ecology*.

Scholars working in this tradition apply the ideas of natural selection that originated with Darwinian evolution to change in organizational populations. Although their point of view has softened in recent years, they originally viewed organizations as unable to alter their portfolios of activities to any meaningful extent.[d] Most firms, proponents argued, are predisposed to seek efficiency rather than undergo the high costs of generating variety in their portfolios through the pursuit of new business models. This is because investing in variety (as in pursuing multiple new opportunities) leads to erratic performance, increasing the probability that key stakeholders, such as investors and customers, will withdraw their support. Enough loss of support, and the firm can't survive.[e]

An alternative perspective is offered by *resource dependence* theorists, who see change as an essential tool for organizational adaptation, which they believe to be possible but also highly political. The role of a strategist is essentially to obtain resources through negotiation. In their view, firms are driven to respond to the external environment in ways that allow them to gain essential resources. They are thus highly constrained in the actions they may take and are continually engaged in political negotiations to acquire more resources. A seminal work in this tradition is *The External Control of Organizations*.[f] More so than in population ecology, resource dependence theory sees managers as capable of mounting responses to challenges from the environment and of trying to shape the context in which their firms do business by influencing those who own important resources.

Christensen argues that patterns of resource dependence stemming from past success can seriously hamper an organization's efforts to respond to those contingencies that will be critical for its future.[g] Burgelman relates a similar finding based on his study of the Intel Corporation. He reports that lower-level operating managers, when given the discretion and incentives to do so, made decisions that had a de facto exit effect on Intel's participation in DRAM technology, even though senior executives were still espousing the technology.[h] The negative consequences of exiting a business are also sometimes so formidable that even the recognition that one would be better off without a particular line of business is insufficient to provoke a change.[i]

At a human level, calling an end to an ongoing project or business is a difficult and often painful thing to do. It can lead to dysfunctional behavior. For instance, managers might persist in throwing good money after bad in a futile attempt to rescue a failing project. This is known as escalation of commitment.[j] McGrath has argued that looking at entrepreneurial ventures as experiments or options instead of as do-or-die business attempts can deliver lower-cost failures with greater learning potential. The powers-that-be in any organization must recognize that both creating and eliminating business models are essential. Those projects or programs that don't work out or that have come to the end of their productive existence need to be redirected. Otherwise, learning is stymied and effectiveness impaired.[k]

a. Nelson and Winter (1982); Miller (1993); March and Simon (1958); March (1991).

b. Levinthal and March (1993).

c. Venkataraman and Van de Ven (1993); Tushman and Romanelli (1985); Romanelli and Tushman (1994); D'Aveni and MacMillan (1990); Bowman (1980).

d. Haveman (1992).

e. Hannan and Freeman (1977); Aldrich (1979); Amburgey, Kelly, and Barnett (1993).

f. Pfeffer and Salancik (1978).

g. Christensen (1997).

h. Burgelman (1996); see also Grove (1996).

i. Harrigan (1981).

j. Staw, Sandelands, and Dutton (1981); Ross and Staw (1986); Ross and Staw (1993).

k. McGrath (1999); Sitkin (1992).

Hewlett-Packard has made similar decisions. Its management decided to divest the measurement devices that had made for one of its earliest success stories in favor of other businesses with greater growth potential, such as their e-service initiative.

Beware here of the argument that marginal aces help utilize fixed capacity or absorb fixed costs or generate volume that is useful in other ways. This can sometimes be the case, but if you have identified many opportunities, why put so much energy into filling volume unprofitably when there may be ways of doing so profitably?

Lucrative Jacks and (Very Rarely) Lucrative Deuces   Lucrative jacks and deuces are gems that deliver highly disproportionate contribution for the revenues they bring in. They are rare because they dramatically outperform larger businesses in a profitability sense. Unfortunately, they are also likely magnets for competition. Anticipate how competitors may be planning to enter your arena and how you intend to defend it. Other things being equal, you will be better off spending your time nurturing and growing these businesses than on desperately defending low-contribution products.

Productive Jacks   Businesses newly arrived into this category from a deuce or marginal category are increasing their contribution and may well be on their way to becoming aces. This is good news. If, on the other hand, they have been hanging around as jacks for some time, someone should be asking whether they are ever going to represent a substantial business for the company. Top priority for productive jacks is profitable growth.

Deuces   Since most new businesses start with small revenue and profit contributions, there is nothing necessarily bad about deuces. Indeed, as we'll discuss in chapter 8, when we talk about real options, low-revenue businesses can help you inexpensively learn about big opportunities. Two issues, however, should be considered: First, how many deuces can you sustain, and, second, are you making sure you understand when a deuce needs to either grow and contribute or be shut down? Many managers find it easier to start new businesses than to bring them to an end when the businesses don't appear to have much of a future. (Chapter 10, which focuses on discovery-driven planning, may be helpful to your thinking here.)

The Usefulness of Stratification Mapping

The usefulness of stratification mapping lies in its simplicity. Almost everyone can understand it. We use stratification maps primarily to get a quick overall perspective on things before spending time on more elaborate analyses. The maps help pinpoint which products and customer segments are the most profitable; which distributors are the most valuable; and which locations, branches, and brokers are making the most substantial contribution.[6]

One entrepreneur even used stratification mapping to form the core of his pitch to a large company interested in buying him out—he showed them how the acquisition would change their business mix and what advantages that would create for them. This brings us to the strategic use of stratification mapping, which is to help you visualize the business going forward so that you can make resource allocation trade-offs.

DEVELOPING FOCUS BY STRATIFYING INTO THE FUTURE

By now, you should have a good fix on how the elements of your existing business contribute (or don't) to performance. Next, consider building a picture of your future stratification map. Start off by reviewing your opportunity register and sorting the opportunities into two categories: arena building and model transforming.

In the first category, arena building, are opportunities to develop whole new future arenas—opportunities that you have identified to introduce significant new offerings, to enter substantial new markets, to develop novel ways of selling or distributing (especially in these Internet times), or to develop major new competences. These opportunities will have come mainly from the work you did in chapters 5 and 6.[7]

In the second category, model transforming, are opportunities that will transform the business model in an existing arena rather than create a whole new arena. These will have come mainly from the work that you did in chapters 2, 3, and 4.

Arena-Building Opportunities

Begin sorting your arena-building opportunities by ranking them in terms of their overall attractiveness. The opportunities with the largest apparent potential should go to the top of the list.

Over the years, many models and frameworks have been developed to assess the attractiveness of business arenas.[8] The trouble is that as uncertainty increases, it becomes less and less easy to anticipate attractiveness. This is a perennial problem for the venture capital industry—by the time it becomes clear whether an arena has a lot of potential, the opportunity to make a killer investment is gone. What venture capitalists do, which formed the starting point for the development of our diagnostic tool in figure 7-3, is look for indicators of high underlying potential rather than to try to measure it precisely.[9]

We liken our approach to trying to tap the inherent genetic code of a business. For example, contrast the potential upside, or advantage, of a drug that dramatically *ameliorates* the symptoms of a widespread, frequently recurring ailment with that of one that cures a disease afflicting one person in 100,000. In the first case, repeated use and high-incidence demand create the potential for a huge payoff. In the second case, use is infrequent and limited, implying a less attractive payoff. Just as geneticists can't exactly predict the characteristics of the mature offspring of a pair of breeding animals, managers can't exactly predict the potential upside of investing in a given arena. It is possible, however, to develop some intelligent conjectures that allow for comparison of alternative arenas.

Indicators of an arena with a potential upside are listed in figure 7-3. These indicators can be used in many ways. The way that we use them is to have people score them on a 1 to 3 scale, and then use the scores as the basis of a formal discussion as a general guide to project

---

FIGURE 7-3

INDICATORS OF SUBSTANTIAL UPSIDE POTENTIAL

- The potential long-run market demand for the solution we offer is enormous.
- Demand will grow for a long time.
- Many critical problems can be solved if we pursue this arena.
- Pursuit of this arena may enable us to tap many potential submarkets.
- The beneficiaries of the final products or services are willing and able to pay or can be easily funded.
- Demand will not be satisfied with only one purchase by the beneficiary—purchase will be repeated.
- The repeated use will be frequent.

assessment. The greater the scores on all or most of these indicators, the more significant the upside potential and, depending on the riskiness discussed below, these are potentially open-ended opportunities. If the indicators are all or mostly absent, the opportunity should be categorized as constrained.

An example of a product with substantial upside potential is Pfizer's treatment for male erectile dysfunction, Viagra. Prior to its market introduction in 1998, treatments for the condition were painful, clumsy, or both. Viagra for the first time offered the convenience of a tablet that could be taken orally and the ability to choose when to use the medication in a discreet and relatively comfortable way. The potential long-run market demand for the treatment is enormous. Millions of men are affected by the condition at some point, with increasing frequency as they age. Growth in demand thus seems assured by the aging of the baby boom population. Viagra has in fact been prescribed more than sixteen million times for over five million men in more than ninety countries worldwide. Many users are more than happy to pay for the benefits of the drug, and since it doesn't cure the underlying condition but only treats the symptoms, repeat usage can be expected. Thus, an opportunity such as Viagra illustrates a highly attractive structure of demand. It is important to note that Pfizer's managers did not know what a blockbuster they had when they first started to explore the product—this was discovered in clinical trials.[10]

One hint: If your technical people are urging you to pursue an opportunity but the marketing types don't seem interested, have a second look. Often, these opportunities represent the disruptive technologies of the future that may have a market impact beyond the vision of those whose job it is to look at current customers.[11]

A different kind of problem is presented by opportunities that have great potential but that may also be vulnerable to risks beyond your control. We are particularly concerned with the risks listed in figure 7-4. To the extent that these risks or others like them are present, the opportunity is constrained rather than open-ended.

An example of a business in which these issues have the potential to cause significant trouble is in the arena of genetically modified foods. In Europe, widespread opposition to genetically modified (GM) foods has taken the U.S. life-sciences company Monsanto by

FIGURE 7-4

RISKS ATTENDING ARENAS WITH UPSIDE POTENTIAL

- The market demographics could shift substantially against us.
- The offering serves an emotionally sensitive market (for example, positing health risks to babies).
- Long-term legal liabilities are a real possibility.
- The ethics of participating in this market are being increasingly debated.
- The market is vulnerable to intervention by a host government.

surprise. In 1999, it launched a $1.6 million advertising campaign in England, stressing the benefits of genetic engineering. The campaign sparked a stunning backlash and revealed several arenas in which the upside opportunity thought to be possible from GM products was severely constrained. The whole question of approving and buying GM products has become emotionally sensitive, leading to legal and ethical concerns and a host of governmental interventions. The considerations in figure 7-4 direct attention to potential issues of this kind.[12]

The next issue we consider refers to how long it will take to turn your opportunity into a revenue-generating business. It is expensive to sit around burning cash while customers slowly make up their minds whether or not they really want the solution you are offering them. Nor can you afford to spend the time or energy educating potential customers all by yourself—all too often your investments in education simply benefit the "me-too," later entrants without conveying any first-mover advantages.[13]

What is most attractive is an opportunity that allows you to create positive differentiation, in which adoption occurs rapidly, little training or prompting is necessary, and the appropriate infrastructure is already in place. Since these conditions rarely occur all at once, it is important to understand which, if any, problems might delay adoption. Indicators of such problems are listed in figure 7-5. We usually score each of these factors on a scale of 1 to 3. If the total score is above 18, you can expect significant adoption delays; otherwise, adoption will be relatively fast.

FIGURE 7-5

INDICATORS OF LIKELY ADOPTION PATTERNS

FACTORS THAT TEND TO SLOW ADOPTION

- The offering does not provide substantial performance advantages over current solutions.
- Target customers are currently quite satisfied with current solutions.
- Those customers who will benefit most from the offering do not control the purchasing decision.
- The final offering will need to undergo a significant regulatory approval process.
- The customer's perception of value will be dependent on the backing of other parties.
- The sale of the product will depend on the efforts and resources of other parties, such as distributors.
- Adoption of the offering will require users, customers, or distributors to change expensive imbedded systems.
- Target markets will have to be educated in how to use the offering.
- Target markets will have to radically change their usage patterns.
- The technical standards in this industry are not yet clearly set.
- The purchasing decision will be risky for target customers.
- Significant sales are unlikely until a critical mass of products is in use.
- Infrastructure or technology must be developed in parallel to get the offering to the market.

As an example of difficulties with adoption, consider the long and checkered history of the voice recognition industry. Although voice recognition technology has been in development for literally decades, widespread use of the technology has been hampered by a host of barriers to adoption. For instance, most applications of voice recognition technology are likely to be embedded in systems, such as in cars and personal digital assistants, that are manufactured by companies other than those developing the voice recognition devices. Truly maximizing the potential of voice recognition will require customers to alter their existing systems, to learn to use the technology, and to bear the risk of being early adopters. In addition, technical standards are not yet clear, only a limited number of products are currently in use, and the major infrastructure components (such as broadband capacity) that will allow voice to become ubiquitous are still not there. Little wonder that it is taking the technology a long time to get off the ground.[14]

At this point, you can begin to roughly categorize the arena-building opportunities in your register, as shown in figure 7-6. Those with strong upside potential and few barriers to adoption clearly have the potential to contribute a big payoff. As upside potential becomes more constrained and adoption rates slow down, the opportunities become less attractive.[15] So flag your arena-building opportunities as lucrative aces, jacks, and deuces.

This process of evaluation allows you to consider whether you have "wide-open" opportunities in your register that have the potential to expand your existing stratification map in substantial ways. Future aces are likely to emerge from opportunities with significant upside potential, low risk, and a reasonably fast route to adoption. Constrained upside potential and the likelihood of slow adoption mean that the opportunity is unlikely to become more than a future deuce (at least in the near term). Although you can argue over the fate of those opportunities housed in the remaining cells, we categorize them as future jacks, unless something happens or can be done to make the upside look even more attractive or someone can conceive of a way to speed up adoption.

You are now in a position to create a map like figure 7-7. This figure maps your current lucrative, productive, and marginal contributors against future aces, jacks, and deuces. Figure 7-7 is built in two stages. First look at your current arenas and their contributions (lucrative, productive, and marginal) and decide whether they will be ace, jack, or deuce revenue generators three to five years from now.

FIGURE 7-6

CATEGORIZATION OF ARENA-BUILDING OPPORTUNITIES

	Upside Scope Wide Open and Risk Low	Upside Scope Constrained and/or Risk High
Adoption Rapid	Future aces	Future jacks
Adoption Slow	Future jacks	Future deuces

FIGURE 7-7

SIGNIFICANT MAP: TODAY AND THREE TO FIVE YEARS FROM NOW

	Lucrative Today	Productive Today	Marginal Today	Arena Building (Doesn't Exist Today)
FUTURE ACE Top 65 percent of revenues 3–5 years from now.	A cornerstone business of today and the future if you can find opportunities to *sustain* a strong competitive position.	A growth business if you can find opportunities to *strengthen* your competitive position.	Rapid growth business if you can find opportunities to *build* a strong competitive position.	Transformational business—likely to change your entire portfolio if you can *create* a strong competitive position.
FUTURE JACK Middle (65–85 percent) of revenues 3–5 years from now.	This may be a business coming under heavy attack or becoming commoditized. Can you find opportunities to rebuild competitive position? Should you harvest?	Think through what this business is really doing for you. Is it a candidate for harvest?	Potential productive growth business, but only if you can find opportunities to *significantly build* your competitive position.	Business extension—likely to extend the reach of your business to new arenas if you can *create* a strong competitive position.
FUTURE DEUCE Last 15 percent of revenues 3–5 years from now.	A business rapidly becoming less attractive. Justify retention and beware of escalation of commitment.	Little contribution and low future revenues. Justify retention; otherwise, firing squad.	Justify retention; otherwise, firing squad.	Only justified as an option for the future or for defensive purposes (see chapters 7 and 8).

Map these in the left-hand column of the figure. Now map your arena-building opportunities in the right-hand column of the figure. Obviously, you won't have exact revenue numbers for highly uncertain new businesses, so for the time being simply put them in the boxes indicated by the labels in figure 7-7, estimating where your existing businesses are likely to fall in your stratification map at the end point of your planning horizon—say, three years or so. To summarize figure 7-7, the columns across the top reflect where each of the businesses are today, at the time you do the analysis. All the new arena-building opportunities will be in the last column. Use figure 7-6 to predict roughly where each arena-building opportunity will be in the future. Future aces go in the second row, then future jacks and future deuces. This is one way of beginning to map the likely dynamic movement of your entire book of business, so that you can see which businesses are likely to contribute significantly to future growth and which are not.

Figure 7-7 gives you and your team a common frame of reference for thinking about the arenas of the future. It also provides a basis for considering where you should focus most of your time and energy, where you might want to avoid making further commitments, and where you want to terminate current efforts. It lays out a strategy for redirection from less productive to more productive arenas. For instance, if entering an exciting new arena means that a stalled contributor will drop into a marginal category, it may be time to be hard-nosed and harvest that product.[16] This pragmatism is as much a part of an entrepreneurial mindset as identifying new opportunities—past contributors must be constantly harvested to make room for the most attractive future opportunities. The idea behind an exercise like this one is to orient yourself toward continual renewal, not only by identifying and pursuing new opportunities but also by eliminating those with limited promise.

The disposable-lighter business at Gillette is a case in point. Although disposable lighters are a core arena for companies like Bic, they were always a relatively small piece of the action for Gillette, whose dominant business has been shaving systems, from the company's founding. As the costs of R&D for each new generation of shaving equipment mounted and the demands of global marketing increased, management at Gillette reasoned that dropping a business such as disposable lighters would help keep people focused on developing the company's core businesses of shavers and other large-scale consumer-oriented products. As we will see in chapter 9, it also encouraged Bic to divert resources away from razors and into lighters. This focus has so far paid off handsomely. The company's latest foray, the Mach III razor, has helped boost the company's share in this core business to 70.7 percent of the U.S. market share, its highest since 1962.[17]

Model-Transforming Opportunities

Now take a look at your model-transforming opportunities, which will play the role of enhancing your position in your *current* arenas. Decide which model-transforming opportunities have the greatest potential to improve the prospects of your existing business arenas. As you go through this list of opportunities, indicate for each the future arena that it relates to. Does it relate to a future ace arena? If so, can the opportunity help you build or sustain or create your competitive position? Or does the opportunity relate primarily to a future deuce arena? If so, is there any point in pursuing it at all? Clearly you will be more inclined to deploy resources to model-transforming opportunities in the most attractive future arenas. Some model transformers may have so much potential that they can move a future jack to a future ace—in which case, shift the arena up one row.

When you are done, you should have a mapping of all your arena-building and model-transforming opportunities in figure 7-7. Now it is time to see what support they will get from your corporation.

WHO ARE YOU TO YOUR COMPANY?

Entrepreneurs should skip this section.

All organizations have resource limitations. When you receive funds and staff for your project, someone else is being denied those resources. Corporate resources are generally allocated after a lengthy, multilevel negotiation process.[18] So before you commit to making bold new moves, it is critical to be realistic about the likelihood that you will be able to command the resources you need.

Before finishing this chapter, then, you need to make a hard, pragmatic assessment of where you stand in relation to the overall corporate terrain.

The evaluation process we discuss here follows the same thought process we went through above; this time, though, you're going to look at the larger organization of which you are a part and identify what your business will be able to deliver to that corporation three to five years hence. Instead of the analysis you did for your own business in figure 7-7, try to do a rough estimate of what the stratification analysis of your entire organization would reveal about the role your piece of the firm will play: Are you currently lucrative? predictive? marginal? Will you be a future ace? jack? deuce? as in figure 7-8.

All kinds of issues (some sensible, some not) influence the internal competition for resources.[19] So by seeing where you fit in the corporate stratification, you are getting to understand how much funding and other types of support you are likely to gain from those who make resource allocation decisions in your organization. Figure 7-8 offers some ideas on the kinds of support (or lack thereof) you might anticipate, depending on how you look to the parent company. The parent company's perception of you will fundamentally influence the number of opportunities you will be able to pursue and the extent to which you will be able to pursue them.

If your business is perceived to be in the top priority category, our experience suggests that you will be able to claim considerable corporate resources. Further, you are likely to enjoy a great deal of discretion in how they are used, with the opportunity to obtain more resources if your program justifiably proves more costly than expected. It's like being given a blank checkbook, allowing you to write checks whenever you need. Remember, however, that you are dealing with a highly uncertain future. Because objective data are not available, your unit's major source of support is the

FIGURE 7-8

CORPORATE STRATIFICATION PROFILE: ACCESS TO AND ACCOUNTABILITY FOR CORPORATE RESOURCE ALLOCATIONS

Future Position	Lucrative for Corporation Today	Productive for Corporation Today	Marginal for Corporation Today	Doesn't Exist for Corporation Today
FUTURE ACE FOR CORPORATION — Top 65 percent of corporate revenues 3–5 years from now.	High priority for corporate resources: Line of credit.	High priority for corporate resources: Line of credit.	Top priority for corporate resources: Blank checkbook.	Top priority for corporate resources: Blank checkbook.
FUTURE JACK FOR CORPORATION — Middle (65–85 percent) of corporate revenues 3–5 years from now.	Moderate priority for corporate resources: Line-item approvals.	Moderate priority for corporate resources: Line-item approvals.	High priority for corporate resources: Line of credit.	High priority for corporate resources: Line of credit.
FUTURE DEUCE FOR CORPORATION — Last 15 percent of corporate revenues 3–5 years from now.	Low priority for corporate resources: Fund yourself.	Low priority for corporate resources: Fund yourself.	Develop exit strategy.	Low priority unless your business is an experiment.

perception that it has good potential. You must be prepared to shape perceptions by communicating and reinforcing the upside potential of your most important projects; it is unlikely that people will arrive at this point of view on their own. This is the critical championing role identified by observers of entrepreneurial activity within corporations.[20]

It will be more difficult to round up support if your unit is in a lower priority category, so you will be able to pursue fewer of your opportunities accordingly. In this case, seek to pursue those high and to the right in figure 7-7. Programs perceived as essential to the future well-being of the company might be considered top priority. Programs that are attractive but not essential are high priority. High-priority programs are likely to result in a "line of credit"—funds and staff will made available in your annual budget, with considerable discretion for you on how to distribute your resources and an accountability simply to keep within your overall budget. If you have moderate priority, you can expect to have to justify funding and staffing project by project and be held accountable for meeting the budget project by project. If your program is perceived as low priority, you'll have to squeeze out the resources yourself. You will have to behave like an independent start-up, being extremely parsimonious with the resources you consume. (We have more to say on being disciplined with resources in chapter 10.)

Depending on how much corporate support you can bank on, revisit figure 7-7 and realistically decide how many opportunities you will get resources to pursue. Even if you have low priority, do not despair: Creative managers find ways to execute initiatives that they believe important without running afoul of internal competition for resources. Some of their techniques are described in box 7-2.

Before we leave the subject of working parsimoniously, a word on skunk works. These are small, separate groups of employees who pursue new ideas, often without the official sanction of company decision makers, often with resources provided through unofficial channels. It has become popular of late to advocate the use of such units to develop new initiatives because they are somewhat protected from competing for resources with "mainstream" businesses. Unfortunately, being left out of the mainstream can also cause skunk works

BOX 7-2

BEGGING, BORROWING, AND SCAVENGING: MINIMIZING THE RESOURCES YOU NEED

The systematic approach to operating with sparse resources is called *asset parsimony*.[a] Following are several ways in which it can be practiced.

Borrowing resources from those who are not currently using them is a great way to avoid having to compete for them. This trick has long been used by entrepreneurs. In Anna Saxenien's book *Regional Advantage*, for instance, there is a great story about the early days of software development, in which Hewlett-Packard was kind enough to lend an aspiring software entrepreneur computer capacity at night, when it was underutilized. The entrepreneur recalls, years later, arriving at the company door with sleeping bags to work through the night on the borrowed resources.

If you are lucky enough to have good relationships with those who have resources to spare, a begging strategy may work, too. They may be willing to let you have a person, a bit of plant capacity, a little marketing time, or some programming help on the basis of mutual goodwill. This is one of the reasons that informal ties within the company and norms of cooperating (i.e., the golden rule) are so important—without them, obtaining these often-critical resources may be nearly impossible.

Scavenging is another great way to save money. Scavenging means finding and using resources that are being thrown away or rejected by other business units. You can often find these by looking around your company (or at your customers!) when it is going through some kind of transition—a move, a change of strategy, a merger, whatever. Often, perfectly good and useful resources, such as filing cabinets, desks, printers, computers, and the like, are simply thrown away because the company doesn't know what to do with them or can't be bothered to make the effort to reassign the resources.

Another aspect of exercising parsimony is processing requests for funds in small pieces, which may enable you avoid the need to obtain formal approvals entirely. Joseph Bower, in his landmark book, *Managing the Resource Allocation Process*, documents how a group of West Coast managers for a manufacturing company built an entire plant out of purchase orders that were individually too small to be passed on to higher-level managers but that were collectively large enough to allow the plant to be built!

The basic rule of thumb when trying to operate parsimoniously is to spend imagination before your spend money. As Zenas Block, a habitual entrepreneur who has started many businesses both inside and outside the corporate realm, says:

Don't buy new what you can buy used.

Don't buy what you can lease.

Don't lease what you can borrow.

Don't borrow what you can beg.

Don't beg what you can scavenge.

a. Hambrick and MacMillan (1984).

that are taking off to flounder. There are many situations in which the use of skunk works is undesirable:

- If the fledgling business needs the know-how or other capability lodged primarily in a mainstream business

- If the opportunity is fleeting and an aggressive launch is warranted—the window of opportunity will close if you launch slowly on account of limited resources

- If the new business will be dependent on distribution, relationships, or channel access that is controlled by a more mainstream business

- If the new opportunity needs to be integrated with mainstream businesses to add value—setting it up as a separate and different entity can lead to enormous culture clashes later on, when you are trying to integrate it

- If the new project has the potential to generate valuable knowledge spillovers for the parent organization or benefit from such spillovers back into its own processes[21]

To finish estimating your chances of receiving the resources necessary for your new business opportunities, go through the list of opportunities and indicate whether you expect each to get a blank checkbook, a line of credit, or a line-item approval or to require self-funding. Step back and look at your register now—many opportunities in unattractive arenas will simply not secure the resources needed for you to pursue them. For each opportunity, decide if you want to polish it up to make it more agreeable to upper management; put it on hold to focus on other, more promising ventures; or toss it out entirely.

The reason we urge you to be realistic about the levels of corporate support you can expect is that at some stage—even though you can get a lot of things started without depending on the largesse of the company—you will need it. Furthermore, over the long haul, you want your piece of the company to represent a legitimate, respected group—a tough thing to pull off if you have burned your bridges in endless squabbling over resources.[22]

Playing Politics—The Legitimate Way

We now come to the issue of internal politics. In our experience, managers are used to characterizing politics negatively—that is, they believe it's a terrible thing that self-interested people do simply to promote their own ends. Usually, though, when you dig a little deeper, what is often called politics is based on some legitimate arguments. It is important to realize that resistance and opposition do not necessarily mean that your opponents are all lunkheads trying to stand in the way of progress. Rather, you need to comprehend and deal with their problems in order to solve your own—how to get your selected opportunities supported in spite of initial resistance.

Political problems require political solutions. The wrong way to tackle politics is to deny its legitimacy and pretend that it won't come up. If you are going to be successful, you must deal with politics; it comes with the territory. The thing to do is to carefully consider your political strategy. A good way to get started is to think through the category in which you would place each person who has an interest (to the good or the bad) in your targeted opportunities. These categories appear in figure 7-9. You need a different strategy for each of these characters.

Heroes need to be given all the visibility and aura of success you can muster. They need to look like winners—the more they win, the more you win. They are your natural allies.

Opponents must be won over, eliminated, or at least neutralized. Some techniques for dealing with opponents are described in box 7-3.[23] We have found that it is critical to understand exactly why you are being opposed—opponents are seldom idiots, and until you can understand deeply why someone opposes you, you have little basis for taking appropriate counter action.

Allies unaware are easy to overlook but can make a critical difference in your political strategy. Often they reside outside your focal company; they may be customers, suppliers, distributors, or regulators, and they can play a key role in supporting you against opposition. Important customers, for instance, can request that your

FIGURE 7-9

ASSESSING POLITICAL POSITIONS

	Perceived Benefit	Perceived Threat
Actively Involved	Heroes	Opponents
Bystanders	Allies unaware	Sleeping dogs

BOX 7-3

STRATEGIES FOR COPING WITH POLITICAL OPPOSITION

Override them: Are you in a position simply to roll over the opposition (that is, they have no power to act against you)?

Preempt them: Can you act before they can react?

Co-opt them: Can you find some common ground on which to align your interests? Maybe your opponents have a pet project that you could bundle with yours. Or maybe you can find a common enemy to rally around.

Change their incentives: Can you somehow change their perceived incentives for opposing you? You need to make the upside smaller and the downside greater.

Bargain with them: Can you cut some kind of a deal? Do you have some product or asset that they need? Do they, in turn, have something you need? Can a swap be made?

Buy them off: Maybe you simply need to pay them to get out of your way.

Isolate them: Try to separate opponents from their sources of support.

Neutralize them: Can you somehow eliminate their power bases? Can you make it impossible for them to legitimately act?

Expose them: If they are foot dragging, hold them to specific, clear, and measurable support requirements, which may cause them to support you out of sheer embarrassment of being exposed.

Settle for a satisfactory, rather than an ideal, outcome: Can you cut a deal or adjust your strategy in a direction that is more acceptable to opponents? Getting most of what you want is better than not getting exactly what you want.

company deliver an enhancement that your operation is working on. You must be comprehensive in your effort to categorize various parties politically. Don't limit your search for sources of support to people inside the company. Anyone who stands to gain by your success, important customers in particular, can be enlisted in your cause.

The first rule of thumb with *sleeping dogs* is to let them sleep as long as possible. Managers are forever creating enormous problems for themselves by bringing unnecessary attention to their activities, stimulating opposition where there had been none. We earlier mentioned Monsanto's entering the European food business. The company spent millions developing competences in creating genetically modified food stocks. In 1998, the company spent $1.6 million in Britain advertising the advantages of genetically modified food, expecting this to smooth the way for entry of its products. The advertising campaign had exactly the opposite effect. Opposition mobilized almost immediately, raising concerns about everything from a lack of nutritional wholesomeness in the genetically modified meats and vegetables to scare stories about their potentially damaging effects on public health.[24]

Even if you don't provoke a response, sleeping dogs are eventually likely to pick up on the issues that your success will raise for them. At that point, the ideal situation is to have preempted them. We call this putting in place a fait accompli—that is, an established situation that they can no longer influence.

SUMMARY OF ACTION STEPS

The action steps that follow are meant to get you started on the concepts and processes discussed in the chapter. Feel free to elaborate in a way that works for your company.

STEP 1: Decide on the appropriate category for stratification maps for the business that you are evaluating (products, services, customers, geographies, or other types of business). Develop your equivalent of table 7-2. Review the basic recommendations for each cell in the map, paying particular attention to how the business categories have shifted in the past.

STEP 2: Revisit the opportunity register and categorize opportunities according to whether their potential is in building new arenas or in model-transforming arenas.

STEP 3: For the most appealing arena-building opportunities, assess their upside potential, risk, and adoption characteristics using the questions in figures 7-3, 7-4, and 7-5.

STEP 4: Determine whether these arena-building opportunities are likely to become future aces, jacks, or deuces within your planning horizon, say, three years from now by mapping them on a figure like 7-6. Now map them into the right-hand column of figure 7-7.

STEP 5: Carry out a stratification into the future by assessing where the categories in figure 7-2 will be in three to five years. Map these into the left-hand columns of figure 7-7. Determine which opportunities and existing business elements are worth further serious consideration and which should perhaps be restructured or sold.

STEP 6: Revisit the opportunity register and identify where your model-transforming opportunities enhance the cells of figure 7-7. Enter those opportunities that appropriately enhance future aces, jacks, or deuces. This will leave you with a list of arena-building and model-transforming opportunities mapped into figure 7-7.

STEP 7: Determine your relative position in the parent corporation by doing a firm-level stratification that incorporates your unit (see figure 7-8). Realistically consider your potential sources of support. Will you get a blank check, a line of credit, or line-item approval, or will you have to go it alone? Depending on this outcome, decide the major opportunities you will pursue.

STEP 8: Identify the people and groups likely to fall into the various categories outlined in figure 7-9. Start planning your strategy for managing the actors in each cell.

CHAPTER 8

ASSEMBLING

YOUR OPPORTUNITY

PORTFOLIO

IN CHAPTER 7, YOU BEGAN TO WINNOW THE OPPORTUNITIES in your register to a few high-potential ones that you could implement within the constraints of your resources. Remember that eliminating activities from your agenda is just as important as adding new ones. Looking at both sets of activities—the new and the existing—is crucial if you are to get control of your entrepreneurial portfolio.

By now you have gained an understanding of which business opportunities would make the most substantial contribution to the future for your organization. The next challenge is to figure out how you are going to appropriately allocate resources to those opportunities that you elect to pursue.[1] You'll use an approach to building a portfolio of projects that draws on real options reasoning, in which you make investments with a limited downside to learn whether further investment is warranted.

Real options reasoning is the thought process underlying the search for many kinds of entrepreneurial opportunities.[2] Many highly uncertain prospects for investment cannot be adequately valued by the net-present-value rule. This rule suggests that all future cash flows (negative and positive) be discounted to their present value. If the result is positive, you should invest. If the result is negative, don't invest. Although it seems logical on the surface (and is still useful when you are not facing major uncertainties), net-present-value thinking will inevitably push you toward short-term investment opportunities at the expense of more ambitious, longer-term ideas.

This is not to say that entrepreneurs spend their resources recklessly. Quite the contrary. What they do is invest in projects that have limited or containable downside risk, in order to test the potential of an idea to deliver substantial returns at some time in the future. Using real options reasoning to guide your investment of people and resources in new opportunities can allow you to pursue attractive opportunities without burning your organization out and without wasting scarce resources.

UNDERSTANDING REAL OPTIONS REASONING

Successful entrepreneurs approach investments in the creation of new businesses the way that investors might approach investing in stock options. To invest in stock options, you buy a contract that costs a small amount of money, relative to what it would cost to make an investment in the underlying security on which the option is written. The contract gives you the right, but not the obligation, to buy (or sell) the underlying asset on or before a specified date at a specific price. Should the deal not make financial sense when the option is due, you simply don't invest. You then forfeit the cost of the option, but lose less than you would have if you had had to buy the underlying asset. The advantage of the option is that it preserves your claim on the opportunity without forcing you to make a commitment to it.

In a similar vein, to explore new opportunities, you might make a limited-downside investment today in the hope of having access to an opportunity in the future. As with financial options, the greater the uncertainty with respect to the distribution of outcomes, the more the option is worth. This is because the cost to acquire the option stays the same, while the maximum potential for upside benefit increases.[3]

If an investment yields information that demonstrates the viability of the opportunity, you can proceed with further investments with more confidence than if the earlier investment had not been made. Because the insight and experience gained by investing in an option is captured only if you make the investment, learning from options investments can give you an edge over competitors, who won't be privy to the knowledge because they haven't experienced the same learning.

Real options reasoning is second nature to firms with an entrepreneurial mindset, like that of the aggressively entrepreneurial Enron Corporation. From its beginnings as a provider of natural gas, Enron has become a leading player in the global energy industry. The company is a leading and obvious user of real options reasoning. This has led the company to make investments that are counterintuitive from a conventional net-present-value perspective, but that make perfect sense given option value.

Go back a moment to the key ratio concept we introduced in chapter 6. In the energy business, a competitive ratio that is often used to compare firms is the incremental cost of megawatt-hours relative to industry standard. In 1999, Enron built three plants in which this key ratio was intentionally well below industry standards—in fact, the energy generated by the new plants costs 50–70 percent more than industry standard. Why would any sensible company do such a thing? The answer has to do with the option value of the new plants. Less efficient plants cost less to build; furthermore, when sitting idle, they cost the company little to be maintained. During periods of shortage, however, when energy prices rise, the plants can be rapidly brought on stream, giving Enron the capacity to meet demand at prices that more than compensate for their higher operating costs.[4] Note that Enron is not required to produce with the less efficient plants unless external conditions—in this case, high energy prices—warrant it. When prices drop again, the plants can be shuttered until the next price spike. The dollar amounts involved are not trivial. *Business Week* reports that in June 1999, prices for a megawatt-hour of electricity in the Midwest shot up from a normal $40 to an astonishing $7,000. By having capacity available, Enron can capture all the upside of that volatility and avoid its downside.

In high-velocity and uncertain environments, using real options reasoning allows a company to keep its options open—literally. Enron can choose to produce or not, depending on energy prices. Other kinds of options allow you to put off the point at which you must make an irrevocable choice. This creates value for a company by allowing its managers to take actions later that enlarge and exploit upside gains while minimizing downside exposure. Options thus offer considerable flexibility compared with investments that incur early, fixed commitments to an uncertain future.

An important distinction seldom explicitly made with respect to real options is that their purpose and nature are not all the same. We distinguish between three kinds of options: positioning, scouting, and stepping-stone options. You will find that you manage them differently and expect different things from them.

Positioning Options

Positioning options create the right to wait and see. Investments that put the company in a position to capitalize on uncertain external events, should they occur—such as the emergence of a hot new market on the Internet or of a successful technology that has been competing for market dominance—are positioning options. Such options are useful when the uncertainty you face is mostly out of your control but you need to be positioned to act in case fortune turns your way.

Positioning is appropriate when several competing outcomes could satisfy high potential market demand, but it is not yet clear which outcome will dominate. Take mobile telephony in the United States. As of this writing, there are three different communication standards and massive uncertainty about which will ultimately become the standard. The plausible scenarios include the following: (1) a lock-in on one of the three standards, (2) preservation of the current multistandard system, and (3) the emergence of some new standard or way of communicating that makes the current mobile concept obsolete. Given such uncertainty, a sensible route for an interested organization may be to make modest investments that will prepare it for any of the three scenarios; committing itself entirely to one or the other would not be prudent. We see this, of course, in practice, as telecom companies engage in a vast array of mergers, acquisitions of smaller firms, and joint ventures and alliances with larger firms while also aggressively lobbying regulatory agencies and investing in the development of standards. The reason to select a positioning option is to make the smallest possible investment and still buy time and flexibility to pursue the best course of action once it becomes clear.

Scouting Options

A second class of options, scouting options, can be considered as entrepreneurial experiments. They are investments made with the intention of discovering and/or creating markets for products and services by deploying capabilities that you have (perhaps recently) developed in potential new arenas. Through these options, you can explore new terrain from a current competence base, gathering information on its most attractive locations.[5]

Scouting options differ from positioning options in that they extend existing competences in directions that you believe will allow you to capture significant market opportunities. This kind of option might emerge from your insights that large opportunities can be within reach if you break a barrier (see chapter 5). Scouting options are also used to discover opportunities to break through barriers. The reason for selecting a scouting option is thus to deploy or develop competences that allow you to ferret out high-potential markets that are highly uncertain.

Scouting options can take many forms. The most familiar is the sacrificial product or probe from which firms seek to determine the market's reaction to a bundle of attributes.[6]

We can't stress enough that these options should be consciously managed as scouts—that is, they are meant to be small investments made without necessarily expecting an immediate payoff. You use them to learn, to gather information. The idea is to send out your scouts using the least amount of fixed investment or sunk cost possible and be ready to redirect your efforts once you find promising paths.

Large companies often do worse at scouting that do small entrepreneurial companies, simply because the large firms have more money to spend. If you load yourself down with heavy fixed costs or massive sunk investment, redirection becomes much more difficult. Even fabulously well-researched and technically brilliant new products can disappoint in the marketplace. Consider the plight of the satellite-communications company Iridium (see box 8-1), which today finds itself bankrupt, its only hope of future success being in markets much smaller and less lucrative than the one it originally targeted.

Stepping-Stone Options

Stepping-stone options mean entering the future one step at a time. They are consciously staged attempts to sequentially discover new competences to pursue highly promising but very uncertain potential markets. They are somewhat analogous to compound financial options, in which the value of a portfolio is a function of a sequence of investment choices.

You choose stepping-stone options when you want to expose your company to opportunities in which there is high uncertainty both about the final shape of a high-potential market and about the likelihood of being able to develop the necessary competences to serve it. Nevertheless, the potential opportunity is so big that it is irresistible. You start with small, exploratory forays into less challenging market niches and use the experiences gained there as stepping-stones to build competences in increasingly challenging and attractive market arenas that you discover as you go.

Investments in stepping-stones are thus made as a series of deliberately staged and sequenced real options. Managing such investments calls for the kind of discipline used by venture capitalists, in which staged funding decisions are made only when key milestones are reached and a great many assumptions have been tested.[7] As each milestone is reached, you have the opportunity to continue or to stop further development or even to sell, trade, license, or otherwise capture returns on investments in technological and market development to that point. The idea is to keep each successive round of investment to an absolute minimum and to reassess the project frequently.

The primary difference between stepping-stone and scouting options is that scouting options involve technology and competences

BOX 8-1

HOW NOT TO SCOUT: THE CASE OF IRIDIUM COMMUNICATIONS

Iridium was conceived in the mid-1980s as an ambitious initiative to provide mobile communications services anywhere in the world through a network of sixty-six satellites. Managers of the Motorola-led consortium supporting the initiative expected huge demand on the part of business travelers for a single phone system that could be used across the globe. In May 1998, Iridium head Edward F. Staiano articulated this assumption: "If you throw our product in your briefcase, you know you can make a call from anywhere on the planet, and people can get to you."[a]

Most prospective customers loved the idea of a global phone. Unfortunately, for many, their enthusiasm for Iridium's solution didn't last long past the product's technically successful introduction in November 1998. For one thing, Iridium phones were staggeringly expensive—the initial cost of the handset alone was $3,000, and calls cost about $7 per minute. For another, although the bulk of business is conducted indoors, Iridium phones work only outside—leading to the sometimes comical sight of executives leaning out of windows or trotting into the street to make calls. The phones, moreover, made it hard to conduct a conversation because of the time it took someone's voice to travel to and from the satellite. The size, weight, and battery life of the phone were also issues—the introductory handset was the size of a brick and weighed more that a pound. In a world increasingly moving toward digital signals, Iridium's analog architecture was outdated.

Most significantly, owning an Iridium phone didn't eliminate the clutter of phones in the globe-trotting executive's drawer, voiding a major assumed benefit. A regular mobile handset was still required to make calls indoors and to access services such as voice mail and local paging. Given the price of the Iridium service, one tended to use it only when there was no alternative. In short, the assumed attribute map for an Iridium phone didn't coincide with the service that customers actually received—the product ended up with a lot more negatives and fewer positives than had been hoped.

By July 1999, the company had by some estimates spent more than $5 billion on the project but had managed to sign on only about ten thousand users.[b] In a desperate bid to redirect in the face of disappointing sales, the company announced that it would slash prices, simplify a complex pricing structure, and redirect its marketing efforts from a focus on global business travelers to industrial customers with employees in remote locations, such as on oil rigs or in distant mines. In 1999, Staiano's resignation was announced and the search for a new CEO begun.[c] The company went formally into Chapter 11 bankruptcy later in that year. By March of 2000, only 20,000 subscribers had signed on, and it seems almost certain that Motorola will soon stop offering the service completely.

The point is not that demand for the Iridium concept doesn't exist in principle. The point is that someone might have asked whether it was necessary to spend $5 billion to test the assumption that this demand would materialize for a high-priced product with significant technological drawbacks. There may have been an overlooked opportunity to deploy scouting options, perhaps by finding or even funding a few customers whose itineraries would allow for a limited road test of the service.

a. Quoted in Crockett and Elstrom (1998), 142.

b. Reinhardt and Yang (1999), 44.

c. "Iridium North America Announces New Pricing Structure" and "Company History," press release reported on <http://www.iridium.com>, June 29, 1999.

that are either in place or that your company is confident can be developed. Stepping-stone options focus on the creation of a new competence base that has huge potential for creating vast, as yet unclear markets. You then use this base to enter into low-cost test markets. You do this deliberately to develop experience and generate cash flows, sometimes with no intention of remaining in the early markets once the competence is sufficiently well developed. Thus you can make deliberately parsimonious resource allocations designed to pursue carefully selected and increasingly challenging opportunities, with the objective of developing a new competence along an increasingly sophisticated trajectory and deploying it in unfolding markets.

The Kyocera Company in Japan used this approach to pursue the industrial ceramics business in the 1960s. Instead of investing to crack high-level applications like automobile engine cylinders or turbine blades (as did many other smart companies, General Electric included), Kyocera initially invested in low-end applications for known niche markets. For instance, the company developed ceramic scissor blades for the textile industry. Through this initial effort, the company resolved considerable technical uncertainty, such as how to process clays and how to make precise edges with consistent quality. This created an initial technological competence which, as it evolved, took Kyocera along a trajectory of increasing technical sophistication. The firm is now a major global supplier of semiconductor chip substrates and other materials for the digital age, spanning entire industries that were still in their infancy when Kyocera began ceramic development.

Building a Portfolio of Options

In highly unpredictable situations, smart companies have learned that the best way to respond effectively to future challenges is to deploy patterns of options.[8] Rather than making a single big bet on a single, attractive opportunity, they have found that it makes more sense to fund several small ventures intended to capture market opportunity in different ways. Thus, established firms such as Intel and Microsoft might take multiple equity positions in start-ups pursuing similar problems with different solutions, research consortia supported by multiple firms might explore various alternative solutions, and joint ventures entered into by a wide variety of players might employ technology-sharing arrangements. Just as you might think of your company as a portfolio of businesses, there is a lot to be said for thinking of the initiatives you are pursuing within a given business as a portfolio of options.[9]

UNDERSTANDING THE ALTERNATIVE: DIRECT LAUNCHES

Despite our obvious enthusiasm for real options reasoning in highly uncertain situations, sometimes it makes more sense to undertake an outright and immediate launch. Intel, for instance, would have been crazy to use any strategy other than an outright launch for each next-generation chip for the bulk of its x86-to-Pentium lines. Why? Because for these products, the company's uncertainty with respect to market demand was low (Intel is a dominant player, people wanted those speedy processors, and manufacturers wanted to put them in the next generation PCs), and technical uncertainty was moderate as well. In fact, there are many situations in which a launch is the preferred alternative to a more cautious options strategy. Cases in point are Gillette's longtime strategy in selling razors (always be the first to market with the most sophisticated shaving technology), most pharmaceutical companies' market entry for approved new drugs, and the plunge by Texas Instruments into all manner of digital signal processing applications.

Launches can be thought of as two types. The first represents improvements in existing products and services and are basically incremental improvements on an existing business model. *Enhancement launches* make existing offerings cheaper, easier to use, of higher quality, or better in some other way. They correspond to many of the model-transforming reconfiguration and redifferentiation opportunities you developed in chapters 3 and 4. *Platform launches* are more uncertain and require more substantial investments. These are launches that a firm can take with some confidence (as does Intel) and that are intended to create a substantial new base of business for the firm. When such launches take you into a new domain, they correspond to the arena-creating opportunities discussed in chapters 5 and 6.

FACTORING MARKET AND TECHNOLOGICAL UNCERTAINTY INTO YOUR OPTIONS

To decide which of the above approaches best suits each opportunity in your portfolio—positioning; scouting; stepping-stone; or outright, damn-the-torpedoes-full-speed-ahead launch—you need to assess the nature of the uncertainty you face. We primarily consider whether the major uncertainties have to do with the market (such as uncertainty with respect to the Iridium application) or with some aspect of the technology (such as Kyocera's uncertainty with respect to ceramic technology) or both.

A simple way to get a feel for market uncertainty is to think through your response to the issues listed in figure 8-1 and score them on a 1 to 3 scale, then assign the project as low, medium, or high market uncertainty. Later on, you'll use these scores to decide what kind of launch or option would best suit your project.

Next comes the assessment of technical uncertainty. Different issues, same idea. Ask yourselves how certain you are about each of the issues listed in figure 8-2. Again, use a simple 1 to 3 scale to categorize the project as low, medium, or high technical uncertainty.

If these procedures seem a little rough-and-ready, it is because they are—and deliberately so. In highly uncertain situations, you need an inexpensive, quick means of sorting your projects into "roughly right" categories. Those projects that survive the screening process can then be subjected to more elegant analysis.

Complete these exercises to determine the certainty level for those arena-building and model-transforming projects that survived your first screening in chapter 7. You are now ready to do a first-cut categorization of the investment strategies you might pursue to capitalize on these opportunities. This categorization scheme is depicted in figure 8-3.

Positioning Options

Choose positioning options when the level of technical uncertainty is high but you have some idea of what markets and segments you eventually want to serve. Your uncertainty may stem from the lack of a dominant design or standard, from a lack of knowledge with respect to the technical feasibility of a given solution set, or from issues such as the regulatory acceptability of certain technologies. Since the major uncertainties have to do with alternative technological solutions, the idea is to take a limited number of positions at the lowest possible cost to hedge against making a single wrong bet, thus containing the damage done by any one position that does not work out.

FIGURE 8-1

ASSESSING MARKET UNCERTAINTY

Enter next to each item the number that corresponds with your degree of certainty about the item. 1 = high certainty, 2 = medium certainty, 3 = low certainty.

_____ Total demand if we invest

_____ Total future revenues from the project

_____ Extent to which we will be able to obtain necessary support from third parties, (e.g., distributors and suppliers)

_____ Stability of the revenue stream generated

_____ Degree of exposure to long-term liabilities

_____ Degree to which pricing can be sustained

_____ Speed with which necessary regulatory bodies will approve the offering

_____ Speed with which we will be accepted in the market

_____ Degree to which parallel investments will be needed to take the final offering to market

_____ Parallel investments can be made in time to support the offering

_____ Degree to which we will have to alter designs

_____ Who likely competitors will be

_____ How aggressive competition is likely to be

_____ Which combinations of attributes will be sought

_____ How many competitors are experimenting with alternative offerings

_____ Whether customers will hesitate because of alternative offerings

_____ If a standard must emerge, and if so, what the standard will be

_____ Length of time it will take for standard-setting groups, such as industry trade associations, to take a position on standards

_____ Length of time we will have to wait for critical decisions to be made by formal standard-setting bodies, such as government regulators

_____ Whether suppliers of complementary products and services (like VCR movies for VCR players) will be willing to invest before standards are in place

Scoring:

20–29: Low market uncertainty
30–44: Medium market uncertainty
45–60: High market uncertainty

FIGURE 8-2

ASSESSING TECHNICAL UNCERTAINTY

Enter next to each item the number that corresponds with your degree of certainty about the item. 1 = high certainty, 2 = medium certainty, 3 = low certainty.

____ Time it will take to complete development

____ Cost of equipment that must be developed

____ Necessary infrastructure will be developed

____ Total costs of development

____ Access to needed complementary technologies

____ Cost of systems needed

____ Type of skills needed

____ Availability of necessary skills

____ Type of equipment needed

____ Availability of equipment needed

____ Cost of equipment needed

____ Raw materials needed

____ Availability of raw materials needed

____ Ability to overcome expected barriers

____ Required level of product quality

____ Required levels of support and service

____ Amount of production capacity needed

____ Ability to recruit the right people

____ Understanding of what could cause the project to fail

____ Understanding of what commercialization skills are needed

____ Ability to assemble a complete team with superior technological skills, relative to competitors

____ Ability to achieve rapid cycle time in development

____ Understanding of breakthroughs needed if the project is to succeed

Scoring:
23–34: Low technical uncertainty
35–49: Medium technical uncertainty
50–69: High technical uncertainty

FIGURE 8-3

CATEGORIZING YOUR REGISTER OF OPPORTUNITIES

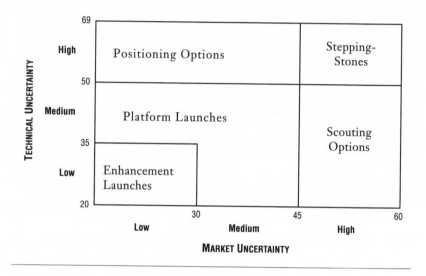

The objective in linking these positioning options is to seek low-cost strategies, such as cross-licensing or technology access deals, joint ventures for commercialization of new technologies, and joint marketing agreements. Of course, if money is no object, one can be a lot more aggressive in staking out positioning options. U.S. telephone giant AT&T, for instance, has spent billions of dollars on taking attractive positions, acquiring cable companies such as Tele-Communications and MediaOne in 1998–1999, entering joint venture agreements with British Telecom and Japan Telecom, and setting up deals with Microsoft for set-top box software.[10] Whatever happens in the telecommunications industry, AT&T is likely to have some options in its portfolio that will position it to participate. The questions in figure 8-4 will help you to manage your positioning options in a disciplined way.

Scouting Options

Scouting options are used when you are not sure what combination of attributes the market will eventually prefer. The core questions

FIGURE 8-4

MANAGING POSITIONING OPTIONS

_____ Have you thought through the possible scenarios that would make this investment worthwhile? Are you making sure that you're not overinvesting in one particular position?

_____ Are the bases covered in terms of the opportunity area—does the number of positions you have targeted cover the range of uncertainties you'll face?

_____ Have you covered the most likely contingencies in some way? (Remember—you don't have to own it all. Some of your positions may be achieved by means of alliances or joint ventures.)

_____ Do you know what data to track to see if you should exercise a positioning option? To let it expire?

_____ Do you have a rigorous intelligence system in place to capture, interpret, and make decisions based on this data?

_____ Does the information get to where it can be interpreted and where decisions are made?

you seek to answer with investments in scouting concern how future markets will be segmented and what would constitute a blockbuster attribute map for these emerging segments. The guiding principle is to put some offering into the hands of customers in order to aggressively get feedback on their reactions to its features.

It pays never to assume that you know what the customer wants. Customers can be remarkably inarticulate about what their real concerns are. Although it is frustrating, you often have to observe the customer in a buying or using situation to gain the insights you need. Review the questions in figure 8-5 when you are considering scouting options.

Stepping-Stone Options

It is wise to use a stepping-stone strategy for opportunities that present both high technical and high market uncertainty, because the organization has a lot of learning to do on both dimensions. A major launch here is generally misguided, since there is absolutely no platform of existing knowledge to go on. Stepping-stone projects should

FIGURE 8-5

MANAGING SCOUTING OPTIONS

_____ Are you being parsimonious enough with your expenditures on scouts? Or have you fallen victim to the notion that you have to develop the whole business to determine whether there is market demand and to decide what the business model is?

_____ Have your assumptions about where you can add value been validated with good evidence? Are you prepared to be surprised?

_____ Do you have a carefully developed set of assumptions that will allow you to learn, no matter what happens?

_____ Have you carefully articulated what you believe the business model to be? Are you prepared to test this hypothesis?

_____ Are you scouting in enough markets that are different from your current segments?

_____ Are you scouting not only for lead users but for the mass market as well?

_____ Are you alert to solutions that may already be in place with lead users that could show you where the real problems are?

be started in small markets that have knowledgeable customers who can provide you with feedback and the opportunity to learn. You should not expect to make a lot of profit from these early forays. They are your sacrificial products, and you need to accept that they are unlikely to be successful right off the bat. The idea is to follow Silicon Valley's famous principle for learning: "Fail fast, fail cheap, try again."

One important point about stepping-stones: If you fix early on a particular design or a particular set of features, you are limiting your future flexibility. Try, if you can, to pursue new designs and applications in a modular way, so that as new information comes in, you can change your design and your plans.[11] Figure 8-6 contains some useful questions to ask yourself before organizing a stepping-stone venture.

LAUNCHES

Finally, there are the two different kinds of launches. These represent opportunities in arenas that you feel reasonably certain about, and so

FIGURE 8-6

MANAGING STEPPING-STONE OPTIONS

____ Have you tried to clearly define a market—even a small market—that will genuinely benefit from what you are proposing to offer?

____ Can you stage and sequence the project? Will you have trouble stopping or withdrawing if you need to redirect?

____ Have you developed metrics to measure success appropriate to an option though it is unlikely to generate substantial independent revenues?

____ Is your company prepared to go through some trial and error with this project before insisting on conventional measures of success?

____ Do you have the patience to let this learning process play out—or will you run out of stamina before critical lessons are learned?

____ Are you constantly looking for evidence and indicators that a major opportunity is opening up?

---

have no need for options investments. Following Wheelwright and Clark's (1995) phrasing, some launches create new product or service platforms from which you can build a substantial business. We will cover recommendations for *platform launches* in depth in chapter 9. The primary goal of a launch is to establish your company in a strong competitive position with a select target market that you feel fairly certain will respond favorably to what you have to offer. It is also worthwhile, as you are launching, to think through the follow-on and enhancement launches that will come later. To the extent that you can launch in such a way that customers have a natural path to either migrate to your next-generation product or to buy a greater variety of products from you, your growth prospects will be better.

The remaining launches are basically enhancements to or variations on an existing platform that help improve your company's attribute map relative to competitors. Many of the model-transforming opportunities covered in chapters 3 and 4 fall into this category. With *enhancement launches*, it is key to be mindful of adding new attributes that will not make a substantial competitive difference at the risk of adding cost or complexity to your offerings. (For a definition of model-transforming opportunities, see chapter 7.)

LETTING STRATEGIC DIRECTION GUIDE RESOURCE ALLOCATION

If we had to pick one of the most common concerns that managers voice when faced with the challenge of entrepreneurial transformation in their companies, it would be their difficulty in balancing the needs of tomorrow's options (the longer-term-growth businesses) with those of businesses that are delivering quarterly earnings per share today. One of the most difficult challenges they face in achieving this balance is figuring out when to put people and resources on a future-oriented project when they are clearly needed on a profitable endeavor today.

The allocation of projects to positioning options, scouting options, stepping-stone options, enhancement launches, and platform launches, as we did in figure 8-3, can be useful to you as you try to sort out these sometimes conflicting demands. The core concept is to let your strategy and available resources guide your choice of how much emphasis to put on each of the categories in the figure. There is no cookbook for how best to do this. In general, though, you want a portfolio of projects that suits the environment in which you will have to compete. Thus, if you are in a fast-moving, highly uncertain industry, you will want to weight your portfolio more heavily toward options. If you are in a relatively stable or asset- and capital-intensive industry, you should probably be investing more heavily in platform launches. Thus, it makes perfect sense for companies like Intel and Hewlett-Packard to invest substantially in options, such as equity investments in small entrepreneurial companies with interesting technology. It makes equally good sense for a company like Boeing to place more emphasis on platform launches, such as its recent successful introduction of the 777 line of aircraft.

Here is the key point: Once you have determined how many projects you can support, and what mix of projects you need to support your strategy, similar projects must compete against other similar projects for budget and staff for the resources dedicated to that category of project. Let's say that you have decided to allocate 20 percent of your available resources to positioning options. Any new candidate for getting resources that is a positioning option should compete for that 20 percent against all the other positioning projects.

They shouldn't compete against other kinds of options or against platform or enhancement launches. This ensures that you will pick only the very best positioning options for your portfolio. What's more important, it gets you out of the constant tug-of-war between short-term and long-term projects. The strategic choice is how many of your resources you will put into each category. Then within each category, the very best projects should compete against one another for consideration.

When allocating resources, a fruitful place to start is by getting a handle on what the portfolio of projects (and ongoing businesses) looks like for you at the moment. Next, determine whether you have the financial and human resource capacity to handle your existing portfolio of businesses and those new initiatives that you want to start. If you are out of capacity, you have two choices: find more resources, or cut back on what you're doing. We've already discussed some ways that you can prioritize the projects in your opportunity register in the last chapter. Understanding your degree of competitive insulation (discussed later in this chapter) will help you further prioritize your opportunities. As part of this process, you will want to establish (at least roughly) what mix of project types are needed to support your strategy and how many you are able to undertake. Most companies, for instance, would be hard pressed to start many platform launches simultaneously—they are terribly draining for the organization.

The first step in designing your ideal portfolio is thus figuring out what your actual portfolio looks like today. Since everything new you want to do will add to the work that people are already doing, you need to look both at your portfolio of new ideas and at the portfolio of work already in the pipeline. In our experience, most firms chase many more projects and ideas than they can execute successfully.

To show how this works, we will walk you through a project we worked on for a technical equipment manufacturer. We began by listing all the projects currently under way in the company. We then worked with the senior executive team to categorize them into the five portfolio categories (positioning option, scouting option, stepping-stone option, platform launch, or enhancement launch). Next, we tried to get an estimate of the effort (roughly in full-time, equivalent-person months) that would be required to bring each project to the next logical milestone at which it would be reevaluated (more on milestones in chapter 10). This gave us a picture of where the company was spending its energy today. On top of this, we then loaded in all the new initiatives that the senior executive had indicated he would like to undertake within the next two years. Finally, we mapped the results on a chart similar to figure 8-3. We show the results in figure 8-7. Each circle in the figure represents a project. The numbers in the circle represent the estimated personnel-months to complete development up to the next milestone. Blank circles represented projects that were on the list, but to which no resources had been allocated when we did the mapping. The idea was to try to get everything that was consuming time and energy mapped in a way that people could identify what was going on.[12]

FIGURE 8-7

A Crowded Portfolio

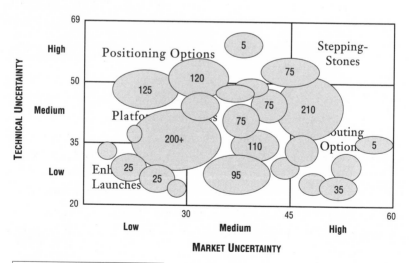

Key
Circle = project
Number = personnel months per project
Blank circle = resources not yet allocated

The visualization exercise was a revelation. After comparing desired with available resources, it became crystal clear that the company was pursuing many more projects than it had people to staff. In particular, by trying to engage in many highly demanding platform launches at the same time, the company was unlikely to do justice to its portfolio of options. Nor was it likely to manage the enhancement launches (as opposed to platform launches) that current customers were demanding, because many of these were still on the drawing board and were competing for the same scarce design and engineering talent as the major platform launches. In short, the company was taking on too much. The results of this overcommitment meant that project deadlines perpetually slipped, promises to key customers were often broken, and people were beginning to feel burned out.

This situation is not uncommon. The processes through which companies take on projects usually lead them to discover that they haven't got the resources to do justice to everything on their plates. In particular, when managers have not clearly thought through which resources for projects will be needed to support their needs to either build new platforms or learn through options, the different types of projects compete with each other, creating confusion. This lack of coordination is also typical of companies that haven't matched their strategy to available resources. A far wiser approach is to pursue a few well-run projects than to chase down a grab-bag of forever-behind-schedule and over-budget initiatives.[13]

If you do a similar exercise, you will now be able to see whether there is any rhyme or reason to the projects that you currently have on the drawing board. The next thing to tackle is to determine your carrying capacity for projects in the first place. Though part of the puzzle is obviously capital budget allocations, most companies seem to have a much higher awareness of the rules by which capital and assets are allocated than they do about how skilled people should be spending their time. There is a lot to be gained by focusing on the skills and talents you will need to cope with the demands of current businesses, to run successful launches, and to manage your options.

The goal of this stage of the opportunity selection process is to ensure that the key people available are not hopelessly overloaded with projects. If you are willing to begin with some educated guesses as to how people are going to have to allocate their time, the process of figuring out how much your organization can handle is straightforward. Start by making rough estimates of the number of different kinds of people who will be needed to work on the projects you have identified in your version of figure 8-7, in the course of the next year, as shown in table 8-1. We like to break it up in six-month chunks. You may prefer shorter or longer periods. There is no need for excessive precision; you need only estimate in broad terms to see the scope of the human resource challenge that you face.

This table allows you to see how many and what kind of staff you will need to do everything you want to do within the time frame specified. Next, consider how many and what kind of skilled people you already have. If your business is anything like our exemplar firm, or indeed like most companies we have worked with, the projects you have committed to complete represent over 100 percent of your carrying capacity. This can have surprising effects on the length of time each project takes to complete. For instance, imagine a project that will take a skilled software developer six months to complete. The lead time to completion if this person is working full-time on the project is six months. Divide this person's time between four projects, however, and three-quarters of the time, each project is being ignored by the person. The lead time to completion of all four projects stretches to two years! Delays like this can be deadly in a world where speed matters.

In planning and then allocating your human resource needs, it's important not to overload people. Putting together a table like table 8-2 will help you begin to flesh out realistic allocations of time for people to pursue new opportunities and to conduct their current ongoing business. We strongly recommend that no more than 90 percent of an employee's time be preallocated. The built-in slack allows for contingencies and breathing space for creativity as well as for the networking that is the heart's blood of entrepreneurial organizations.

It may seem trivial to account for employee time to this degree, but it is absolutely vital, particularly if you plan to take on a number of projects with different time demands, different levels of uncertainty, and different requirements from the people you are working with.

TABLE 8-1

APPROXIMATE HUMAN RESOURCE DEMAND

Key Contribution	Project 1: Jan.–June	Project 2: Jan.–June	Total: Jan.–June	Project 1: July–Dec.	Project 2: July–Dec.	Total: July–Dec.
Development staff	1	1	2	1	—	1
Engineering staff	1	2	3	2	1	3
Software staff	—	1	1	2	2	4
Marketing staff	—	1	1	—	2	2
And so on . . .						

TABLE 8 - 2

KEY HUMAN RESOURCE ALLOCATIONS

	Functional Contribution	Time on Current Business	Time on Project 1	Time on Project 2	And So On . . .	Total Time (Maximum 90%)
Person 1	Development	0%	90%	0%		90%
Person 2	Development	0	0	80		80
Person 3	Engineering	60	20	10		90
Person 4	Marketing	70	20	0		90
Person 5	Marketing	75	0	15		90
And so on						

This much being said, don't get trapped into microallocating people's time. Allocating personnel-months is sufficient for most projects of any strategic significance. Regularly reviewing a chart like this can also clear up a lot of misunderstandings. Absent information about how many other projects colleagues are working on, it is easy to misinterpret absences (or sheer exhaustion) as a lack of commitment.

Once you have made a realistic assessment of the human resources required for each project, you can further adjust your portfolio of opportunities to accommodate this assessment. The effort to group projects by type really pays off here. You have already given some thought as to what an ideal portfolio of projects would look like for your firm. Now you can be specific about the number of each kind of project you want and have the resources to pursue.

For the company we were advising, we suggested that it cut back the number of projects in its portfolio mix to include only one stepping-stone project, the three most important platform launches, five enhancement launches, five positioning options, and seven low-budget scouting options. This project load did not exceed the capacity of the organization. At the same time, it attended to the firm's need to generate growth through platform launches, to meet the enhancement needs of current customers, and to support a number of positioning options that would allow it to react swiftly should it be taken by surprise.

We didn't suggest that they completely kill off other good projects. Most of those could be deferred without undue damage, so they were kept in the opportunity register for future use if resources or opportunity emerged. You can also consider spinning off projects you don't have the capacity to handle, either through joint venture or other mechanisms (such as licensing).

Making comparisons within each category of launch or option allows you to make project trade-offs without having to worry about trading off between the different categories—that is a separate decision that gets made when you determine how many projects you want in each category. This can be a big relief, as it is common corporate practice to put people in the position of having to choose between an essential enhancement launch (a short-term goal) and a stepping-stone that is thought to be crucial to the firm's future viability (a long-term goal). Using the categories and your target number of projects within each category, you can compare launches to launches and options to options.

Naturally, your freedom of choice is also going to be constrained by your parent firm's strategy, if you are part of a larger organization. This is a good time to revisit figure 7-8, to make sure you know how free-flowing a pen the resource allocators in your company are apt to wield. If you are in the blank-checkbook category, you have considerable latitude with respect to resource access. Your big challenge then will be not to overestimate what can be accomplished by overloading people with too many projects. Just because the resources are there doesn't mean that they should be spent. So make sure you put each venture you're considering through a rigorous analysis. The other funding categories (line of credit and line-item approval) put more limits on spending and therefore on the number and extent of the opportunities you will be able to pursue.

Also make a realistic assessment of what else is going on in your corporate environment. If your company is in the midst of a major reorganization, merger, business crisis, or other significant change, the amount of time and attention people will have for new initiatives will be limited.

USING COMPETITIVE INSULATION FOR SELECTING PROJECTS WITHIN A CATEGORY

In addition to prioritizing projects on the basis of your company's interests and needs, you also want to get a sense of how big the window of opportunity is for your various projects within a category (e.g., within all stepping stones or all enhancement launches). This is a core element of real options reasoning that we haven't touched on yet: namely, timing. You can safely defer the "exercise" (active pursuit) of an option with a long expiration date. Those with near-term expiration dates, however, have to be either exercised or allowed to expire. In the world of real options, competitive behavior is the primary driver of expiration. Let's turn now to consider how competitor activity might suggest which options to actively pursue and which can be postponed.

Like their financial analogues, real options expire. Most of the time this has to do with competitive actions that close your window of opportunity, shorten the period during which you can exploit your advantage, capture significant first-mover advantages for the competitor, or create a strong cost position for the competitor. The extent to which you are insulated from competition of this nature should also affect decision making on which projects to pursue with urgency and which to postpone. This logic applies even more so to prospective launches—to the extent that the launch is well positioned competitively, it is more likely to yield attractive returns than if competitive action undercuts it rapidly.

Imitation shortens the opportunity to exploit a good idea. In traditional strategic decision making, barriers to competition (or market entry) play a big role in a firm's determination of where it should try to build a competitive position. The goal was to create a competitive advantage and then sustain it by relying on barriers that keep out competitors. Most young, small firms are extremely vulnerable to competitive attack, and hoping to hide behind entry barriers such as superior scope, scale, or cost advantages, is unrealistic. Instead, entrepreneurial thinkers try to determine where they can compete in such a way that they enjoy early insulation from competitive attack. In other words, competitors are prevented from copying them or otherwise driving out profits. Other things being equal, opportunities with potential protection from early attack are more attractive than opportunities in which rivalry is likely to be immediate.

The items in figure 8-8 represent a compilation of the most common sources of insulation. The more you have, the longer your potential advantage, and the more priority the project deserves, other things being equal.

The figure covers three types of insulation: Technical insulation results from barriers you create to prevent competitors from imitating your moves. Competence-based insulation stems from your firm's particular capabilities and will take competitors time to emulate. Relationship-based insulation stems from your unique relationship with customers and distributors, something that will take competitors some time to match.

FIGURE 8-8

SOURCES OF COMPETITIVE INSULATION

Answer yes or no to each of the following questions.

TECHNICAL INSULATION

____ The offering is an extension of a protected business you already have.

____ The offering uniquely leverages other proprietary assets.

____ Formal mechanisms are available (patents, trademarks, etc.) to protect the offering.

____ Commercialization will embody formally protected process or trade secrets.

____ Avenues to enforce formal protection mechanisms are available in your most important markets.

____ The firm will take advantage of these avenues of enforcement.

____ Patents, trademarks, or copyrights will cover key aspects of the offering.

____ It will take a long time for competitors to invent around or substitute the protected offering.

____ You will have access to inputs (e.g., raw materials) not available to your competitors.

____ You will have exclusive contracts with key suppliers and/or distributors and/or customers.

____ Customer costs to switch from your offering to another will be high.

____ The opportunity requires substantial initial investment.

COMPETENCE-BASED INSULATION

____ You will be farther down the production/operations learning curve than your competitors.

____ Your technology will be difficult to reverse-engineer.

____ Competitors will not have a comparable distribution channel.

____ Competitors will not have a comparable sales force.

____ Competitors will not have a comparable service capacity.

____ You will have a unique location advantage.

____ Your employees will be uniquely trained in the work required to create this offering.

____ You will have special know-how that will be hard for competitors to discover.

FIGURE 8-8 (CONTINUED)

SOURCES OF COMPETITIVE INSULATION

____ You will have developed special systems and procedures that competitors will find hard to replicate.

____ Competitors will find it difficult to replicate your systems and procedures without your talent.

____ This offering would not be successful without the development team in your firm.

RELATIONSHIP-BASED INSULATION

____ You will have a unique, good relationship with the purchaser of the offering.

____ You will have an unusually strong reputation in this area.

____ Your offering will capitalize on brand loyalty.

____ Your customers will trust you.

____ Your products have cachet—your target market will not accept imitations.

Matching is nearly as bad as imitation. It is another way in which competitors can eliminate your profits. It occurs when competitors, having observed your success in solving an important customer problem, address the same problem but do it using technology or other resources proprietary to themselves. They find a different path to what is essentially the same end, as far as the customer is concerned.

Matching is a particular problem for industries in which customers neither know nor care much about the inputs to the product or service but evaluate it simply on the basis of what they perceive or observe. Many service industries—from insurance, to banking, to commercial lending—fall into this category. Often unable to judge the real quality of the product until long after the purchasing decision has been made, customers are forced to choose on the basis of those attributes they can observe. The situation creates the opportunity for matching. A current example of the hazard of matching is in the development of the personal digital assistant industry. Pioneered by Apple's Newton and successfully captured by 3Com's Palm Pilot handheld device, the market is now being contested by firms such as

Philips and Casio, each of which offer a new twist on the core functionality introduced in the original PDAs.

Matching can be intentionally, and sometimes even unintentionally, destructive. Drastic price cutting by incumbents that drive your profits through the floor and intimidation of your suppliers or distributors by large-share players are some ways in which firms that play hard ball can match you without even coming up with a comparable offering. How vulnerable are you to the threat of matching? Consider the items in figure 8-9. As with imitation, a project that has little risk of matching tends to be more attractive—other things being equal— than a project in which matching poses a substantial threat.

Blocking activities are actions taken by your competitors that prevent or considerably delay your ability to execute your opportunity. Since it serves no purpose to launch an opportunity only to have it stopped in its tracks, opportunities at high risk of being blocked should be returned to the opportunity register unless you can come

FIGURE 8-9

HOW SIGNIFICANT IS THE POTENTIAL FOR MATCHING?

Respond "agree" or "disagree" with the following statements.

____ The target arenas are ones that many companies think are exciting and worth entering.

____ You anticipate many competitors in your target arenas.

____ You expect intense response from existing competitors in your target arenas.

____ You expect a competitive response from firms with substantial resources.

____ There are many firms with the degree of competence needed to respond to your introduction.

____ Competitors have recently hired some of the talent associated with the target arena.

____ Competent players in other industries are aggressively pursuing similar offerings with alternative technologies.

____ The competitors you will be affecting are very competent.

____ The competitors' key staff members have very good track records.

up with a creative way of removing or circumventing the barriers. Look at the issues listed in figure 8-10 when trying to determine how forceful a blocking effort is likely to be.

Having thought through how vulnerable your options are to blocking and how rapidly your advantages from launch may be competed away by imitation or matching, use these insights to inform your project selection. Clearly, any opportunity in which blocking is a big deal should be postponed until you've figured out what to do about blocking. What you don't want is to burn cash while waiting for a block to be removed after you've gone to the trouble of developing the idea. The only time you should move immediately on a project with a high blocking risk is if the project is otherwise difficult to imitate or match and you can envision a fairly sure way to overcome the blocking hazard.

FIGURE 8-10

HOW LIKELY IS BLOCKING?

Respond "agree" or "disagree" with the following statements.

____ Entry barriers are high in most markets you will seek to access.

____ The potential offering is socially or politically controversial (e.g., the "abortion pill").

____ You can expect organized resistance to your entry into the arena.

____ There are many existing or potential regulatory barriers.

____ Competitors have preexisting relationships with key value-chain partners that you will need.

____ Your competitors have more influence with regulators than you do.

____ Competitors command more respect from the public eye than you do.

____ Competitors have a better relationship with the media than you do.

____ Competitors may use leverage over customers, distributors, or suppliers to block your entry into the market.

____ Competitors can prevent you from developing the contacts you will need to succeed.

____ Potential arenas are dominated by exclusionary business networks that prevent newcomers from entering.

Summary of Action Steps

The action steps that follow are meant to get you started on the concepts and processes discussed in the chapter. Feel free to elaborate in a way that works for your company.

STEP 1:   Get out the list of arena-building and model-transforming opportunities that you listed in chapter 7. The arena-building opportunities represent future aces and jacks, with perhaps some deuces for which technological developments are worth tracking. The model-transforming opportunities represent actions you can take to build future aces and jacks from current arenas.

STEP 2:   For each attractive opportunity on the list, assess the market and technical uncertainty by using the questions in figures 8-1 and 8-2. Plot each opportunity to the appropriate option or launch category in figure 8-3.

STEP 3:   Decide on what proportion of your resources you will allocate to each kind of initiative you might want to take—positioning options, scouting options, stepping-stone options, platform launches, and enhancement launches. The greater the uncertainty and amount of change in your arenas, the more resources you should allocate to options as a proportion of your overall portfolio. (Think of this as your initial rule of thumb—you can adjust it later as warranted by experience.)

STEP 4:   Estimate the number of personnel-months to months to completion of each project in your portfolio. Plot both your new and current initiatives in a format similar to that in figure 8-7. Assess how realistic you are being, and decide on the maximum numbers of each type of option or launch.

STEP 5:   Determine the personnel load on your organization for executing new initiatives and current ones, using the method demonstrated in table 8-1. Assess your capacity to carry this load for the next two years.

STEP 6: If you have more projects than capacity, consider which should be postponed or dropped, or how you will increase your capacity. Your objective is to manage your portfolio of projects so that they fall within the carrying capacity of your organization. Compare projects within a category with other projects within that category (e.g., compare launches with launches). Within a category, use the competitive assessment questions to determine how durable any advantage emerging from these projects is likely to be. Projects with good competitive insulation from imitation and low threat of matching should receive higher priority. Projects at high risk for blocking should receive lower priority, unless you can identify a way out of the block hazard.

STEP 7: Assign specific responsibilities to specific people and make a record of it, so that there is no future confusion as to who is supposed to do what, using a table like table 8-2.

STEP 8: Make it a point to regularly review capacity, the portfolio of opportunities, and the match of people to projects.

CHAPTER 9

SELECTING

AND EXECUTING

YOUR ENTRY STRATEGY

YOU ENTER THIS CHAPTER HAVING BUILT A PORTFOLIO OF entrepreneurial opportunities. You have gone from identifying opportunities to screening them, to focusing in on those that are now incorporated in an attractive portfolio of projects that will build your competitive position. In this chapter, and in chapters 10 and 11, we take up the challenges of adaptive execution of your ideas.

Adaptive execution involves three main activities. First is deciding on an entry strategy. This will depend in large part on what you anticipate competitive response will be. We will spend considerable time in this chapter demonstrating how to anticipate competitive behavior and response. Second (discussed in chapter 10) is planning to learn, rather than planning to meet objectives identified in advance, an essential practice when uncertainty is high. We will discuss a technique called discovery-driven planning that allows you to convert assumptions to knowledge at the lowest possible cost. Third (in chapter 11) is assessing project progress as it unfolds.

Anticipating competitor's responses is crucial to defining an entry strategy. If the new business models you put in place have significant impact on current competitors' performance, they will have no choice but to respond to you. To some extent, however, your choice of entry strategy can help shape the nature and impact of their reaction. Our goal is to help you avoid debilitating competitive interactions by using speed, skill, and surprise to outmaneuver competitors. The idea is to use your imagination rather than the organization's physical resources to compete successfully.[1]

No Sales Until the "First Five Sales"

The starting point for designing your entry strategy is to identify a few seed customers for each opportunity you seek to pursue. We ended chapter 8 by having you select a number of different initiatives with the potential to add significant value to your firm, whether they were ready for full-scale launch or not. For each of these, you should be able to identify one or more distinct customer segments. You should also be able to map a fairly accurate consumption chain and link attributes of your offering to an attribute map for each segment. The challenge now is to go out there and secure a commitment to purchase from your first few target customers.

We studied a small group of habitual entrepreneurs to see how they do this. One skill they seemed to possess was the ability to get customers to make some kind of commitment to a given set of attributes that they hoped to deliver, sometimes even before the product or service had been developed. These entrepreneurs see this commitment as affirmation of market acceptance of their new business model. One goes so far as to say that if he does not have some kind of commitment from several key stakeholders, he won't proceed, but will rather go back to his register and select another opportunity.

To keep our explanation of the process simple, we have focused on customers. Your opportunities may be dependent on other types of key stakeholders—distributors, suppliers, key skilled employees— each of which can be critical to your success.[2] In each case it is vital that you find a way of eliciting their support.

Obviously, all potential customers are not equally attractive. Nor are you equally attractive to them. The central challenge in creating that first set of customer transactions is zeroing in on those few customers on whom you can rely to get your business going. Be specific.

When entrepreneurial wanna-bes come to us with business plans, we actually insist that before they even think about spending a dollar on assets or expenses, they provide us with the names of at least five customers with a demonstrated willingness to buy. If they can't get an order, they should be able to get a letter of intent. If they can't get a letter of intent, they should be able to get a written expression of interest. If they can't even get an expression of interest from a living, breathing customer, they had better rethink their business model. (For some products it is first-time distribution rather than customers.)

Where should you look for these all-important first few sets of customers? A logical place is to look to those you are already serving well and with whom you have built a good relationship. Often, though, the real beneficiaries of a project in your portfolio will be customers who are new to you—either because you are resegmenting a market (as in chapter 3) or because you have achieved a breakthrough that will reconfigure the relations between players. In the latter case, the target segment doesn't even exist yet (as discussed in chapter 4), and you need a strategy to bring these new customers on board. If your existing customers won't see the value in what you are doing, avoid them until the business is off to a good start.[3]

A good place to begin is with what are sometimes called lead-steer customers.[4] *Lead-steer customers* are opinion leaders in their industry and/or are highly regarded by their peers. Corporations like those on the "most-admired" lists regularly published by the business press might qualify. Individuals who represent a segment that is highly desirable to you might do as well. The objective is to use these customers' enthusiasm about what you are doing to simultaneously test your assumptions about attribute maps and use their success with your offering to sell to others. Testimonials and actual experiences with real customers are critical if buying from you involves any kind of perceived risk.[5]

In trying to sell to these customers, bear in mind that the buying decision may be complex. If you are trying to market to consumers, then a distributor or another channel partner will usually be involved. If you are trying to sell to companies, they invariably have multiple employees who are involved not only in making the purchasing decision but also at many different—and potentially crucial—links in the company's consumption chain.

When planning your launch, you need to know the people involved in making the critical decision on whether to buy from you. You also need to get a feel for their needs and interests as far as the offering is concerned. Try to articulate to yourself, as best you can, your assumptions about how the sale will be closed. What will stop the sale? Who will try to stop the sale? Why should they stop the sale? What will clinch the deal? The idea is to be prepared to overcome obstacles to closing the sale before they arise.

You should be so familiar with these customers' consumption chains that you will have a good idea of how risky and difficult it will be for them to buy from you. How hard will it be for them to switch to your offering? How much will it cost them? If they need to learn to work with or operate your product or service, what is the training and adjustment burden? The greater the effort they must put into implementing your solution, the more you must convince them that the effort is worthwhile.

You might find it helpful to prioritize potential customers according to the extent to which you believe they will generate substantial benefits by adopting your offering and to which they perceive it to be a risky, effortful move. Figure 9-1 shows the resulting matrix, which you can use to help set priorities.

To illustrate how crucial understanding risk is to an entrepreneurial start-up, let's take the case of a young entrepreneur in the chemicals business. He had licensed some exciting catalytic technology from a former professor and was attempting to get refinery managers in the edible oil industry to switch to what he hoped would be a revolutionary, barrier-breaking product. His proposal was to sell a new kind of catalyst that would allow his customers to hydrogenate oil at a much lower cost than that incurred by current catalysts. Although his proposal made sense, it didn't offer much in the way of exciter features to his target audience.

This was because the annual savings for a refinery manager to switch to the new catalyst were modest—perhaps $15,000 per year per converter. Moreover, the refinery manager wouldn't personally benefit from the savings, which would appear on the plant expense budget and were not part of the criteria on which refinery mangers were evaluated.[6] Should a batch of oil be lost, on the other hand, the manager would be held responsible and the cost could exceed

FIGURE 9-1

PRIORITIZING THE FIRST FEW SALES

	Risk Low	Risk High
Benefit Low	SECOND PRIORITY Try to make the risk of not buying greater than the risk of buying, perhaps by using peer examples.	LOW PRIORITY Postpone the attempt to sell unless you can increase value or decrease risk.
Benefit High	FIRST PRIORITY Easy sell.	THIRD PRIORITY Credibly underwrite the risk for these customers. Your message might be "Don't worry, if it doesn't work out, send me the bill."

$150,000 per batch. This high-risk/low-reward proposition to switch to the new catalyst was a predictably hard sell, and our entrepreneur got nowhere with his "I'll save you money—trust me" pitch.

Finally, in desperation, the entrepreneur called on an old college friend who was running an oil refinery for the Unilever Corporation. The entrepreneur brought with him the professor who had developed the catalyst and who could credibly attest to its safety and quality. He even volunteered to donate the first batch of catalyst at no cost, just so his friend could try it out. His friend was persuaded to make the order. The catalyst worked well, and Unilever made the switch. In this industry at the time, the Unilever plants set the standard for what was considered cutting edge. Once it became known that Unilever had adopted the product, nearly every other plant in the region switched over as well.

The entrepreneur had achieved two critical outcomes. First, for the individual refinery managers, he had removed the risk of switching to his catalyst; in the event something went wrong, they could credibly argue that they were simply following the best practice in their industry. Second, he had increased the downside of their not switching to his product, because a leading manufacturer was using it. This first sale led rapidly to the next few sales required. With momentum well established, the entrepreneur went on to convert the bulk of his target customer segment to the new catalyst within eighteen months.

The most important deals, in short, are those that secure the critical first few sales. You do not have sales of a thousand units until you have sold a hundred, and you can't sell one hundred units until you have sold the first five. (We use the idiom "find the first five sales" to keep the idea fresh in people's minds.) The front end of the initial marketing plan should focus on how to target customer for these first few sales and how to reduce their risk of purchase.

ASSESSING COMPETITIVE RESPONSE

Having thought through who those first few buyers will be, you must next decide how aggressively you are going to move. To make this decision, you need to get a sense of the competitive terrain. In the rest of this section, we are assuming that you are entering a market where there are established competitors. (If you are entering into an entirely new market, you need not invest effort in analysis of past competitive behavior.) A critical variable is the response of likely competitors. Our research indicates that the success of any new business proposition is critically dependent on the venture's insulation from early, nasty, competitive attack.[7] Unless you have overwhelmingly powerful sources of competitive insulation (such as patents in the pharmaceutical industry), the response you get will be shaped in part by the initial moves you make.

Research conducted by us and by colleagues shows that two major factors dominate competitive response. The first relates to a competitor's motivation to challenge you in that arena. The second concerns its capacity to challenge you.[8]

Motivation has a lot to do with whether managers in competing organizations will feel threatened by your entry and feel that they must respond urgently. The degree of threat depends on how they view the competitive significance of the arena. If they have a sizable commitment to a competing solution for the customers you are going to start selling to, they will have a greater motivation to respond.

To gauge their level of commitment to the arena, you need to get a sense of their stake in it. Recall the stratification analysis explored in chapter 7. Using publicly available information, you can often get a rough estimate of which business areas fall into which category for your competitors, at least on a revenue basis. If your sought-after segment is in an "ace" or a "lucrative" category for your competition, the competitor probably has a considerable stake in preserving its position. In addition, businesses to which a competitor has made a long, accumulated psychological and resource commitment are more likely to be highly valued than new businesses. Another indicator of corporate commitment by your competitors is their relative effectiveness in a target arena. You can gauge this by assessing a competitor company's performance on the key drivers for that arena—if the firm regularly outperforms its competitors, it has a strong position and is more likely to seek to defend it. Intel, for instance, is widely known and respected for its control of competitive interactions in the microprocessor industry. Over the years, it has also shown that it is both capable of defending itself against new entrants in its core business, and motivated to do so. As a result, one does not lightly make a move against the company without being prepared for a vigorous response. Whatever the indicators, the level of competitor commitment should provide you with a basis for judging the amount of energy, attention, and resources that the competition is likely to pour into defending against your move or expanding its position.

Capacity to respond is also important to a competitor's propensity to react to your move. Even with all the motivation in the world, a competitor without the resources, or without the appropriate skills or technologies, cannot do you much harm. On the other hand, a competitor with lots of free cash flow (or cash reserves), lots of sunk costs in assets that could be mobilized against you, or a strong position with respect to distribution, supply, or standard-setting networks is going to be formidable.

Figure 9-2 summarizes some indicators of competitors' propensity to respond to your entry into a market. If the total of the commitment scores is 4 or less, categorize the competitor as having low commitment to respond; above 4 means it is highly committed to

FIGURE 9-2

INDICATORS OF COMPETITORS' PROPENSITY TO RESPOND

Score each item a 1 if the answer is no, a 2 if the answer is maybe, and a 3 if the answer is yes.

Questions

Indicators of commitment	What would you look at to make the judgment?
Is this arena important to them? Score: _____	Stake and position, such as percent of their sales or profits that stem from their participation in the arena. The higher the stake and the stronger the position, the more important the arena is likely to be.
Have they been increasing commitment in this area? Score: _____	Look for the following signs of increasing commitment: new product announcements, increases in publicly known resource allocation, and increasing fixed-asset commitments to the arena. The greater the increase in commitment to the arena, the more likely the competitors are to defend it.
Have they invested heavily in this arena? Score: _____	Examples are plant and equipment investments, considerable advertising expenditures, training investment.

Commitment total: _____

Indicators of capacity	What would you look at to make the judgment?
Do they have lots of slack? Score: _____	Look for this evidence of available slack: cash on hand, excess capacity, demonstrated ability to take on new challenges, and absence of distractions such as mergers or acquisitions. The greater the slack, the more they will be able to mount a response.
Is their current position strong? Score: _____	Evaluate their performance: Have they demonstrated an ability to consistently achieve superior performance on key ratios in their chosen competitive arenas? Are the best people working in the arena choosing to work for these competitors? Do they have a good reputation in this arena? The stronger their current performance, the more they will be able to mount an effective response.

FIGURE 9-2 (CONTINUED)

INDICATORS OF COMPETITORS' PROPENSITY TO RESPOND

Indicators of capacity	**What would you look at to make the judgment?**
Can they match our move easily? Score: _____	Evaluate how difficult it would be for the competitors to match the move: Is our move poorly protected? Can competitors easily access the same infrastructure and enabling technologies we use? Are there any customer switching costs or risks to using the competitors' offering? If our move is easy to match, the competitors will be more capable of doing so.
Is their cost of defense largely sunk? Score: _____	Do competitors already possess assets, plant, and equipment that may be used to mount a response? If so, they will be more able to defend (and more motivated to defend, since they might have to write off some portion of their assets if our move succeeds).

Capacity total: _____

respond. If the total of the capacity scores is less than 6, categorize the competitor as having low capacity to respond to your challenge; otherwise, categorize it as high capacity.

Use figure 9-2 to think through the likely competitive response you will have to cope with. You can then estimate how threatening the competitor is likely to be, based on its capacity and commitment to the arena. Figure 9-3 depicts a rough first cut. This should give you some idea of the scope and intensity of response that you can expect from moves you make against various competitors.

The information in figure 9-3 gives you some idea of what your initial strategy might be. Obviously, if you anticipate facing a combatant, you don't want to make a move that is likely to precipitate a knee-jerk response, such as massive price cutting. This brings us to the question of what specific moves you should consider as you enter. There are several alternatives, ranging from direct attacks to multiple-arena maneuvers.

FIGURE 9-3

LIKELY COMPETITIVE RESPONSES

	High Capacity	Low Capacity
Low Corporate Commitment	SLEEPING DOGS Make sure you are tracking them—should they decide the arena is attractive, they can mobilize fast.	BYSTANDERS For now, anyway, you don't need to worry too much about these competitors.
High Corporate Commitment	COMBATANTS Capable and motivated to pour significant effort into combating your moves. Expect a forceful response if you engage in a direct, visible attack.	SKIRMISHERS Determined but have to depend on limited resources to cope with your move; tend to be selective in their responses.

COMPETITIVE ENGAGEMENT

You may want to skip this section in your first pass through the book.

No competitor has exactly the same customers, product lines, geographic coverage, and so on that you have. Because of these differences, certain customers, subsegments, product lines, or some combination of these, will always be more interesting or important to your competitors than they are to you. This gives you the opportunity not only to establish a position yourself but to influence how competitors will try to compete with you.[9] You can influence their responses.[10] Four distinct kinds of competitive moves will be available to you: onslaughts, guerrilla campaigns, feints, and gambits.

Onslaughts

An *onslaught* is a direct, aggressive entry in a target arena. It typically involves a relatively expensive, high-commitment move to capture a significant position of the market for yourself. With an onslaught, you are hoping to capture an arena by establishing first-mover lockout, persuade incumbent competitors to withdraw, consolidate a fragmented industry, or at least deter competitors from expanding their presence. You will have accomplished your purpose when you succeed in deterring competitive entry or when existing competitors reduce their commitment to the target arena.

A well-known example of an onslaught occurred when Japanese semiconductor makers advanced on the Intel Corporation's DRAM (dynamic random access memory) business in the mid-1980s. The Japanese firms used what they termed a 10 percent rule, which meant that they would cut prices on DRAMs for every target customer by 10 percent until Intel gave up on the customer.[11] The eventual result of these cumulative attacks was Intel's complete withdrawal from the DRAM market.[12]

The principle danger with onslaughts is that they can precipitate a major counterattack by combatants (see figure 9-3). This can result in a war of attrition that leaves both the victor and the vanquished debilitated. The conditions under which you may want to undertake an onslaught are listed in figure 9-4.

If you are an entrepreneur or a small player, aggressive onslaughts may do you as much harm as they do to the competition, because you will generally be more vulnerable to a sustained struggle and more likely to have to give up first. A more subtle alternative is the guerrilla campaign.

Guerrilla Campaigns

The objective of a guerrilla campaign is to build your position by moving into an arena piecemeal, starting in one niche and then progressively expanding into other niches as your position consolidates. We use the term *guerrilla* because it calls to mind Mao Tse Tung's admonition that toppling a better-financed, larger, and entrenched opponent cannot be accomplished by means of conventional warfare.[13] Mao was among the first to put forth a documented set of principles for the conduct of a guerrilla campaign. These principles emphasize fluid positions and dynamic thrusts and retreats. Thus, rather than seeking to dominate a mainstream market, a competitor using a guerrilla strategy might selectively sell to a

FIGURE 9-4

WHEN DOES AN ONSLAUGHT MAKE STRATEGIC SENSE?

Respond "agree" or "disagree" with the following conditions.

_____ The competitor has much lower corporate commitment to the area than you do.

_____ Your assault is seen by informed observers as highly credible. (The greater the investment you make in a move, the more credible it will appear to others. Highly credible onslaughts often exacerbate competitors' weaknesses—both physical and psychological—dampening their will and their capacity for retaliation.)

_____ The competitor has attractive opportunities elsewhere and hence may be inclined to seek these opportunities.

_____ You can draw off support from allies prepared to commit resources to your effort. (These allies may be other stakeholders—such as distributors, customers, suppliers, and/or government agencies—that would like your onslaught to succeed.)

_____ You can deploy a disruption strategy along the lines discussed in chapter 5 to completely change the rules of the game, leaving your opponent at a serious disadvantage.

_____ The competitor would normally fight back but is in the midst of an internal crisis (acquisition, merger, divestiture, leveraged buyout, etc.) that is preoccupying management.

Scoring: If you don't have at least three "agree" responses, you should not even consider engaging in an onslaught. The ensuing response is likely to be ugly. The more "agree" responses that you have beyond three, the more an onslaught might work. Before making the move, however, you should validate the assumptions underlying your responses to the statements here and make sure that you have considered all relevant competitors, including those not currently engaged in the arena.

niche, then abandon it if their activities should attract the attention of a major player. Mao's principles also cleverly describe how to use an opponent's scale against them by forcing them to defend positions with heavy sunk costs and also to use their existing commitments to lock them into undesirable positions. A smaller player can thus be much more flexible with respect to pricing and product modification than a large player can afford to be. These ways of competing would strike a familiar chord with many a beleaguered manager today.[14]

The essence of the guerrilla campaign is to identify a niche in the market, preferably one that is underserved, and create a block-buster attribute map for this niche that competitors will be reluctant to match. This niche then serves as a guerrilla base from which you move into another niche, then another, and so on. If you are able to identify such niches, you may avoid the highly costly alternative of a full onslaught on the target arena. Niches are particularly useful for new entrants because they tend to be less visible and less threatening than an onslaught. The ideal reaction, especially from an incumbent combatant, is one that suggests the competitor doesn't perceive you to be a threat worthy of its concern. You will have the opportunity to build a substantial position before the competition notices that you are there. Figure 9-5 lists the conditions under which a guerrilla campaign is likely to succeed.

A classic example of a firm that pursued a guerrilla strategy is that of Progressive Insurance, described in chapter 3, which moved into the high-risk niche in automobile insurance. This niche move was actually met with relief on the part of some competitors. This is characteristic of a great guerrilla strategy—if established competitors find your chosen niche difficult to serve or a poor fit with their capabilities, they are unlikely to do anything to stop your progress. For several years, Progressive built its capabilities. Eventually, the company used the competences that evolved from serving its niche base to begin expanding into more attractive niches. Today, fully 15 percent of Progressive's portfolio of customers are in the standard (i.e., low-risk) segment, and the company ultimately hopes to mirror the industry at large, in which only 15–20 percent of all drivers are in its initial nonstandard segment.

An entire industry being reshaped by guerrilla competition is Internet business-to-business commerce. Many of the most promising of today's Internet start-ups began by serving as distributors or access points for small customer segments. Customers in these segments have found that they can create considerable scope when they consolidate their numbers globally, making serving their needs valuable for the first time. Thus, a segment that ordinarily would not be

FIGURE 9-5

WHAT MAKES A GUERRILLA CAMPAIGN SUCCESSFUL?

Respond "agree" or "disagree" with the following conditions.

_____ Consumption chain and attribute analyses have uncovered an initial seed niche and follow-up niches that are poorly served by existing offerings.

_____ You are able to focus your initial effort on the seed niche.

_____ You can rapidly achieve a decisive result in each of the target niches, which you can defend from later competition.

_____ Customers in the niche are vocal about being underserved or overcharged. They have negative attributes to complain about, and nobody seems to be listening.

_____ Competitors are reluctant to match—particularly if matching means that they must extend the additional attributes to their entire market at great cost.

_____ Customers in the niche are willing to pay a premium if you meet their needs.

Scoring: If you don't have at least three "agree" responses, you should not even consider engaging in a guerrilla campaign, because you do not have the right conditions to be able to grow from your initial base. The more "agree" responses that you have beyond three, the more a guerrilla campaign might work. Before making the move, however, you should validate the assumptions underlying your responses to the statements here and make sure that you have considered all relevant competitors, including those not currently engaged in the arena.

---

well served because it is too small can leverage low-cost Internet transactions to become a potentially valuable niche globally.

One example of such a niche consists of laboratory scientists. Formerly, obtaining the sometimes esoteric chemicals that they require was an extremely laborious process of hunting through voluminous catalogs and manuals that listed every chemical stocked by the supplier. The reason was that under a manual system, it was not cost-effective for specialty providers to tailor their catalogs to the needs of a given subset of scientists. Internet player Chemdex, however, has begun to address the needs of this under-served niche by allowing fast, accurate searching for chemicals on a Web site that can be tailored specifically to the user community looking for materials. On the supply side, Chemdex can work with suppliers to obtain favorable pricing by consolidating many small orders into larger-volume buys.

Another example is eBay. The company found a loyal following among collectors and other consumers who realized enormous benefit in being able to access a vast number of potential buyers for their goods; another benefit to customers was the time they could save in searching for items of interest. From this initial niche, eBay seems poised to pursue ever more challenging and aggressive incursions into the mainstream; it has purchased high-end auctioneer Butterfield and Butterfield to reach the market for luxury goods more systematically. This move finally caught the attention of dominant incumbents and prompted a hurried alliance between upscale auctioneer Sotheby's and Amazon.com.

Feints

If the competitors that worry you most are engaged in multiple arenas (this could mean multiple industries, products, or even individual customers), you have the opportunity to use a feint to help influence how they react. A *feint* involves two arenas—the focal arena, to which you attract the focus of the competitor, and the target arena, which is your true strategic objective. (These terms are also used in the discussion of gambits, below.) The feint is a direct attack on a focal arena that is highly important to your competitor. Unknown to this competitor, your true target arena lies elsewhere. The purpose of the feint is to force your competitor to attend to the arena you are attacking rather than continue committing resources to your target arena.

We observed a small, scrappy candy manufacturer in an emerging economy using feinting to great advantage. Although his primary business was manufacturing hard candy and chewing gum, he also ran (basically at break-even) a toffee candy plant. In reviewing his portfolio of businesses, we asked why on earth he would run a small-scale, funds-consuming toffee plant when the rest of his business was highly profitable and enjoying strong regional growth. "Simple," he replied. "I'm not worried about local competition in candy, and I'm not really interested in the toffee business. But every so often, managers at a giant multinational toffee company, which sells massive amounts of toffee in my country, get the idea that they would like to enter the candy business here. The minute I get wind of it, I drop my toffee prices in a hurry. I may lose money for a while, but for every dollar I lose, the international giant, which is fifty times my size, loses fifty dollars, which they have to explain to their head office overseas. It doesn't take long before they get the message and back off from the candy business." The interesting thing about this story is that this entrepreneur is actually using the giant company's size and competitive success in toffee against it.[15]

With feints, you also have timing choices. You can feint and then move into your target arena afterward, or you can feint and move into your target arena at the same time. You can reduce pressure after the feint has succeeded, or you can keep up the pressure to keep the competition distracted. What you decide to do will be a function of the resources you have at your disposal. If you can keep up the pressure, increasing it (or reducing it), depending on your competitor's behavior, you can use the feint as a tormenting factor that keeps the competitor constantly distracted. Our candy manufacturer offers an excellent example of how tormenting a major opponent can keep the opponent boxed in.

Feints can succeed with relatively little investment, but the threat must be credible. In addition, they tend to work well only when the focal arena is of considerable interest to your competitor. Your competitor is likely to perceive the feint as a significant threat in any arena in which it has substantial commitment or that drives a lot of its profitability. Your feint's credibility is a function of your perceived intentions: The greater the apparent amount of your investment, the more hostile and credible your competitor will consider your attack. An example of a strategy of combined feints and onslaughts is illustrated in box 9-1.

Gambits

Gambit is a term taken from chess, in which a player knowingly sacrifices a piece to gain strategic advantage. In competitive exchange, a *gambit* means visibly retreating or even withdrawing from a sacrificial arena with the express intention of prompting your competition to expand into it. Meanwhile, you use this diversion of attention to the sacrificial arena to build a position in another arena—your target

BOX 9-1

WHO WILL FEED FLUFFY?
HOT CONTESTS IN THE PET FOOD BUSINESS

In the late 1980s, a new segment of affluent, diet-conscious pet owners emerged. This segment tended not to have children but did have both money and strong emotional attachment to their pets. Ralston Purina, the dominant player in pet foods, with nearly 30 percent market share and the well-known Purina brand name, initially didn't bother much about this emerging segment. Start-up companies instead targeted it, introducing brands such as Iams and Hill's Science Diet. These foods were initially sold in specialty pet shops or through veterinarians.

At the time, the distribution channels for pet food were changing significantly. Pet supermarkets such as PETsMART and PETCO eroded the market share of supermarket channels. These category-killer superstores positioned themselves as offering the same or superior products at lower prices. Among other things, they started stocking specialty foods such as the gourmet pet products made by Iams.

Ralston wanted to prevent the entry of the high-end competitors into supermarkets and to consolidate the Ralston position there, making the supermarket Ralston's target arena. Ralston feinted by developing and launching its Pro Plan line directly into pet shops and specialty stores. It was positioned as a high-end food but priced slightly below Iams and Hill's. This precipitated a major defensive reaction from the two companies, who introduced new, even-higher-quality lines in the specialty channels, coupled with in-store promotions to pet owners. This defensive move consumed all their available resources and reinforced the positioning of these foods as superpremium products that could not be bought in supermarkets. In defending their focal arena for fear of compromising their brand image, Iams and Hill's locked themselves out of the Ralston's target arena—the supermarket mass-merchandising channels.

The feint having succeeded, Ralston next executed an onslaught. It introduced to the supermarket a product called Purina O.N.E. (Optimum Nutrition Effectiveness). This was a premium-brand pet food of a quality almost the same as Ralston's Pro Plan line but offered at a still lower price. Ralston's mass distributors now had a premium-image, lower-cost product to offer in competition with the pet superstores. This competitive interchange left Iams and Hill's locked out of the traditional Ralston channels, while Ralston retained a foothold in the specialty stores with its ProPlan product.

Note: Data on the pet food industry are taken from David Collis and Toby Stuart, "Cat Fight in the Pet Food Industry (A)," Case 9-391-189 (Boston: Harvard Business School, 1991) and from additional published material collected for this book.

arena. Gambits can be used to signal competitors that you are willing to give up position in the focal arena in exchange for position in the target arena. If a competitor has already become competent in the focal arena, it would probably prefer to expand there rather than put much energy into fighting for position with you in your target.

As in chess, you sacrifice a playing piece of low value to establish a stronger position or to defend a piece of higher value. By purposefully and visibly retreating from your position in the focal arena, you entice your competitor to increase its investment. Your true objective is to build position in your own target arena. If the gambit works, your competitor is kept busy building position in the focal arena while you develop your position in your target arena. Note that you need not withdraw completely—if you do, you are giving up future opportunities to feint. The greater your withdrawal, the more credible your gambit and the more opportunity opened up for your competitor.

A gambit features prominently in the long rivalry between Bic and Gillette. Bic and Gillette have competed with each other for decades in multiple markets. Two arenas in which they clashed are disposable lighters and razors. Gillette's traditional competitive strategy for razors was to focus technology on increasingly sophisticated cartridge-based shavers. Bic, on the other hand, developed formidable abilities to manufacture inexpensive, disposable products. Bic's aggressive entry into the disposable-razor market in 1975 forced a similar entry by Gillette. Gillette's entry into the disposable business cannibalized its highly profitable cartridge-razor business, which might have been a disaster for the company, since razors are the core of its business.

After ten years of razor warfare, with low profits for both Gillette and Bic, Gillette executed a gambit in lighters, as we described in chapter 7. Bic had a strong position in lighters and was making much better profits there than in razors. In 1984, Gillette withdrew entirely from lighters and redirected its resources into razors.

Bic accepted the gambit and diverted razor resources to build its lighter division. Meanwhile, Gillette focused on building position in razors. Within two years, Gillette had a 50 percent share in razors and was diverting the profits generated into a string of new razor products, particularly in the high-priced, cartridge segments. Although its position at the lower end of the market eroded, six years later Gillette executed an onslaught in the premium-priced razor market with the 1990 introduction of the Sensor razor, a stunning success for the company.

Note that as a result of feints and gambits, both parties can end up better off—in effect, they allow both parties to expand position, you in your target arena, and your competitor in its focal arena.[16]

Combinations of Moves

The three stratagems of onslaught, feint, and gambit can be combined into more complex moves. In one fascinating case, Philip Morris used combined onslaughts and feints to recapture its position in the U.S. arena and to position itself to build a dominant position in the Eastern European arena. These moves came to be known as the Marlboro wars. In the early 1990s, R. J. Reynolds (RJR) was using discount and low-priced brands to erode share for premium-brand cigarettes in the United States. Philip Morris had seen its leading premium brand's (Marlboro's) 30 percent share of the U.S. segment erode significantly. On April 2, 1993 ("Marlboro Friday"), Philip Morris executed an onslaught by announcing a 20 percent price reduction on Marlboro cigarettes in the United States. Two weeks later, instead of cutting back on advertising, Philip Morris increased it substantially. RJR responded by matching prices and boosting advertising in the United States.

Although the cost was great, the price-cutting onslaught allowed Philip Morris to recapture share that had been lost to discount brands. In November 1993, RJR signaled a truce—the company announced a 10 percent increase in U.S. prices for its premium brands. Within three days, Philip Morris increased the price of Marlboro by the same amount, leaving Marlboro back at a 30 percent share of the U.S. market, albeit at lower prices. The onslaught, in other words, accomplished its purpose.

This adventure of Philip Morris in the United States turned out to be a feint in the global game! Philip Morris could afford to incur losses in the United States, but RJR could not. Prior to the Marlboro wars, RJR had been establishing a strong position in cigarettes in Eastern Europe, where, as of 1994, about 700 billion cigarettes were sold per year and sales growth was rapid. At the time, the U.S. market was roughly 500 billion cigarettes, representing a 15 percent decline over the previous decade. Defending RJR premium brands such as Winston and Camel in the United States diverted resources that the firm could otherwise have used to continue building position in Eastern Europe.

By the end of 1993, RJR had let 10 percent of its U.S. workforce go. Philip Morris, in contrast, was flourishing: completing factories in Krasnodor, Volna, and St. Petersburg and continuing a three-year plan for the acquisitions of other Russian factories. It had also invested $800 million in acquisitions and joint ventures with local cigarette companies in Russia, Lithuania, Kazakhstan, Ukraine, Poland, Hungary, Czech Republic, and former East Germany.[17] Thus, while RJR was defending its eroding position in the U.S. arena, Philip Morris was building its position in the higher-growth Eastern European arena.

DESIGNING ENTRY WITH COMPETITIVE RESPONSE IN MIND

You may want to skip this difficult section in the first pass through this book. Let's now apply these concepts to market entry, using the pet food industry in the mid-1990s as an example.[18] The pet food industry is a straightforward example for illustrative purposes because factors such as new technologies, patents, and proprietary systems don't muddy the picture. In the 1990s the pet food industry entered a period of slowing growth after enjoying several years of strong growth and profits. We'll examine the U.S. pet food industry from the perspective of the Purina division of Ralston, which in 1986 was delivering 27 percent of the Ralston's total revenues.

In the mid-1990s, Ralston had three major competitors: Heinz, Nestlé, and Mars. The U.S. pet food division management of Ralston was facing the problem of how to develop its positions in seven subsegments of the pet food business: dry, moist, and canned dog food; dry, moist, and canned cat food; and a new product category called snack dog food. We use the situation these managers faced to illustrate how you might go about analyzing your own competitive situation.

Step 1: Assess Corporate Support   The first step in applying to market entry what you have learned is to assess the level of corporate support that each player can expect. Table 9-1 shows the contribution to revenues of four of the major players. Combined, these four players account for 55 percent of sales in this industry. Column 5 shows that the pet food divisions of Ralston and Mars are strong contributors to revenue and so are highly attractive to their parent companies and can expect high commitment from the parent. Heinz's pet food division is of medium attractiveness to its parent and can expect medium commitment. Nestlé's is low and so cannot expect much corporate commitment. Using the same logic that we discussed in chapter 6, we can anticipate the support that each of the competitor's divisions can expect from their corporation (figure 9-6). For example, if the target pet food product of Mars is in a strong position, it will get a blank checkbook; Nestlé will get only line-item approval.

Step 2: Assess the Motivation and Capacity of the Competition   Using figure 9-2, you can also assess the motivation and capacity of each player to aggressively respond to your potential moves (figure 9-7). For example, Mars and Ralston are likely to be highly combative, but Heinz and Nestlé will have far fewer resources to aggressively respond to Ralston's moves so will tend to be skirmishers.

TABLE 9-1

DATA ON TOP FOUR U.S. PET FOOD MANUFACTURERS

Company	1 Brand	2 Market Share of U.S. Pet Food	3 Share of Largest Competitor	4 Relative Share[a]	5 Pet Food Percentage of Company Revenues	6 Attractiveness to Parent
Ralston	Purina	27	12	2.25	33	High
Nestlé	Carnation	12	27	0.44	4	Low
Heinz	Nine Lives	8	27	0.30	9	Medium
Mars	Kal Kan	8	27	0.30	20 (estimate) Low U.S. share but no. 1 worldwide	High

[a]Column 2 divided by column 3.

FIGURE 9-6

CORPORATE RESOURCES SUPPORT AVAILABLE TO MAJOR PLAYERS IN THE PET FOOD BUSINESS

Competitive Position of the Target Pet Food Product	Corporate Commitment High	Corporate Commitment Low
Strong	Blank checkbook • Ralston • Mars	Line-item approval • Nestlé
Medium	Line of credit • Ralston • Mars Line-item approval • Heinz	Self-funded • Nestlé
Weak	Line-item approval • Ralston • Mars Self-funded • Heinz	

Step 3: Map Arena Attractiveness   First specify the criteria by which you will categorize the attractiveness of each of your arenas. Select what you consider to be key strategic variables that drive arena attractiveness in your business. In our analysis of the different pet food segments, we developed a score that combined attractiveness variables such as segment growth rates, product margins, shipping and materials costs, and trends in customer appeal to come up with the attractiveness ratings in figure 9-8.

The objective is to identify the arena attractiveness criteria of each of your industry's major categories. Next score each product category on industry attractiveness, then allocate the category into high, medium, or low attractiveness, as shown in figure 9-8 for pet foods.

Step 4: Map the Competitive Positions of Each Player   You now need to get a sense for how strong each player's position is in each category.

FIGURE 9-7

LIKELY COMPETITIVE CATEGORIES IN THE PET FOOD INDUSTRY

	High Capacity	Low Capacity
Low Motivation	None	
High Motivation	COMBATANTS	SKIRMISHERS
	Ralston	Heinz
	Mars	Nestlé

FIGURE 9-8

ARENA ATTRACTIVENESS OF MAJOR PRODUCT CATEGORIES

Arena	Dry Cat	Dry Dog	Moist Cat	Moist Dog	Canned Cat	Canned Dog	Snack Dog
Attractiveness	High	Medium	High	Medium	Medium	Low	High

Decide which criteria you will use to determine business positions. Then score and allocate each player's position for each product category, as is done in figure 9-9. We used the stratified revenues for each of the four major players as a proxy for a more detailed analysis of their business position. (If you don't have detailed data, be pragmatic; use the best representative data at your disposal, and be careful not to overinterpret.) We use A, B, and C instead of strong, medium, and weak to remind ourselves that we are using revenues as a proxy for business position. Note that the arenas in our illustrative pet food industry are product categories. You might end up with other categories, such as market segment, customer type, or geography.

In figure 9-9 the following patterns can be observed: Ralston is strong in dry products, Mars in canned products, Heinz only in canned cat products, and Nestlé in cat food products.

FIGURE 9-9

COMPETITIVE POSITION OF FOUR TOP PET FOOD PRODUCERS

	Ralston	Mars	Heinz	Nestlé
Dry dog	A	B		B
Dry cat	B	C	C	A
Moist dog	C			
Moist cat	C		C	
Canned dog		A		C
Canned cat	C	A	A	A
Snack dog	C	C	B	

Note: A = strong, B = medium strength, C = weak.

Step 5: Decide on Your Organization's Preferred Strategic Inclinations
Recalling your own probable access to corporate resources from your
corporate resource profile (see chapter 7), you now need to decide
what strategic moves you would prefer. To illustrate, we'll look at the
pet food industry from Ralston's perspective. It is number one in the
industry (27 percent share) and dominates the dry food segments
(with its famous Chow brand name).

The pet food division contributes 33 percent of company revenues but 45 percent of its profits. This is a very profitable, attractive
business from Ralston's point of view, with margins of 20–25 percent.
A simplified depiction of Ralston's portfolio of pet food products
appears in figure 9-10. For example, compared to its competitors,
Ralston has a strong competitive position (position A) with dry dog
food, which is considered a medium attractive arena, and a medium
strength position B in the highly attractive dry cat arena. Since Ralston does not produce canned dog food (a low attractive arena), the
squares across the "Low" row are blank. Ralston's management will
likely support any moves that will build dry cat, snack dog, and moist
cat positions and spend aggressively to consolidate/defend the dry
dog position. The canned cat and moist dog arenas are not core to
Ralston, but that they might be useful for strategic maneuvering.

Step 6: Assess the Strategic Inclinations of Each Key Competitor You can anticipate what your competition will want by assessing its current position as you have done for Ralston in figure 9-10. Where they can, competitors will want to strengthen their positions from right to left, starting at the top row, where the industry attractiveness is highest. They want little movement in the bottom row, except perhaps to exit. This should give you some ideas on what kinds of moves your competitors will find most desirable.

For the sake of example here, will conduct this analysis only for Mars, which is Ralston's only *combative* competitor. Normally we would (as you should) do the analysis for every major player. With $3 billion in sales, Mars is the number one manufacturer of pet food worldwide. The company has strong positions in canned pet products of all kinds and a strong advertising presence in all the large global arenas. Interestingly, Mars is privately owned, which means that it may have a lot more strategic flexibility than a does firm that has to answer to shareholders. Mars might seek to play by different rules.

As we can see in figure 9-11, Mars would probably like to build positions in dry cat and snack dog foods, which means that it could go head-to-head with Ralston. And it may have a lot of resources with which to do this. Another valuable aspect of its dry cat food position is that aside from being an attractive segment in its own right, it also has potential for use as a feint against Ralston. Mars managers are likely to also seek to hold and consolidate their position in canned cat

FIGURE 9-10

CURRENT STRATEGIC POSITIONING OF RALSTON'S PET FOOD PRODUCTS

Attractiveness	Position A Strong	Position B Medium	Position C Weak
High		Dry cat	Snack dog Moist cat
Medium	Dry dog		Canned cat Moist dog
Low			

FIGURE 9-11

CURRENT STRATEGIC POSITIONING OF MARS'S PET FOOD PRODUCTS

Attractiveness	Position A Strong	Position B Medium	Position C Weak
High			Dry cat Snack dog
Medium	Canned cat	Dry dog	
Low	Canned dog		

and dog food, because these are arenas in which they have already established strong positions with considerable sunk assets, excellent brand image, and solid distribution access. Dry dog food is another potential feint because Mars does not have a huge position in the arena whereas Ralston does.

Step 7: Map Each Competitor's Business Position against Your Own   Map every point at which your firm (in this case, Ralston) shares arenas with each other firm. Start with a chart similar to figure 9-12, listing your competitors' positions in rows and your own in columns. Make one chart for each competitor. (Again, we have done this only for Mars here.)

Notice that each cell is numbered. For instance, cell 3 shows that canned cat and canned dog are in position A (strong) for Mars and C (weak) for Ralston. A single asterisk indicates that Ralston does not currently produce the product. A double asterisk indicates that Mars does not currently produce the product. Thus cell 9 shows that Mars offers neither moist cat food nor moist dog food.

As you inspect figure 9-12, you can make the following interpretations:

1.   Canned cat in cell 3 is important to Mars but not to Ralston, thus providing an ideal feinting or tormenting arena for Ralston. If Ralston were in canned dog (cell 3), it, too, would be a good tormenting arena.

FIGURE 9-12

MAPPING OF IMPORTANCE OF SEGMENTS FOR RALSTON VERSUS MARS

	RALSTON		
	A	B	C
MARS			
A	1	2	3 Canned cat Canned dog*
B	4 Dry dog	5	6
C	7	8 Dry cat	9 Snack dog Moist cat** Moist dog**

*Ralston does not offer this product.
**Mars does not offer this product.

2. Mars depends heavily on canned pet foods (cell 3) and will be highly sensitive to moves against these segments.

3. Snack dog, moist cat, and moist dog (cell 9) are virtually unattended by Mars and Ralston.

4. Finally, Ralston is highly dependent on, and therefore vulnerable to feinting by Mars in, dry dog food (cell 4).

Now let us add another layer of insight by using typestyles to indicate attractiveness (figure 9-13). Cell 8 shows that dry cat food (in bold type) is a highly attractive segment. Cell 3 shows that canned cat food (in italic type) is a moderately attractive segment for both companies and that canned dog food (in plain type) is a fairly unattractive segment.

Before going on to interpretation, we finally insert the level of support that Mars can expect for the various segments (figure 9-14). Using figure 9-6, the corporate support potential for each product is shown in the left-most column. The figure shows that the Mars pet

FIGURE 9-13

MAPPING OF SEGMENT ATTRACTIVENESS FOR RALSTON VERSUS MARS

	RALSTON		
	A	**B**	**C**
MARS			
A	1	2	3 *Canned cat* Canned dog*
B	4 *Dry dog*	5	6
C	7	8 **Dry cat**	9 **Snack dog** **Moist cat**** *Moist dog***

Note: Bold type denotes products with a high degree of attractiveness. Italic type denotes products of medium attractiveness. Plain type indicates products with low attractiveness.
*Ralston does not offer this product.
**Mars does not offer this product.

food unit can probably expect a blank check for any Mars A-position products. Mars B products will probably have to appeal for a line of credit, and Mars C products will have to get line-item approval.

If we review the competitive positions in figure 9-14, we see the following important patterns:

1. Mars is particularly strong and therefore sensitive in canned food for both cats and dogs (cell 3) and will get a blank check-book to defend/consolidate its position.

2. Dry cat (cell 8) is a highly attractive segment that could be a future focus of Mars. Unless Ralston can keep Mars out, Mars may be in a position to move aggressively here and can do a lot of damage by cutting price or otherwise increasing rivalry in the arena. Mars may be able to drum up line-item approval from Mars corporate to attack this segment.

FIGURE 9-14

MAPPING OF RALSTON VERSUS MARS

	RALSTON		
	A	**B**	**C**
MARS	1	2	3
A **Blank** **Checkbook**			*Canned cat* Canned dog*
	4	5	6
B **Line of** **Credit**	*Dry dog*		
	7	8	9
C **Line-Item** **Approval**		**Dry cat**	**Snack dog** **Moist cat**** *Moist dog***

Note: Bold type denotes products with a high degree of attractiveness. Italic type denotes products of medium attractiveness. Plain type indicates products with low attractiveness.
*Ralston does not offer this product.
**Mars does not offer this product.

3. From Ralston's point of view, canned cat (cell 3) is a feint opportunity. It is highly important to Mars, while not important to Ralston. As an A category for Mars and Ralston's fourth biggest segment, canned cat feints will tend to be credible.

4. Snack dog is a growth opportunity for Ralston because it is a highly attractive segment yet only a small part of the Mars current portfolio (cell 9). Mars may be able to get line-item approval to build this segment, so highly visible moves by Ralston are likely to be contested.

5. Moist cat is also a growth opportunity. It is highly attractive, yet Mars (cell 9) is not yet in the game. A launch via onslaught by Ralston is worth considering.

6.   Ralston's major vulnerability is dry dog. It is currently a medium-position product for Mars (cell 4) but is of high importance and medium attractiveness to Ralston. If Mars cuts prices in this segment, it could degrade the entire segment to a low attractiveness category.

7.   At this point in time, moist dog (cell 9) is unlikely to become a focal arena. The danger for Ralston, however, is that other players such as Heinz and Nestlé can use this segment to build their positions in dog foods, which are important to Ralston. There is also the risk that advances in the production technique for moist foods might challenge the dominance of cans, which are expensive to ship and often awkward to use.

8.   Aside from the existing business positions, it is also interesting to observe where the combatants are not currently engaged. Ralston, for instance, might have gained considerable strategic value with a canned dog product that it could use for feinting against Mars in the event that Mars attempts to make inroads in the dry dog segment.

Having completed an analysis like this one, you are now in a position to begin working through various combinations of competitive moves. One combination of plays for Ralston would be the following (there are, of course, other combinations you may wish to consider):

Offensive Plays by Ralston

1.   Use a guerrilla campaign approach to systematically build the attractive dry cat segment, using the opportunity inventory to identify niches that focus on model-transforming opportunities for enhancing attributes or extending the attribute map for each niche. It may be worthwhile to do a stratification analysis by geography and by distribution channels to find key distributors and regions where you can do this.

2.   Simultaneously feint in canned cat, which will help divert Mars away from dry cat. Use feinting rather than tormenting because we want to avoid provoking Mars into an unnecessary war of attrition.

3.   Since Mars's strength lies in canned products, an onslaught on moist cat to secure a strong position early on might be worth launching, particularly since Mars would probably need a line of credit to develop a product here.

4.   Since Mars can only get line-item approval for its snack dog position, use the model-transforming opportunities from the opportunity register to launch a guerrilla campaign that will help to build in this segment selectively.

Defensive Plays by Ralston

1.   Consolidate and prepare to defend potential attacks on dry dog, using the model-transforming opportunities from the register to aggressively and continually enhance or extend attributes. By continually redefining the most favored attribute set, Ralston can minimize price-eroding, reactive responses to feints, or attacks by Mars on this segment.

2.   Seriously consider developing a canned dog product line to use as a feint against Mars.

In hypercompetitive conditions, one of the single biggest considerations, after knowing that you can create an attribute map that targets customers, is how your competitors are likely to respond and what you can do about it. The techniques we have presented in this chapter should help you think through how you want to launch each of your initiatives into the market and how your competitors might react.

SUMMARY OF ACTION STEPS

The action steps that follow are meant to get you started on the concepts and processes discussed in the chapter. Feel free to elaborate in a way that works for your company.

STEP 1:   Identify the first few customers for your new business model (using the "first five sales" as a guiding principle). Determine the priority that you will give them, using the risk/benefit trade-offs depicted in figure 9-1.

STEP 2: Articulate the strategy you will use to persuade them to begin transacting with you by mitigating any risks that they may anticipate. Make sure that you have clearly identified all the parties in the client organization that will need to be positively involved in the purchase.

STEP 3: For each major customer arena that you intend to pursue, identify the major competitors that will be affected, as in table 9-1.

STEP 4: Assess the level of corporate support that each player can expect, illustrated in figure 9-6.

STEP 5: With their potential corporate support in mind, assess the commitment and capacity of the players to respond to your potential moves aggressively. Use the questions in figure 9-2 as a guide, as illustrated in figure 9-7.

STEP 6: Specify the criteria by which you will categorize arena attractiveness. Analyze and map the arena attractiveness of each of your industry's major categories, as in figure 9-8.

STEP 7: Specify the criteria you will use to decide on your business position and map competitor positions, as in figure 9-9.

STEP 8: Map the competitive positions of each player, one map per player, as in figures 9-10 and 9-11. Use these figures to do a first-cut assessment of the strategic inclinations that you and each major competitor will have.

STEP 9: Systematically build a competitive mapping of your business categories versus those of each competitor (figure 9-12); then use bold, italic, and plain type to depict arena attractiveness (figure 9-13); and finally add the resource support that the competitor can expect (figure 9-14), one for each competitor.

STEP 10: Use figure 9-14 to decide what strategic moves to make and anticipate responses.

CHAPTER 10

PUTTING

DISCOVERY-DRIVEN

PLANNING TO WORK

IN THE PREVIOUS CHAPTER, YOU TRIED TO PREDICT HOW competitors would respond to your moves to reconfigure business models. Your choice of entry strategy was influenced by your assumptions about their responses. Because you don't know for sure what they will do, you have no choice but to make assumptions about competitive reaction. Assumptions are just that—you can't be sure that the competitors will act as you expect. Nor can you be sure that the markets, products, distribution, or supply system changes that you intend to introduce will pan out as you hope. The more uncertain the project, the more you must rely on the best assumptions you can make for your decisions.

In effect, you can be certain only about the uncertainty, which pretty much guarantees that the outcomes of your new initiative will be different from what you have planned. As discussed in chapter 4, Bob Goergen never dreamed that the small religious-candle-making firm he acquired for $200,000 in the early 1980s would have a market capitalization of $1.5 billion in mid-1999. Nobody who supported the Iridium project over the course of its decade-long development phase would have dreamed that it would go bankrupt within a year of launch. Who would have thought that a technology leader like Intel would have been virtually forced out of its core DRAM business just a few years after having completely capturing a dominant position?

This brings us to a central question we pose in this book: How do you plan and manage an initiative whose direction and outcomes are not yet known? In this chapter, we tackle that question, picking up on the theme of adaptive execution that is so characteristic of habitual entrepreneurs. You will be exposed to the adaptive planning methodology that we developed from work originating from the wisdom of Zenas Block, a habitual entrepreneur who provided us with many key insights. We call this adaptive planning method *discovery-driven planning*. It reflects the habitual entrepreneurs' propensity to stop over-analyzing and get started, aggressively using the outcomes of their early efforts to redirect and learn their way to the real opportunity.

Discovery-driven planning is vastly different from conventional planning. In conventional planning, success means delivering numbers that are close to what you thought you would deliver. In discovery-driven planning, success means generating the maximum amount of useful learning for the minimum expenditure. We'll show you how to use this process and illustrate how it can help you create discipline and control without imposing inappropriate requirements on your projects.

WHY DISCOVERY-DRIVEN PLANNING?

The concept of discovery-driven planning had its beginning in frustration. In one company after another, we saw managers in charge of major new initiatives who were miserable in the straitjackets of conventional planning. This often led to dysfunctional behavior. To meet the planning requirements imposed by their management, people would come up with numbers based on untested assumptions. Even worse, they would come up with numbers based on what they thought would get their projects approved. The ink would barely be dry when unfolding experience revealed the numbers to be wrong. Then, six or twelve months down the road, a senior executive would come barging in, demanding to know why the project managers were "off plan": "Why didn't you make your numbers?" What followed could be nasty, with senior management's insisting that such variances are symptomatic of incompetent management, when in fact having outcomes that were not expected is typical in high-potential ventures. An organization in which this is happening is an organization deprived of permission to learn.

Plans in which success is judged by the lack of deviation between plan and outcome are fine for working in well-understood contexts. They are toxic in situations in which little is known. Like real options reasoning, discovery-driven planning is most useful when the situation is highly uncertain.

In conventional planning, you extrapolate to the future from a well-understood and predictable platform of past experience. With a project that has high uncertainty, there is no such platform. In the absence of hard knowledge, plans must necessarily be made on the basis of assumptions.

THE ASSUMPTION-TO-KNOWLEDGE RATIO

In any highly uncertain venture, the proportion of assumptions you need to make relative to the knowledge you have is considerable. We refer to this proportion as the assumption-to-knowledge ratio. Managing when most of your decisions are based on assumptions is a completely different proposition from running an operation in which you know what is going on. You will find yourself making decisions about people, assets, markets, technologies, risks, revenues, and other critical project elements on the basis of assumptions. Under high levels of uncertainty, the data simply don't exist. Nobody knows, and you won't be an exception.

While you search for some breakthrough insight, such as GEFS's insight into debt-delinquent behavior (chapter 6) or Citibank's revolutionary view of the credit business (chapter 5), your primary challenge is to maximize the conversion of assumptions to knowledge at the minimum possible cost. Remembering that you are working with assumptions can be especially difficult given the way we tend to surround assumptions with a cloak of reality. People are hired, computers bought, marketing materials prepared, and so on, all on the basis of the best assumptions you have available at the time. Before long, what you originally knew were assumptions start to look, feel, and smell completely real to you. The problem is that the reality you are experiencing is self-constructed and self-sustaining.[1]

Consider the Iridium system discussed in chapter 8. From a technical point of view, the project is a stunning success. Yet the project got nowhere near enrolling the 500,000 subscribers it needed to succeed. In its first year of business, only about 10,000 people demonstrated that they truly wanted an expensive, heavy phone with poor sound quality that must be used outdoors. Assumptions that global access would outweigh these concerns did not materialize. Iridium may yet find the right market and come up with a package of solutions that good customers find irresistible, but the assumptions regarding the initial launch strategy were certainly off the mark.

Even smart companies can find themselves facing unpredictable outcomes when they operate in unfamiliar environments. Stories of corporate mistakes in moving to foreign cultures are legion. McDonald's effort to move its fast-food franchise to China is an example (box 10-1).

So, how do you plan under such fundamentally uncertain circumstances? Clearly, a method of planning appropriate to new situations has to acknowledge the challenge of high levels of assumptions relative to knowledge. Faced with this challenge, many well-intentioned managers throw up their hands and suggest that projects to create new business models are fundamentally unplannable. Nothing could be further from the truth. Indeed, done properly, planning for a new initiative takes as much, or even more, conscious, hard-headed discipline as planning for any other kind of business.

DISCIPLINES OF DISCOVERY-DRIVEN PLANNING

We have divided discovery-driven planning into the following six areas in which discipline is paramount: framing, competitive specification of deliverables, benchmarking, assumption testing, managing to milestones, and parsimony. In a conventional, platform-based business, managers generally approach planning and control as a problem of

---

BOX 10-1

McDonald's Goes to Beijing

McDonald's is not a company run by dummies. Yet managers of the store in Beijing forgot to check their assumptions regarding the nature of a McDonald's experience—after all, fast food is fast food, right? Fast food means fast turnover, and this premise guided the design and construction of the Beijing restaurant. It turned out, however, that for the average Chinese citizen, a McDonald's meal is not a low-budget nosh but a big chunk of disposable income. So customers came in droves, and they lingered to enjoy what was from their perspective an exotic, perhaps even gourmet experience. Imagine the managers' dismay when they realized that they had designed the restaurant for fast turnover and that the customers wanted none of that. McDonald's eventually solved the problem in Beijing by expanding the size of the restaurant.

In its early days in Moscow the company used a different strategy. Here, a gate on one side of the restaurant would admit a number of diners waiting in line. After a predetermined amount of time had passed, a gate on the other side would open, everybody in the place was asked to leave, and the process would be repeated for the next group.

---

pattern recognition and replication.[2] The patterns that have repeated themselves in the past are often a good guide to those patterns yet to come. The learning that works in a conventional project involves extrapolating expected results based on some kind of past history, measuring outcomes against those results, and making adjustments to bring the projections and the actual outcomes into closer convergence.[3]

In discovery-driven planning, in contrast, you are not looking for convergence (at least not at first) but rather at creating entirely new patterns. The process does not involve analysis of a reality that exists but *enactment*, that is, the creation of a new reality.[4] That is not to say that we encourage the wholesale abandonment of common sense. If left unguided, then creative enactment is as likely to produce interesting but uneconomical outcomes as it is to result in a successful entrepreneurial business. The key problem for the entrepreneurial manager is to balance the tension between creativity and novel thinking and the need for businesslike attention to costs, potential losses, and upside gains. The six disciplines we use to create the discovery-driven framework help to achieve this balance. They embody real options reasoning in a highly disciplined planning and control process.

Framing

Discovery-driven plans begin with a sense of purpose. Just as no profit-minded entrepreneur would dream of getting into a business in which the potential for significant gain was not part of the package, no company should launch a new business model without being clear on what would make it all worthwhile if things worked out. You have already taken the first step of developing a discovery-driven plan if you developed a frame for your piece of the business, as we discuss in chapter 2.

Be hard-nosed. Any new initiatives you take on must be worth the toll they take in effort (sometimes to the point of exhaustion) and risk. What this means is that any strategic action should have the prospect of substantial, quantifiable impact on the firm. By *impact* we mean bottom-line impact—a project targeted at improving efficiency should have at least the potential to save significant bottom-line dollars. A project aimed at enhancing revenues should at least have the prospect of adding substantial profits. Otherwise, why bother? Find something else in your opportunity register that does have this promise.

There is a big difference between discovery-driven plans and conventional ones in this respect. Discovery-driven plans begin with where you want to end up and drive the plan from the future backward. Conventional plans tend to begin with where you are and try to depict a path to a successful future.

Use the frame you developed in chapter 2 (or one you will start now) to begin your planning process. Our inspiration for this approach came from studying the way habitual entrepreneurs take on or abandon business ideas. They do not ask, "How big is the market?" but "Is it big enough to deliver the profits that I must have and the profitability that my various constituencies expect?"

Part of the challenge of framing is to specify the business model. You must be clear about what you expect the unit of business to be and how this relates to the cost and asset architectures of the proposed business, that is, how the business is configured to deliver that unit. By *unit of business*, we mean the product or service that actually triggers a revenue-generating event. In insurance, a typical unit of business is a policy; in banking, the yield from a particular loan or account. In investment banking, it's a deal. In consultant work, it's usually a unit of time (such as a day) although it can also be a project. For most manufacturing businesses, a unit is a product. Units of business on the Internet are still largely undefined—in some models, it's an advertisement to be shown to so many eyeballs; in others it's a transaction.

Whatever your unit of business, you must be clear on what it is, because understanding your unit is essential to defining your business model. A change in business model virtually always implies a change in unit of business. GE's Locomotives Division, for instance, went from selling locomotives (in which the unit was a locomotive, a product) to selling locomotive traction as a service (in which the unit is the service contractor). Often new business managers give insufficient thought to what units they are actually selling and how many they will need to sell over what period of time to generate the profits they require.

Different business models can have completely different cost and revenue flows. For instance, software has often been sold on a give-away-and-upgrade profit model. Common practice has been to spend a considerable amount up front on development, give the initial package away, then make profits on the upgrade stream. In this business model, revenues and expenses don't track each other at all—they flow at completely different times and rates over the life of the product.

In a professional services model, in contrast, revenues and expenses tend to correlate pretty well: You incur costs to do business, and you receive revenues to do the same. The key ratio for a professional service business is leverage—how many of what David Maister, an industry expert, calls *grinders* (workers) do you have versus the number of *minders* (key managers) versus *finders* (rainmakers) on any given project?[5] If the ratio of grinders is high relative to the others, you have a more profitable business model than if it is lower.

Different from software and consulting is the unit of business in the insurance industry. With insurance, you receive revenues before you incur the bulk of costs (consisting of claims). Costs are incurred sometime after a stream of premium revenues. Indeed, many insurance companies make no money on their underwriting at all—they make their profits by investing the money they hold during the time between receipt of a premium and presentation of a claim.

We often find that even at this point in discovery-driven planning, many ideas can be screened out because their business model and earnings logic is fundamentally not profitable enough. Service businesses without the potential for leverage are a typical example.[6]

Competitive Market Reality Specification

As enthusiastic entrepreneurs formulate plans to do great things, it is very easy for the plan on paper to take on an unrealistic quality. Markets appear larger and more profitable than they are, and required performance relative to competition recedes into the background as a limiting consideration. Specifying the market reality forces you to acknowledge that in competitive conditions, your firm will be pressed by talented, aggressive competitors to uphold the benchmark standards for basics and to differentiate on others. This part of the planning process forces you to understand what the key ratios are in your arena. As discussed in chapter 6, *ratios* are the components of your business model that allow your business to be compared to others and that give you an early warning of where you should be competing. With this understanding, you can articulate exactly how you plan to achieve and exceed the competitive standard on these ratios.

You don't need an in-depth market analysis at this stage. What you want is a grasp of what the benchmark parameters of the project must be for the venture to succeed competitively and what the scope of the market must be to make it worthwhile at all. You also need to understand where you might have a competitive advantage—say, because you have a superior technology or production process—and where you might be at a disadvantage.

It isn't unusual for a lot of initially plausible ideas to reveal themselves as inadequately profitable or impractical when you assess market reality. Consider the story about a new business that we were asked to evaluate (box 10-2). Ironically, the purpose was to demonstrate the power of discovery-driven planning—the power it revealed got us fired!

Specification of Deliverables

The specification of organizational deliverables involves translating your broad strategy into the daily operating activities that must be delivered if your opportunity is to become a reality. The difference again is that in a discovery-driven plan, the frame dictates what this translation will look like. For instance, the number of sales you need to close will dictate the size of your sales staff and in turn the cost of the selling process. The more realistic these deliverables are, the greater your confidence that the plan is feasible.

There are four reasons why it is important to specify in operational terms what the organization must be able to deliver. First, it translates strategic objectives into language that everybody can understand. Just as the attribute mapping and consumption chain exercises we discussed in chapters 3 and 4 clarify customer needs for employees throughout the organization, specification of deliverables clarifies how everyone fits into the strategy.

Second, specifying deliverables provides a focus for competence creation (discussed in chapter 6). It isn't enough to know that you must telephone delinquent customers within ten days of their learning that they are late in paying their bill (as GEFS had to do). You have to know what it will take to make those phone calls in terms of number of telephone operators and stations, computer support systems, tracking systems, and financial information systems.

Third, it is in the operation of a business that many of the business's most dangerous assumptions reside. For instance, we have seen many otherwise insightful venture managers assume that the incumbent sales force will be delighted to sell their brand-spanking-new

BOX 10-2

IGNORE THE REALITY OF THE MARKET AT YOUR PERIL (AN EMBARRASSING, BUT TRUE, STORY)

We were invited a few years ago to give a major presentation on discovery-driven planning to a new ventures group in a premier U.S. corporation. The organizers suggested that we apply the technique to one of the businesses they were incubating that was still in its prelaunch period.

A day or two before the meeting, we were given the most recent business plan for the venture. The proposition was for a textile manufacturer to vertically integrate into clothing sales. We were asked to mirror this plan with a discovery-driven plan so that the participants could clearly see the differences between the two approaches. The organizers got a lot more than they bargained for.

After less than one hour of research, we learned that to meet plan numbers by year five of the business, the operation would have to be making one in eight of *all* garments sold to women in department stores in the United States annually, at premium prices, no less. We were now confronted with a dilemma. Discovery-driven planning had worked and was posing a serious reality check to the feasibility of this business design. Our hosts felt that presenting these conclusions would make for a great learning experience, so we went ahead with the presentation (albeit somewhat gingerly).

What happened next is an object lesson in how not to practice a discovery-driven approach. The venture manager refused to entertain the idea that the company might not have the skills to achieve a dominant share position, let alone succeed, in an industry in which the company had never participated: retail clothing, an industry in which companies that do know what they are doing regularly fail.

Despite our misgivings and against our advice, the project was launched. Six months and $12 million down the tubes later, it was shut down without ceremony and declared an unconditional flop.

offering. In fact, most of the time the sales force would rather go on selling products whose quirks they have worked out for commissions they know they will get. Even taking the time to learn about the new offering is time spent *not* selling and for which they are seldom appropriately compensated.

Finally, the more richly intertwined and integrated your deliverables are, the harder it is for a competitor to come along and copy them. We gleaned this wisdom from Jim Bailey of Citibank, who for many years directed the company's highly profitable credit card business. "Competitors might be able to hire our people and copy our procedures," he would argue, "but they can't duplicate our organizationwide ability to deliver without taking over our whole operation."[7]

You can build a bottom-up specification of organizational deliverables on a simple spreadsheet without spending a nickel. Flaws and unwarranted assumptions often become glaringly obvious, affording you the luxury of being totally wrong without having to pay the price of failure.

Assumptions Testing

Documentation and testing of your assumptions makes for the single largest difference between discovery-driven plans and conventional ones. In discovery-driven plans, the whole plan is organized around converting the maximum number of assumptions to knowledge at minimum cost. Most firms fail to document and test their assumptions.

The specification of deliverables lays out the assumptions of all the operating activities that it will take to actually deliver the business. Together with the deliverables specification, you will also develop a key assumptions checklist, which will be revisited as planning proceeds. Testing assumptions is crucial in situations where new information emerges piecemeal. What can seem like small negative differences from expectations can be devastating when their cumulative impact is finally seen.

Managing to Milestones

Milestones are critical, identifiable points in time at which key assumptions are tested.[8] We have incorporated this discipline here, linking the specification of milestones to be tested and assumptions to be checked at each milestone with the rest of the planning process. The idea is that you plan in detail only as far out as the limits of current knowledge suggest is sensible, then stop, revisit your assumptions, and replan at each milestone.

In highly uncertain situations, you can't plan to validate your previous expectations, because they are largely assumptions. In such circumstances, it is more important to plan to learn. As box 10-3 demonstrates, the only way to accomplish your objectives is to learn your way to them.

BOX 10-3

HOW PLANNING TO LEARN GOT ASTRONAUTS ON THE MOON

The history of the space program in the United States is a vivid illustration of the power of planning to learn. NASA, the National Aeronautics and Space Administration, was created in 1958 in the midst of consternation about the Soviet Union's successful launch of an artificial satellite, *Sputnik 1*, on October 4, 1957. Between the time the United States launched its first artificial satellite, *Explorer 1*, on January 31, 1958, and Neil Armstrong first set foot on the moon on July 20, 1969, the agency faced an unprecedented challenge under conditions of extreme uncertainty.

On May 25, 1961, President John F. Kennedy committed the nation to landing a man on the moon before the end of the decade. When he made the announcement, the farthest a person had gone in space was a fifteen-minute suborbital flight, made by Alan Shepard. Through three programs—the manned Mercury program, Project Gemini, and, finally, the Apollo missions, which eventually led to the successful lunar landing, NASA's rocket scientists faced a massive, ongoing learning challenge.

The way NASA organized its learning is illuminating for all organizations dealing with uncertainty in facing a challenge. NASA systematically identified, in advance, the major milestones for each program. Before an astronaut could go to the moon, he would have to go into orbit. Before he could go into orbit, technologies for a reliable launch and recovery would need to be developed, and so on. Next, NASA specified for each of these stages what its staff would have to learn to acquire maximum confidence to go on to the next stage. The organization specified, in other words, what assumptions needed to be tested and validated at each stage so that NASA staff would have the knowledge needed to go to the next stage. NASA would then plan in detail to the next major milestone.

As each milestone was reached, the staff revisited their assumptions and replanned according to what they had learned. NASA literally learned its way to the moon and back, by systematically converting assumptions to knowledge and by redirecting its activities in the face of emerging understanding.[a]

a. National Commission on Space (1986).

To identify milestones, start with the major events that might occur as your project unfolds. Common events for manufacturing projects are concept test, model development, focus group test, prototype, market test, pilot plant, full-scale plant initial run, initial sales, initial returns, redesign, and so on. Even if you are not in control of the outcome at each milestone, it is still a point at which major assumptions will be revealed to be correct or not. For example, the first competitive response should be identified as a milestone, even though you don't know when it will occur or what will cause it to occur.

The next challenge is sequencing. You want a sequence of events that will minimize cash burn and corporate expectations while you are engaged in learning. For instance, don't promise senior management a rollout date until you have successfully completed all the invention required for technical development. Don't build a full-scale plant before you have thoroughly analyzed the evidence from a pilot plant. Don't staff up your service and delivery operation before you know how the selling will occur.

The output of milestone planning is a milestone/assumption map. In its simplest form it looks something like figure 10-1. Look for a connection between your assumptions and your milestone events. If there is such a connection, mark the appropriate box with an X. For each milestone, instead of a vague assumption, you should have in place either a specification (as in "the battery life has to be at least x hours") or a calculation (as in "the expected market penetration in Boise is 20 percent, giving us an initial market size of x").

One iron-clad rule: No milestone event should occur without triggering the test of an assumption. If this does happen, you should keep thinking, because you have probably overlooked an important assumption. The second iron-clad rule: Never allow an assumption to enter your plan without knowing when you are going to test it in milestone terms. If you find that you have to make the assumption, but there is no current milestone at which to test it, then perhaps you need to invent a milestone. Many assumptions will be tested over and over again at various milestones—assumptions such as price, features, and required performance should be carefully reviewed multiple times.

Every good story needs a hero, and this one is no exception. The hero in discovery-driven planning is the "keeper of the assumptions." This is the person who at every milestone gathers information on the most critical assumptions and, more important, gauges their effect on the business model as a whole. This information forms the basis for a critical review of the project, which should take place at each key milestone. A key milestone is one that reveals evidence about many assumptions. The longer you delay in conducting such a

FIGURE 10-1

MAPPING ASSUMPTIONS TO MILESTONES

Assumption	Milestone 1	Milestone 2	Milestone 3	Milestone 4
A	X		X	
B	X	X	X	X
C			X	X
D		X		

review, the greater the amount of investment at risk, should you decide later on to redirect the project. The questions that should be asked at such a review include the following:

- What new evidence do we have about the validity of our assumptions?

- What assumptions need revision?

- What new assumptions need to be made?

- Does the new upside gain still justify downside risk?

- Can the objectives be accomplished, or should we revise them?

- Have new opportunities been uncovered?

- What will it take to move to the next milestone?

- Do we need to redirect, scale up or down, speed up or slow down, put on hold, form a joint project, license, sell, or abort?

The discovery-driven approach to planning not only is realistic but is also much more motivating than the conventional approach to planning for new businesses. It gives people permission to learn instead of making them feel obliged to justify the differences between what was planned and what the reality is.

Parsimony

The discipline of parsimony (mentioned briefly in chapter 7) comes directly from real options reasoning. This discipline charges the people in the organization with finding imaginative ways to minimize investments and commitments until critical assumptions have been tested.

Parsimony requires you to find ways of avoiding investments in assets and commitments to fixed costs until there are revenue streams to justify them. The philosophy is that assets and fixed costs are earned by evidence of income. This makes a difference in which milestones you pursue first—the ones that might make you commit to assets and lose flexibility are the ones to postpone. Assets should be bought only as a last resort. To the extent possible, fixed commitments should be kept variable by paying per use or by subcontracting. As long as you bear this in mind, you won't find yourself in the thankless position of having to explain to investors why you decided to close down your facility after having earnestly persuaded them to invest in it. Further, you might elect to spend a little money to validate assumptions that have a significant downside component.

The principle of parsimony calls for you to challenge people to spend their imagination before spending your money, including incurring small losses in order to avoid big losses.

CREATING A DISCOVERY-DRIVEN PLAN: A CASE STUDY AND EXAMPLES

To demonstrate the development a discovery-driven plan, we will refer to a major strategic foray made by Japan's Kao Soap Corporation.[9] The Kao venture serves as a good illustration for several reasons. It was a venture that took the firm far from its core business, it was highly uncertain, and public data was available from which we could reconstruct the initial business model. In addition, this example is useful because at many points it shows how planning for a new area differs from planning for an established one. Using this example, we will also show you how to create five sets of documents that form the tangible core of a discovery-driven plan: the reverse financial statements, the key ratio comparison, the deliverables specification, the key assumptions checklist, and the milestone/assumption map.

Kao, a centuries-old manufacturer of soap and toiletries, had become a successful supplier of surfactants to the magnetic-media (floppy disk) industry in the late 1970s. In 1981 the firm began to study whether it could become a player in this industry by leveraging its surfactant technology. By the end of 1986, the demand for 3.5-inch floppy disks was about 500 million units in the United States, 100 million in Europe, and 50 million in Japan, with future growth rates assumed to be 40 percent per year compounded. This meant that by 1993, the global market would be approaching 3 billion disks. Of these, about one-third would be in the original equipment manufacturer (OEM) market, where industry prices were expected to be about 180 yen (or about \$1.44 at the prevailing exchange rate of 125 yen to the dollar on January 1, 1993) per disk.

Quality and reliability were particularly important product characteristics for OEM producers such as software developers. Before the advent of CD-ROMs, these disks were the primary vehicle on which software products were shipped. Defective disks have a devastating impact on customer perception of the quality of the software (not of the disk). Kao's management believed that the process knowledge the company had gained from supplying the floppy-disk industry could be combined with its skills at surface chemistry to produce higher-quality floppy disks that would sell at a much lower cost than the current offerings. For a firm in largely mature industries, this opportunity to deploy its current process insights into the information technology/computer industry was highly attractive.

Framing

Let's now introduce the reverse financial statement, which makes the discipline of framing highly operational. As the name of this tool implies, with a reverse financial statement, you do your financials from the bottom line up rather than from the top line down. Instead of starting with estimates of revenues and working down the income statement to derive profits, you start at the bottom line with target profits, target return on assets, and subsequent sales required. You then determine the required level of revenues and finally allowable costs and allowable investment. This is how it looks:

Required profits = required revenues minus allowable costs

Required return on assets = required profits divided by allowable assets

Required unit volume = required revenues divided by allowable price.

You saw the beginning of a reverse income statement in chapter 2. The reverse income statement brings a sobering clarity and reality to the challenge facing the business. It causes you to clearly specify how the new business will make a real difference to the bottom line. As we discuss in chapter 2, absent a better idea, we use the guideline of a 10 percent increment in profits as the minimum necessary performance goal when the business is operating at a steady state.

Above we mentioned units of business—the Kao floppy-disk venture had a very straightforward model. The unit of business is individual disk sales. This allows us to develop the reverse income statement for Kao as of 1988 (table 10-1).

What would a frame derived from these data look like? To be worthwhile, a high-risk venture into a new technology such as floppy disks would have to enhance Kao's bottom line substantially. If we assume that 10 percent is enough, this represents profits of 4 billion yen when the business reaches a steady state. As we mentioned in chapter 2, if you want to drive your business to increasingly attractive strategic arenas, increases in profitability should also be specified. If we assume a 2 percent premium in return on assets (ROA), the floppy-disk business would have to deliver 10 percent ROA (at minimum to compensate for the increased risk), since the firm is already achieving 8 percent ROA. We also specify that the new business has to achieve better return on sales than the existing one—say, a 0.5 percent increment. That means the floppy-disk venture must have the potential to achieve a 10 percent return on sales. (Note that the incremental profits and profitability are matters of your strategic choice.)

Without investing a dime in the business, you can now begin to scope it out. To enhance Kao's total profits by 10 percent, the floppy-disk project needs to deliver 4 billion yen in profit to Kao's bottom line. You then project from this to see what revenues are required. For a 10 percent return on sales, required revenues would be 40 billion yen. At 10 percent margins, the total allowable cost to manufacture, sell, and distribute the disks worldwide cannot exceed 90 per-

TABLE 10-1

1988 PERFORMANCE DATA FOR KAO CORPORATION

Net sales	490 billion yen ($3.93 billion)
Income before taxes	37 billion yen ($296 million)
Return on sales	9.5%
Return on assets	8%
1993 forecast OEM price per disk	180 yen ($1.44)

cent of revenues, or 36 billion yen. To make its target of 10 percent ROA, Kao can't invest more than 4 billion divided by 10 percent, or 40 billion yen in assets.

The same logic applies to the number of disks the company has to sell. The first assumption concerns price. If Kao is to break into an established market, even with superior quality, it is not likely to succeed by charging standard prices. Consequently, entering an established business will require the company to sell its disks at lower prices. Suppose Kao were to anticipate selling below the estimated 1993 price of 180 yen per disk and offer its disks at 160 yen per disk. So to make its required revenues of 40 billion yen, the company would have to sell 40 billion yen divided by 160 yen per disk, or 250 million disks. Table 10-2 summarizes the challenges.

Having established the required scope of the project, you can also sketch out the first-cut reverse financials. The numbers for Kao are listed in table 10-3. With the project clearly framed, the next step is a reality check.

Checking Market Reality

It is critical to understand whether the market space you plan to enter will support the kinds of volumes you need. Here, you might want to do a little research, with the emphasis on keeping it simple. Let's see how this might have worked for Kao.

From the frame for the business, we know that Kao must sell 250 million disks to achieve the volume that will generate the profits

TABLE 10-2

Challenges for Kao's Floppy-Disk Project

Required profits to add 10 percent to total profits	4 billion yen ($320 million)
Necessary revenues to deliver 10 percent sales margin	40 billion yen ($3.2 billion)
Necessary unit sales at 160 yen per unit	40 billion/160 = 250 million units

TABLE 10-3

INITIAL REVERSE FINANCIALS

Reverse Income Statement

Required profits to add 10 percent to total profits	4 billion yen
Necessary revenues to deliver 10 percent sales margin	40 billion yen
Allowable costs to deliver 10 percent sales margin	36 billion yen

Reverse Balance Sheet

Allowable investment to deliver 10 percent ROA	40 billion yen

required. In Kao's case, there were three major markets for floppy disks. The first was end users and consumers, who bought the disks to back up data and to share data between machines. They typically bought their disks at computer stores or through office supply outlets. Next was the business segment, which bought disks—usually through the business's conventional suppliers—for the same purposes as the consumer segment. A final segment was the OEMs, who bought disks to load them with software and then ship them with related computer hardware or sell them as stand-alone software products.

Which group to target? Consider the "search" link of each major segment's consumption chain (see chapter 4). Kao had no access to the search link in the consumption chain for either consumers or distributors in electronics, especially outside Japan. Moreover, the consumers who did know Kao were likely to associate the name with its soap and detergent brands—the company had no legitimacy whatsoever in the minds of consumers as a floppy-disk manufacturer, meaning Kao would be at a disadvantage at the "selection" link. Similar concerns existed for the business market: it isn't easy to try to sell a product you've never made before to risk-averse production managers.

The OEM market, on the other hand, had none of these drawbacks. Not only was it big enough, but these customers made their purchasing decisions on the basis of technical specifications, and they had the technical capacity to test the disks. Furthermore, both price and quality were critically important to them. Meet the quality at a lower price than what they pay, and the orders are yours. The next question is whether this was feasible.

To justify entering the floppy-disk industry, Kao would need to capture 25 percent of the total world OEM market by the firm's anticipated steady-state revenues date of 1993. This meant that Kao would have no choice but to go global. The necessity of going global, in turn, further reinforced the assumption that the company would have to enter at a lower price than established incumbents, because such an inroad into market shares of global competitors is almost certain to lead to major price perturbations. This lays out the marketing challenge—can you capture 25 percent global share with much higher quality but at only a 10 percent discount?

Next comes the discipline of identifying key ratios, as discussed in chapter 6, and specifying how you will create a better business model than competitors have. Some illustrative operations specifications of key ratios—the key ratio comparison—for Kao are shown in table 10-4.

Notice that Kao is not anticipating advantages on every dimension. It has no reason to believe that it will achieve better asset utilization, productivity, or equipment depreciation than its competitors. Kao's only real advantage resided in its superior quality and lower price derived from its knowledge of surface chemistry and surface physics. These insights could be deployed to improve quality and reduce materials costs. Laying out the challenges in this way clarifies the marketing, technical, and operational challenges.

Specifying Deliverables

The next step for the floppy-disk venture would be to develop a deliverables specification. To do this, Kao managers would need to make assumptions about the logistical activities necessary to sell, manufacture, deliver, and administer the project. As with the key-ratio exercise in chapter 6, initial assumptions can be derived from a variety of sources at this stage. The point is not to seek detailed numbers but to build a reasonable model of the project's economics and logistics.

TABLE 10-4

KEY RATIO COMPARISON FOR THE FLOPPY-DISK BUSINESS

	Industry	Kao
Shares of OEM market	1 billion unit demand split between 8 major players	25% (dominant share)
Fixed asset investment/sales	0.8:1	0.8:1
Effective production capacity per line (after allowing for scrap, rework, maintenance, and setup)	25 disks per minute	25 disks per minute
Effective life of equipment before technological obsolescence	3 years	3 years
Sales margins	12% on sales	10% on sales
Surfactant material cost/sales	27 yen per unit	20 yen per unit
Expected selling price per disk to OEMs	180 yen	160 yen

The most significant assumptions are not necessarily the easiest to assess. We make this point because most people are inclined to analyze things that are easy to assess and that may not be important at all. For instance, we saw one multimillion-dollar corporate business plan in which per-unit energy and materials costs for the plant were spelled out to decimal-place accuracy, while projected sales were simply spreadsheet extrapolations from a guesstimated number for the first year of sales.

As you are creating your deliverables specification, it is helpful to document your thought process as we did in the last column of table 10-5: Did the number come from a calculation you did? Some information you looked up on the Internet? Is it an assumption? Table 10-5 shows what a portion of Kao's deliverables specification would look like.

TABLE 10-5

DELIVERABLES SPECIFICATION

Specification	Estimate	Source of Estimate
Required profit margin	10% of sales	Management requirement
Unit selling price	160 yen	Assumption based on share capture needs
Required unit disk sales	250 million disks	Calculation
Fixed asset investment/sales	0.8:1	Industry norm
Effective production capacity per line (after allowing for scrap, rework, maintenance, and setup)	25 disks per minute	Industry norm
Size of world OEM market by 1993	1 billion disks	Consultant projection

Sales Expenses

Average OEM order size	10,000 disks	Calls to IBM and Hewlett-Packard
Required disk sales (from above)	250 million	Calculation
Sales orders required (250,000,000/10,000)	25,000 orders	Calculation
Number of calls to make a sale	4	New hire's previous experience
Annual number of sales calls needed	100,000	Calculation
OEM sales calls per day per salesperson	2	New hire's previous experience
Annual salesperson-days needed (100,000/2)	50,000	Calculation
Salespeople needed: 250 selling days per year = 50,000/250 selling days	200 sales staff	Calculation
Annual salary per salesperson	10 million yen	Assumption
Total sales salaries (200 × 10 million yen)	2 billion yen	Calculation

continued

TABLE 10-5 (CONTINUED)

DELIVERABLES SPECIFICATION

Specification	Estimate	Source of Estimate
Shipping Expenses		
Order size of 10,000 disks requires one container	2.5 billion yen	Assumption based on shipper's current price list
So 25,000 orders shipped per year at an average shipping cost per container of 100,000 yen		
Manufacturing Expenses		
Effective production line capacity of 25 per minute = 12.5 million disks per 350-day year	12.5 million disks per line	Calculation
Number of production lines needed (250 million disks/ 12.5 million disks per line)	20 production lines	Calculation
Number of people to support one manufacturing line (including all functions): Assume 10 per line for 3 shifts per line = 30 per line	600 manufacturing staff	Assumption based on current industry experience
Manufacturing salaries = 5 million yen per manufacturing person annually (600 × 5 million yen)	3 billion yen	Calculation
Raw materials costs: Assume 20 yen per disk	5 billion yen	Assumption based on analyzing competitors' costs
Packaging: 40 yen per package of 10 disks	1 billion yen	Assumption
Depreciation Costs		
Assume high-tech plant replaced every 3 years. Depreciation = 32 billion yen investment in 3 years	10.1 billion yen annual depreciation	Assumption—industry norm

The idea is to build a picture of all the commercial activities that are needed, document the assumptions about how they will materialize, and (most important) document both how the activities connect and how the assumptions will be tested. It is in making this connection that companies characteristically err—they will set up the model and then forget to test the linkages between activities and assumptions as new information comes in. For instance, if your estimates of how many sales calls the sales staff can make in a day or how many calls they need to make to secure an order are off, your entire budget for sales costs may be wrong. The unfolding logic of the business should thus be repeatedly looped back into the reverse income statement and reverse balance sheet. Table 10-6 shows how these would look for Kao.

TABLE 10-6

REVISED REVERSE FINANCIALS

Reverse Income Statement	Billion Yen
Required profit	4.0
Required revenues at required margin of 10%	40.0
Allowable Costs (90% of sales)	36.0
Sales force salaries	2.0
Manufacturing salaries	3.0
Variable manufacturing	5.0
Packaging	1.0
Shipping	2.5
Depreciation	10.1
Maximum allowable administrative and overhead costs	6.4
Total allowable costs	36.0
Reverse Balance Sheet	
Allowable investment	40.0
Fixed assets at 0.8 times sales	32.0
Total allowable other assets (inventory and receivables)	8.0

At this point, the job of project execution is made much clearer. In Kao's case, the project is worthwhile only if the firm can accomplish some major challenges:

1. Capture 25 percent of global market share with a superior-quality disk and a 20-yen-per-disk discount relative to competitors' expected prices

2. Maintain at least the same asset productivity as the average competitor's

3. Use superior materials technology to produce disks for 20 yen per unit materials cost instead of 27 yen per unit

4. Support a global business with no more than 8 billion yen total in inventory and receivables

Documenting Assumptions

As we were preparing the deliverables specification for Kao, we became alert to the assumptions we would be making if the plan were a real one.[10] We captured the most important of these in an assumption checklist. The checklist should provide the background for vigorous, disciplined debate. For instance, in the plan so far, we have made the implicit assumption that prices will hold at about 160 yen even if Kao gains share of 25 percent against well-established competitors. Knowing the desire of asset-intensive incumbents to hold onto market share even at the expense of profitability, this may well be a fatal assumption.[11]

At this point, you can begin to determine how robust your business model is by evaluating its sensitivity to changes in certain underlying assumptions. To do this, we recall a basic principle from our discussion of real options. Some uncertainties are relatively easy for the organization to influence. Setting price, for instance, is a decision you can make. Other uncertainties are beyond your control, which implies that you have no option but to react to them. We apply the same logic to the assumptions we make. Some are internally derived and reflect what we think we will do—we call these *internal assumptions*. Others—*external assumptions*—are externally derived and reflect what we think is going to happen in the environment beyond our control. Kao, for instance, has little control over the number of sales calls required to get an order, but it can to a much greater extent control the number of sales calls it expects the sales staff to make in one day. In your checklist, specify assumptions as either internal or external (figure 10-2).

FIGURE 10-2

ASSUMPTION CHECKLIST

Assumption Number	Assumption	Type of Assumption	Range
1	Profit margin	Internal	±10%
2	Unit selling price of 160 yen	Internal	−25%
3	Fixed asset investment/sales	External	±20%
4	Effective production capacity/line	External	±15%
5	1993 world market	External	±20%
6	1993 world OEM market	External	±20%
7	Average OEM order size of 10,000 disks per order	External	+100%
8	Sales calls per OEM order	External	+100%
9	OEM sales calls per salesperson per day	Internal	±50%
10	Selling days per year	Internal	±5%
11	Annual salesperson's salary	Internal	±5%
12	Containers required per order	Internal	100%
13	Shipping cost per container	External	±25%
14	Production days per year	Internal	±5%
15	Workers per production line (10 per line for 3 shifts per line)	Internal	±10%
16	Annual manufacturing worker's salary	Internal	±10%
17	Materials costs per disk	External	±10%
18	Packaging costs per 10 disks	External	±15%
19	Average life of high-tech plant	External	±25%
20	Allowable administrative costs	Internal	Calculated
21	Competitive price cuts	Internal	±25%

To get at the model's sensitivity to changes in assumptions, either manually calculate sensitivities to change in variables or set up for simulation by estimating possible ranges. If you don't have a clue, the range should be pretty large. If you feel reasonably confident, you can use a smaller range. For instance, in the assumption checklist for Kao, shown in figure 10-2, the range for order size (assumption 7) and sales calls per order (assumption 8) reflects much greater uncertainty than that for the number of production days and selling days per year. Note also that prices are specified as a range from 160 yen down to 25 percent less, whereas order size is specified as from 10,000 up to 100 percent more.

Having established the ranges, you can use simulation techniques to gauge the sensitivity of the entire model to changes in the values of the component variables. It is a relatively simple matter to run software simulations, in which a computer program takes a number of random draws for the variables in the model from a probability distribution you specify, and estimates what results the model would return over a number of repeated tries of the model.[12] This allows you to identify the assumptions for which the required performance parameters are most sensitive. These assumptions, and any others you think are critical, are those that you should select for careful testing as your plan progresses through its major milestones.

It makes sense to run separate simulations for internal and external assumptions.[13] The external set suggests how turbulent your environment is, whereas the internal set suggests how much discretion you have. Although every business will have its own set of core assumptions, at minimum, you should address those listed in figure 10-3, or their equivalent for the particular industry you are entering.

Planning to Learn at Key Milestones

The heart of discovery-driven planning is replanning. Replanning will be vastly facilitated by keeping your lists of milestones and assumptions short. By the time you've invested the energy to come up with hundreds of assumptions and milestones, you won't have the heart to toss them in the shredder or the energy to replan, so hold the number of milestones to less than twenty.

FIGURE 10-3

CRITICAL ASSUMPTIONS FOR ANY NEW BUSINESS

WHAT IS OUR PROFIT MODEL?

- Unit of business
- Cost, asset, revenue architectures, and timing
- Major obstacles and feasibility of breaking through them

WHO ARE OUR CUSTOMERS?

- Who will buy and why: quantity, continuity, and frequency
- Forces producing or reducing resistance to use of the product/service
- How do our different market segments behave?
- Market growth rate
- Cost and time to achieve target volume and/or share
- How will we get to the customer? What are our distribution channels? How will we access them?

HOW ARE WE COMPETING?

- Functional characteristics related to market need
- Advantage compared with competitive products
- Duration of product advantages
- Product costs and quality controllability
- Service requirements and costs

WHO IS OUR COMPETITION?

- Different categories of competition call for different actions
- Likely responses: price, product, functionality, service, marketing strategy
- Capacity to respond
- Motivation to respond

WHAT DO WE HAVE TO DO?

- Ability to produce at required scale
- Proprietary advantage—lead time
- Availability of people with required knowledge and skills
- Development time and cost
- Can the business stand alone without "borrowed" or cheap resources?

continued

FIGURE 10-3 (CONTINUED)

CRITICAL ASSUMPTIONS FOR ANY NEW BUSINESS

WHAT ARE OUR ECONOMICS?

- Cash required to reach cash breakeven
- Daily, weekly, monthly, breakevens
- Numbers broken down into actionable pieces
- Investment required to profit and loss breakeven, to reach profit objectives
- Gross and net margins
- Time required to achieve above
- Costs, profit/loss at varying volume levels

WHAT INTERNAL ISSUES SHOULD WE EXPECT?

- Support of key players
- Availability of qualified management
- Ability of venture to survive firm's management practices: planning, performance evaluation, and controls

---

Milestones in hand, you now want to link them to the most critical assumptions. Again, less is more here—stick with the twenty to thirty most important assumptions. Try to include more hard-to-test assumptions than easy ones. As mentioned, the easy ones are usually the least important of them all. Also try to make sure that high-impact, low-probability assumptions stay on your list—these are the factors that can do a business in.

Critical assumptions are those with one or more of the following properties:

- They affect many elements of the project.

- They have the greatest effect on key outcomes.

- They make or break basic feasibility: If they are wrong, you can't deliver the business.

- They precipitate significant investment commitments.

- Small deviations or changes have huge impacts.

Figure 10-4 lists the critical milestones for Kao and the assumptions likely to be tested at each one (figure 10-2 shows what the assumption numbers refer to). From this information you can create a milestone/assumption map like figure 10-5.

Notice in figure 10-4 that milestones can be designed explicitly as tests of assumptions. An example is milestone 3, the creation of a prototype disk. Before Kao entered the manufacturing phase, it tested assumptions with respect to acceptable price and quality using prototype disks whose manufacture the company subcontracted.

FIGURE 10-4

KAO MILESTONE EVENT AND ASSUMPTION TEST CHECKLIST

Milestone Number	Milestone Event	Assumptions Tested
1	Market study	1, 2, 3, 5, 6, 17, 18, 19
2	Feasibility study	2, 3, 4, 7, 8, 11, 12, 13, 14, 15, 16, 19
3	Prototype disks	17
4	Technical testing by customers	2, 7, 17
5	Subcontracted production	1, 3, 4, 15, 16, 17, 18
6	Sales of subcontracted production	1, 2, 7, 8, 9, 10, 11, 12, 13
7	Purchase of small existing plant	3, 4, 13, 14, 15, 16, 17, 18
8	Pilot production at purchased plant	3, 4, 13, 14, 15, 16, 17, 18, 20
9	Full-scale plant construction	1, 2, 3, 4, 13, 14, 15, 16, 17, 18
10	Competitor reaction	5, 6, 21
11	First major distributor signs on	2, 7, 9
12	Repricing analysis	1, 2, 17, 18, 19

FIGURE 10-5

KAO MILESTONE/ASSUMPTION MAP FOR FLOPPY-DISK VENTURE

		Milestones										
Assumptions	1	2	3	4	5	6	7	8	9	10	11	12
1	X				X	X			X			X
2	X	X		X	X	X	X	X	X		X	X
3	X	X			X		X	X	X			
4	X	X			X				X	X		
5	X	X								X		
6	X			X		X						
7		X				X					X	
8		X				X						
9						X					X	
10							X					
11		X				X						
12		X				X	X	X	X			
13		X					X	X	X			
14		X			X		X	X	X			
15		X			X		X	X	X			X
16		X			X		X	X	X			X
17	X	X	X	X	X		X	X	X			X
18	X											
19	X	X							X	X		
20								X				
21										X		

Even though Kao had to pay quite a lot for the subcontracted disks, offering them as prototypes to prospective customers allowed the company to make sure that it didn't build an expensive plant only to find that it had erred in making some critical assumptions. Through this process, the firm tested several crucial assumptions: whether, on the basis of technical specifications, customers would in fact buy a disk that said "Kao" on it; whether quality mattered; and what features customers regarded as important.

Exercising Parsimony

Throughout this process, remember that your main objective is to maximize learning while minimizing costs. Applying real options reasoning, sometimes you might even spend a little to avoid a huge downside.

To succeed, Kao had to maintain at least the same asset productivity as key competitors. This was a difficult challenge indeed for a company in an asset-intensive industry that had never made disks before. The final investment called for was 32 billion yen in fixed assets alone (a key ratio of 0.8 assets to sales).

Could Kao justify this asset-intensive investment by gathering strong evidence of potential success? The test has a real options flavor to it. Before going ahead with the construction of a full-scale plant, Kao first acquired production capacity by buying a single line plant from a small existing floppy-disk manufacturer. The company then learned from the original owner of this established plant, rather than try to start up a full-scale operation. Once Kao engineers could demonstrate their ability to produce disks with the required quality and cost on a single-line plant, Kao could move toward building full-scale plants with far greater confidence.

The benefit of parsimony is that it allows for strategic experimentation. To the extent that one can keep the costs of pursuing each one low, many more experiments can be afforded.

Box 10-4 tells what happened with Kao's floppy-disk business. A strategic concern that Kao management missed is that they had no insightful mechanisms to differentiate their product other than high quality at low cost. The trouble with competing primarily on the

BOX 10-4

POSTSCRIPT: A TALE OF ECSTASY AND AGONY FOR KAO

Kao did decide to launch its floppy-disk project. It became the top U.S. producer of disks in 1990. By 1992, the company had achieved U.S. sales of 30 billion yen ($240 million) at a cost per disk of just over 100 yen ($0.80). By 1994, when we were writing the original *Harvard Business Review* article on discovery-driven planning, it had the leading world market share in the floppy disk business and was by far the largest single supplier to the OEM market. As of 1997, Kao was the world's single largest producer of floppy disks (and it was also manufacturing other media, such as CD-ROM devices), with disk production of 400 million units per year.

Unfortunately for Kao, it wasn't the only player to recognize that opportunities in disk making could be lucrative. The company fell victim to a common fatal assumption, namely, that prices would hold, even in the face of competitive entry as players fight over share.

Because there was no competitive insulation on the disks aside from whatever process and manufacturing skills a manufacturer could bring to bear, other companies began an eager pursuit of the disk business. The most damaging entry from Kao's point of view was that of firms from mainland China. These firms, desperate for revenues and foreign business, gladly bought used and inefficient disk-making equipment. They then used their inexpensive labor costs to make massive numbers of disks at little profit, putting extreme price pressure on the industry worldwide. It was dramatic, and it happened quickly. In January 1992, the manufacturer's price of a floppy disk was about seventy-five cents. By December of that same year, the price had collapsed to twenty-five cents per disk, with no sign of a rebound in sight.

On April 23, 1998, Kao announced that it would end its floppy-disk production altogether. It sold its information technology operations in Canada, Germany, Ireland, and the

United States to Zomax Optical Media for about $37.5 million. Despite this setback, Kao continues to be admired as one of the most successful and entrepreneurial Japanese companies.

Source: Data from Hoover's On Line (www.hoovers.com) as of July 2, 1999.

basis of quality and cost is that such a strategy is all too easy to replicate—there will always be some competitor out there with high fixed asset costs and lower labor costs or a willingness to settle for slimmer margins just to get the business.

SUMMARY OF ACTION STEPS

The action steps that follow are meant to get you started on the concepts and processes discussed in the chapter. Feel free to elaborate in a way that works for your company.

STEP 1: Specify a clear frame for each project you wish to plan. You may wish to return to chapter 2 and review the mechanics.

STEP 2: Identify what you consider the key ratios and key market specifications for each project. Benchmark against competitors and against the market for the key drivers of profits.

STEP 3: Develop reverse financial statements.

STEP 4: Identify deliverables specifications to achieve the benchmark objectives; document your assumptions as you go through the process.

STEP 5: Develop an assumption checklist, and assign the assumptions to the category of internal or external. Set ranges on the assumptions that reflect your uncertainty.

STEP 6: Run a sensitivity analysis to see how sensitive your plan is to changes in assumptions and to identify which assumptions seem the most critical. (If you wish, use a simulation package.)

STEP 7: Develop a list of milestone events, and sequence them so that you will burn the least cash while converting key assumptions into knowledge. Don't put more than twenty milestones on the list—you won't want to replan if it means rewriting dozens of milestones.

STEP 8: Identify the thirty (maximum) most critical assumptions and identify milestones to test them. Create a key milestone/assumption map to make sure you aren't forgetting to do your testing. Appoint a keeper of the assumptions.

STEP 9: Throughout, be parsimonious. Find ways to drive down initial investment and fixed costs until you test the most critical assumptions. If you have to, make modest investments to test key assumptions before making big, fixed-cost investments.

STEP 10: Revisit the assumptions at each milestone and replan on the basis of emerging knowledge.

CHAPTER 11

MANAGING PROJECTS

WITH UNCERTAIN

OUTCOMES

IN THIS CHAPTER, WHICH CONCLUDES OUR TREATMENT OF adaptive execution, we turn to the assessment and management of project progress when the outcomes are highly uncertain.[1] We hope to give you ways to encourage a disciplined approach to learning by doing.

Your challenge in managing projects intended to capitalize on new opportunities is to guide the group in such a way that they can discover new competences and customer solutions, without forcing them to cope with the conceptual straitjacket that conventional project management can create. Just as discovery-driven planning relies upon a different kind of discipline than does conventional planning, discovery-oriented project management requires a different discipline than does conventional management, which deals with familiar territory.

The biggest problem, in our view, is that it is devilishly difficult to find good measures of progress for projects with a high assumption-to-knowledge ratio. Consider three categories of measures that you might use to evaluate performance. You could use *lagging* indicators, which reveal the results of actions and decisions already taken; *current* indicators, which inform you about where things are today; or *leading* indicators, which give you some idea of where you are going. Unfortunately, most corporate performance management systems systematically focus on lagging indicators—those that give you great information about what has already happened and about which you can do nothing. Leading indicators are far harder to come by. As figure 11-1 suggests, most companies have absolutely no problem obtaining information about things that have already happened or even about things as they are. The hardest numbers to get are the leading indicators—the numbers that suggest where things are going.[2]

The purpose of this chapter is to give you an approach to developing leading indicators of your project's progress, to help you figure out where things are going. The diagnostic technique we recommend is based on surveys. We call it a process of accelerating competitive effectiveness (ACE) because the idea behind it is to enhance your ability to identify project problems at the earliest possible time, when the least amount of resources have been expended. The earlier you can redirect the project, the better.[3]

DEVELOPING LEADING INDICATORS FOR UNCERTAIN PROJECTS

The bottom line in the entrepreneurial projects you have launched is to end up with a new business model (or a more effective business, in the case of efficiency-oriented projects) capable of creating a competitive advantage.

We started looking for leading indicators that might help you to tell if a project was heading in the right direction, long before the numbers that are the stuff of most corporate performance-measurement systems would be available. We used a medical analogy.

What if we were to tackle the problem of emerging competitive effectiveness the way doctors are trained to diagnose the state of their patients' health? Instead of being able to directly measure as complex and poorly understood a phenomenon as health, doctors are trained to evaluate indications of illness or well-being. By comparing growth rates and weight gains in children over time, for instance, they can make inferences about the health of the children's underlying metabolic system, even if they cannot measure its functioning directly. By

FIGURE 11-1

INDICATORS

Lagging Indicators	Current Indicators	Leading Indicators
Current resources	Market share	Trend in market share
Past profits	Operating ratios	Trend in backlog or advance orders
Most "hard" numbers	Current profitability	Trend in profitability

analogy, we thought, perhaps we could come up with something like a height/weight chart for developing effective new businesses.

We have since found that even when the end point is unknown, progress toward developing new areas of competitive strength can be monitored and obstacles to progress diagnosed. This is because new competitive strengths—or competences—develop by means of a definable set of processes. These processes occur partially in sequence, but they also influence each other, so they are mutually dependent.

Business Drivers

Typically, creating a successful new business begins with the definition of the business model concept. Rough at first, the concept becomes more and more refined over time, until eventually you clearly understand the real drivers of future business model success and resolve critical uncertainties. By drivers, we mean those activities that will become visible in a key ratio for the business (see chapter 6). For instance, until you understand how credit and payment flow within a credit card business or how payments affect cash flows in a distribution business, it's nearly impossible to create superior performance on a key ratio over time. Your discovery-driven plan (chapter 10) explicitly or implicitly spells out the key drivers of the business based on the best assumptions you have available. When your group understands these key drivers and how to measure them, you have successfully reduced a major source of uncertainty and laid the foundation for the future business.

Team Effectiveness

As the team learns more about the key drivers, the people involved are also learning more about each other, about the roles that need to be taken on, and about how to get things done in the context of the project. Early on, when drivers are unclear, most groups will operate ineffectively—you'll see a lot of checking up on things, a lot of excess paper shuffling, and a lot of time spent simply learning to work together. As the understanding of the business starts to improve, in a project that is headed in the right direction, the effectiveness of the group working on it will improve as well. They will work more in a coordinated way and be more effective.

Increasing Competence

With growing confidence about the business drivers, and improving effectiveness at working together, your team will find themselves increasingly able to accomplish what they set out to do. This expanding ability to achieve objectives reliably and consistently is the hallmark of an emerging new competence for your firm, which we defined in chapter 6 as a combination of skills, assets, and systems that allow you to reliably achieve your objectives.

Emerging Distinctiveness

As we have stressed throughout this book, it isn't enough to deliver the basics and tolerables to your customers (or future customers). To make a competitive impact, you have to offer new differentiators and exciters, or eliminate tolerables, dissatisfiers, and enragers in some meaningful way for future target segments. We refer to the ability to deliver these attributes as evidence of emerging distinctiveness.

Emerging Advantage

Over time, your group will put emerging distinctiveness to work in the creation of blockbuster products and services for selected customer segments. If the characteristics that create distinctiveness can be insulated from immediate competitive attack, your group will have created a significant competitive advantage.

In real life, of course, things are never this smooth and orderly. Unexpected discoveries are made, paths open and close, and groups iterate back and forth in emphasis between the processes we described. What seemed to be a high-profit-potential project can turn out to be a dud; and what looked like a loser can suddenly become a great opportunity. Consider the path followed by the group developing Viagra. We all know now that the product has become a very popular and profitable treatment for impotence. When Pfizer first started working on the drug, however, the original idea was to use it to treat heart patients, an indication for which the drug failed miserably. It wasn't until the discovery of its other side effects that the product had any hope of commercial success. In entrepreneurial terms, tests to determine whether the product had the potential to create exciters initially failed, leading to a redefinition of the drivers of the business and redirection toward a new and different type of business. We think about this as an *advantage chain* to communicate the idea that competitive advantage does not flow from one project element, but many, and that they influence one another.

DIAGNOSING YOUR PROGRESS

We have developed a set of survey instruments that you can administer to the group working on a project, in order to understand where they are with respect to each of the underlying building blocks of competitive advantage. In effect, the survey results give you leading indicators of where your group or team is headed, which is useful even in the very early stages of a project, before you have sorted out what other measures will be useful. We named the process of administering and analyzing the surveys accelerating competitive effectiveness (ACE) because using the surveys allows you to take the earliest possible action to improve the processes in a project, thus accelerating your progress.

Getting the Data

To conduct the ACE analysis, assemble a group of people working on the initiative whose progress you want to diagnose. The rule of thumb is to include everyone who has significant responsibility for meeting one or another project objectives. If you can, get them together as a group and review the questions in figures 11-2 through

11-7. There are often differences in interpretation of what some questions mean, which you should clarify as a group before you fill out any of the surveys. You want everyone to have the same image in mind when thinking about *the client, the offering, the user,* and *the customer*—words that often cause confusion. The next task is to complete the questions, following the instructions on the top of the survey pages. Individual responses should be given to someone who is committed to keeping who answered what confidential for analyzing. If you can't assure confidentiality, you can't be sure that you are getting unbiased results. Your firm's accountant or legal officer can serve this function well.

With the responses in hand, next average the responses for the entire team for each item. Thus, if three people answered a question, and one scored it a 2, one scored it a 4, and one scored it a 5, then their average response as a team to the question is 3.67 (2 + 4 + 5 divided by 3 responses and rounding to two decimal places). Once you have the item averages, also calculate the overall average for all the items in each figure. For example, there are 18 items in figure 11-3. You should thus have 18 team item average scores to add up and divide by 18. This will give you a grand average for all the items in a given measure. As a measure of variation, you should also calculate the standard deviation for each item. This gives you a measure of agreement—if the standard deviation is low, it means your respondents answered similarly. If it is high, it means they don't agree, which can sometimes be valuable information in itself. A less accurate but still useful measure of variation is to calculate the range for each item, which is simply the highest minus the lowest score of the group. High ranges mean low consensus, and vice versa.

Obviously, your initial focus will be on the items with the lowest averages and/or highest variation in scores, since these signal places in which the process of building competitive advantage is bogging down, or places in which people do not share a common view of what is happening. We suggest getting the group together to go over the analysis and the implications of their responses. Never take the position that the scores that respondents provide are a "grade." This can destroy the effectiveness of the whole exercise. The scores are simply scores—no more value laden than a thermometer's report of today's highs and lows. It is what the scores mean in the context of a particular project and in light of underlying assumptions that will give you useful information.

The responses of the group can signal the presence of issues worth spending some time on, usually long before they would be addressed in the normal course of events. For instance, respondents commonly indicate that the project will add value for customers, increase responsiveness, and improve quality but that the company will not capture this added value in the form of price premiums. This can spark a strategic discussion of why you should do all this for customers if there is little to be gained in margins or profits. Sometimes, there are good reasons (to regain market share or to lock customers into the next-generation upgrade, for instance). Other times, the results suggest that you need to rethink the value of the project. Occasionally, the process has brought up issues that led groups to conclude that their projects were fundamentally flawed and that the talents of the people involved could be better spent on something much more valuable to the firm.

Next, let's examine each of the processes through which competitive advantage emerges. We will suggest how you can interpret the responses of your group to each set of questions.

Building Group Understanding of What's Driving the Business

In a highly uncertain environment, projects, particularly options projects, are often initiated before there is real clarity as to who the ultimate customer is, why this customer might want an offering like the one being developed, or what the organization must do to deliver on customer expectations. More often than not the business model that emerges is not the business model the group had in mind to begin with. For this reason, it is critical that the group redirect to pursue the real opportunities that unfold as the project progresses.

Let's offer some examples. A financial services firm originally envisaged that the primary customers for its line of asset securitization products would be financially sophisticated clients. These clients would welcome the opportunity to unlock the cash value in assets such as accounts receivable in exchange for a securitization charge. The financial services firm assumed that its customers would eagerly use its products as one of many financing techniques.

As the project team gained experience with the sales cycle for these products, they learned that they were dead wrong about clients' willingness to give up legal ownership of their assets. It turned out to be a more emotional decision than expected. Instead, the real primary customers (their "first five" sales) were from firms that found themselves in a cash crunch, often as much as two or more years after the first discussion with a salesperson. A delightful surprise to the team was that unlike the sophisticated down-to-the-last-basis-point negotiations they had anticipated, clients under pressure turned out to be relatively price-insensitive to the fee charged. The business flourished, despite its being based on a business model much different from that articulated in the original business plan.

Sometimes, teams learn that the capabilities they have developed are more valuable than they had thought. Like many Japanese companies, a systems integrator we worked with assumed that price would be the major issue when the firm was competing for a paperless-document-transfer product. After reviewing the target customer's consumption chain, the firm determined that a considerable cost component for the customer would be integrating the document-transfer system into its existing operations. What turned out to create an advantage for the systems integrator had little to do with price and a great deal to do with the ability of the new system to integrate with existing hardware. The integrator's system excelled at this feature, but it had never previously been viewed as an exciter capable of delivering competitive advantage.

In another example, a commercial bank had developed a computer system that integrated information on clients' cash balances in accounts all over the world. Although the system had many useful features, what sold it to the chief financial officers, who were the primary target customers, was not so much the access to information. They liked the easy-to-program instant printing and downloading feature that allowed them to obtain and manipulate information without having to wait around for the management information system (MIS) department to develop a special report. The excited reaction by these customers was astonishing. One can only guess at how difficult they found it to do business with Central MIS!

In each of these cases, teams started projects without clearly understanding what would motivate customers to buy and which attributes would be considered most valuable. As you convert your assumptions to knowledge, your group should increasingly hone in on the cause-and-effect relations that will drive your new business model. The questions in figure 11-2 are designed to help you ascertain your progress. Each question gets a score of 1 if the team member believes "We have no idea at this point" and a 5 if the respondent believes that the team knows exactly what's going on. The lower the score, the greater the assumption-to-knowledge ratio, and the greater the projects' uncertainty with respect to the eventual profit drivers of the business model.

Note that the right-hand column of questions pertains to projects not intended to generate revenues—projects such as major information-technology (IT) systems development, process changes, human resource development programs, and so on. These processes do not involve external, revenue-paying customers, but they do have internal clients.

The customer-oriented questions in the figure are designed to indicate how much progress your group has made in developing insights in the consumption chain and attribute mapping exercises in chapters 3 and 4. If they can't answer these questions, they might need to revisit these exercises with potential target customer segments. The second major set of items measures the organizational deliverables portion of your discovery-driven plan. Does the team understand the cost drivers in the business model? What could cause operational or quality problems? Are you taking on risks or legal/regulatory challenges that you don't understand?

And, most important, does the team feel confident about pricing? Let's say that your team has completed this survey. You are now staring at a feedback report indicating that of the sixteen items, the lowest-scoring item concerns price. Remember, the score is not generated by some consultant with a running meter—it represents your team's view of what is going on right now. The low score suggests that this issue needs discussion. The discussion might take the form of debating the implications of various pricing decisions and fleshing out the assumptions underlying each person's position.

FIGURE 11-2

UNDERSTANDING BUSINESS DRIVERS

To what extent do you believe that your team understands each of the following aspects of your project? Circle 1, 2, 3, 4, or 5, with 1 being the least extent and 5 being the most. Note that a lack of clarity is expected in some areas, especially early on. If an item does not apply, please check the N/A column.

The left column is intended for revenue-oriented projects, the right for non-revenue oriented projects.

Projects Intended to Generate Revenues Directly	We Have No Idea at This Stage			We Know Exactly at This Stage	N/A	Projects Not Intended to Generate Revenues Directly
Key sources of revenue	1	2	3	4	5	___	Key sources of funds
Who key customers are	1	2	3	4	5	___	Who key clients or users are
The customer's needs being satisfied	1	2	3	4	5	___	The client/user's needs being satisfied
The competition you face in filling this need	1	2	3	4	5	___	The internal competition you face in filling this need
Where, when, and how customers will use your offering	1	2	3	4	5	___	Where, when, and how customers will use your offering
Risks to the customer in buying your offering	1	2	3	4	5	___	Risks to the client in using your offering
How to price your offering	1	2	3	4	5	___	How to assess the value of your contribution
Legal or regulatory matters affecting your business	1	2	3	4	5	___	Legal or regulatory matters affecting your business
The main sources of risk to your firm	1	2	3	4	5	___	The main sources of risk to your firm
Necessary support services	1	2	3	4	5	___	Necessary support services

FIGURE 11-2 (CONTINUED)

UNDERSTANDING BUSINESS DRIVERS

Projects Intended to Generate Revenues Directly	We Have No Idea at This Stage			We Know Exactly at This Stage		N/A	Projects Not Intended to Generate Revenues Directly
The cost of resources	1	2	3	4	5	___	The cost of resources
How key operations need to be carried out	1	2	3	4	5	___	How key operations need to be carried out
Factors that interfere with operations reliability	1	2	3	4	5	___	Factors that interfere with operations reliability
Factors that interfere with output quality	1	2	3	4	5	___	Factors that interfere with output quality
Cost of operations	1	2	3	4	5	___	Cost of operations
Major bottlenecks preventing improved operations	1	2	3	4	5	___	Major bottlenecks preventing improved operations

Make note of the key points of the discussion—it's a great way to capture the implicit assumptions made by advocates of different approaches. We often recommend that clients expand these discussion notes into what we call *issue papers*, for discussion with higher management. To write an issue paper, someone is appointed to set forth short, simple statements that outline the problem and propose alternative solutions (you can sometimes pull the statements right out of the operations specifications in your discovery-driven plan). This allows you to explore alternatives and gives everyone involved with the project a common point of reference.

Becoming aware of areas with a high assumption-to-knowledge ratio can focus attention on crucial issues early. With a major customer-service initiative in an insurance firm that we worked with, it became clear from the first round of postsurvey discussion that the team had a lot of confusion on how to price, among other aspects of the project. The issue paper the team put together suggested that the team was on the brink of offering a service that could fundamentally change the company's overall strategy for distributing products through brokers. Figuring out the answers to the low-scoring items eventually required a board-level decision about the ultimate purpose and objectives of the project.

The survey served as an early warning to the project leader—he became aware of the need to get a decision on the project's pricing and distribution strategy months before he would have otherwise made a board-level presentation. Had those months gone by, changing the strategy to reflect the board's final decision would have wasted a lot of time, money, and effort and, worse, created dreadful credibility problems among both brokers and customers.

The items outlined in figure 11-2 measure how much your discovery-driven plan includes knowledge of the business drivers. Low scores suggest that you are still dealing with a great many assumptions. Questions about business drivers handle the "what" of the business. The next set of questions concerns the "how"—specifically, how effectively is the project team working together?

Building the Deftness of the Team

Despite the considerable attention given to the vital issue of how people work effectively in a group, popular interpretations of a lot of research indicate that teamwork is often misunderstood. As people who do research on teams will tell you, creating the conditions under which a team can flourish is a challenging task.[4] Unclear goals, a context in which the objectives of individuals are not aligned, or a structure in which authority, responsibility, and communications do not support the objectives of the team will dampen performance, no matter how many rah-rah team-building workshops the organization sponsors.

When we looked at real organizations building new strategic competences, our findings often bore little resemblance to the intensely engaged, close-working groups popularly associated with teamwork. In reality, while we did observe teams that behaved that way, another pattern seemed equally prevalent. In this second pattern, we observed a fluid, constantly reconfiguring assemblage of people united in the pursuit of an emerging purpose but not necessarily united in their sense of belonging to a permanent team.

We were working with a very successful reinsurance company and luckily obtained its consent to test the early version of our methodology on one of their most significant new ventures. When it came time to report the results to the project "team," we had a terrible time getting everyone together. For one thing, they were seldom in the same geographic location at the same time. They spent a lot of their time working independently and, when they did meet, tended to confer in subgroups rather than engaging in full-blown meetings. Little in the popular team literature prepared us for this situation, yet the project went on to become a major source of growth for the reinsurer. We had a very similar experience with a commercial bank team working on developing a global presence—in this case, team members were scattered across the planet and could hardly spend large amounts of time in conference.

The surprises got us thinking. Once a new business development effort is well launched, perhaps the people working on it have fewer—not more—reasons to meet. Perhaps, in fact, too much "teaming" diverts attention from the task at hand. The misconceptions that many people hold about the relationship between teamwork and team competence are listed in box 11-1.

Groups that function smoothly and effectively operate with what we call deftness. The dictionary defines *deft* as characterized by "facility and skill" using "sureness of touch and handling."[5] Such a team has a minimal need for coordination or relationship building (and their attendant costs). Deftness is a second indicator of emerging competence, building on the first, which is an understanding of the key business drivers.

There are four components of emerging deftness in a group:

- Interpersonal confidence, or the extent to which everyone is confident that all the others both know what to do and are able to do it

- Confidence that others are willing to do what is needed

- Information flows, or the extent to which people receive needed information of the appropriate quality at the right time. Sometimes crude information received early is superior to perfect information too late

BOX 11-1

SOME MISCONCEPTIONS ABOUT TEAMWORK

1. **Effective teams work together a lot.** We found instead that smoothly functioning groups work just as well when individuals are able to work independently, yet confidently.

2. **Conflict between group members is bad.** Many researchers agree that this is dangerous.[a] But constructive conflict is essential to prevent such dysfunctions as individual apathy, groupthink, and the so-called Abilene paradox, in which members agree to agree, even if they have qualms.[b] What makes conflict constructive is controlled disagreements over ideas (not personalities) and a common commitment to, and mutual confidence in, execution after a decision is made.

3. **Teams are better off when members like each other.** True, it's tough to work with someone when you have an overwhelming urge to throttle the person. On the other hand, there are plenty of groups whose members would not care to spend any time together on a personal basis but who do leverage each other's experience and skill effectively. The key seems to be mutual respect rather than affection.

4. **Team satisfaction produces performance.** We found no necessary correlation.[c] When a group puts more energy into its own good feelings than into the task at hand, performance suffers. In one extreme example, an IT project manager was so concerned about morale that she would hold pizza parties when deadlines were missed so that people didn't feel discouraged.

a. Coser (1956); Eisenhardt (1989).

b. Harvey (1974); Janis (1972).

c. Nerkar, McGrath, and MacMillan (1996).

- Feedback, or the extent to which those involved can give or receive important feedback

Figure 11-3 asks your team members to position your project between two statements. A position closer to 1 indicates less deftness, and a position closer to 5 indicates greater deftness.

Suppose that your group's lowest scores relates to dissonance—in particular, item 5 ("On this project there are many hidden agendas") and item 17 ("Individuals tend to pursue their own interests in execution of the project"). This might well allow issues that generally lurk unmentioned beneath the surface to be brought into the open and addressed. Sometimes, the solutions are surprisingly straightforward.

For instance, one manager charged with implementing a major systems overhaul faced exactly this pattern of low scores. She gathered her group together to go through the responses and find out why they were so suspicious of one another's motivations. After about twenty stilted, uncomfortable minutes, a key member in charge of the whole customer service operation started talking about the pressures she felt. "Every time you guys need me," she said, "I have to drop what I'm doing with my people and come running over here. And while I'm here with you, my regular staff feel like second-class citizens—as though all I want to do is work on the glamorous new system while they get stuck with all the problems it generates!" Her comments opened a floodgate. As it turned out, everyone (except the full-time dedicated systems staff) was feeling overwhelmed by trying to do both a good job "at home" and for the project, in an organization whose culture made it difficult to admit such problems.

What was really going on, we realized, was a manifestation of the increasingly common problem of multitasking, not of a lack of commitment to the project. The customer service manager's absences from the team and her obvious resistance when she was asked to participate were interpreted by others as a lack of commitment, when in reality she was desperately trying to cover two demanding sets of conflicting obligations.

The senior manager in charge immediately implemented a policy of setting aside time during every significant project meeting during which she asked people to discuss the implications of project

FIGURE 11-3

ASSESSING DEFTNESS

Instructions: Circle the number that most accurately positions your project between the two statements made for each item. Note that there are no right or wrong answers to the questions below and that each question is independent of the others.

1. Few others on the team know what to do	1	2	3	4	5	All the others on the team know what to do
2. Few others on the team are competent to do what is needed	1	2	3	4	5	All the others on the team are competent to do what is needed
3. Few people on the team can depend on one another to do what is needed	1	2	3	4	5	All people on the team can depend on one another to do what is needed
4. Few people on the team know what information is important to the others	1	2	3	4	5	All people on the team know what information is important to the others
5. On this project, there are many hidden agendas	1	2	3	4	5	On this project, there are few or no hidden agendas
6. Important information often gets held up	1	2	3	4	5	Information flows quickly
7. Important information often gets withheld	1	2	3	4	5	Information never gets withheld
8. Important information is often distorted	1	2	3	4	5	Information is always accurate
9. New people joining the project find it difficult to be accepted	1	2	3	4	5	New people joining the project are easily assimilated
10. Few people on the team understand one another	1	2	3	4	5	All people on the team understand one another—we "speak the same language"
11. Few people on the team can depend on one another to implement decisions	1	2	3	4	5	All people in the team can depend on one another to implement decisions
12. Information needed to move the project forward is simply not available	1	2	3	4	5	We have all the information that we need to move the project forward

FIGURE 11-3 (CONTINUED)

ASSESSING DEFTNESS

13. The project is short on key skills	1	2	3	4	5	All key skills are in place
14. Team members are uncomfortable challenging one another	1	2	3	4	5	Team members are comfortable challenging one another
15. There is little agreement that correct decisions are being made	1	2	3	4	5	There is general agreement that correct decisions are being made
16. I get little feedback regarding my contribution	1	2	3	4	5	I get rapid and open feedback regarding my contribution
17. Individuals tend to pursue their own interests in execution of the project	1	2	3	4	5	Individuals suppress their interests in favor of project interests
18. I am given no opportunity to provide open feedback regarding the contribution of others	1	2	3	4	5	I am given a great deal of opportunity to provide open feedback regarding the contribution of others

work on other obligations and the impact of these other obligations on their project work. By making the topic first visible, then discussable, the group was much better equipped to find solutions. In this particular case, the entire group figured out ways to get the job done without driving the operations and service people crazy; this had the beneficial side effect of interfering less with customers as well.

Problems of conflicting roles pop up all the time in companies today because the slack time that used to give people time to catch up is gone. The time to make decisions is shrinking, and managers are overwhelmed with inputs. E-mail, voice mail, telephone calls, and other forms of communication that seem to demand instantaneous responses are taking their toll on managerial time. The issues raised from the responses to the questions in figure 11-3 should help you decide whether the people on your team are becoming more deft. People can chart responsibilities in a straightforward way, reinforce the distinctions between the urgent and the important, and clarify goals, all without help from consultants or counseling. If people continue to be unable to cope, you may be facing the need to drop some projects, as we discussed in chapter 8.

Having obtained a sense of what the business model is and how deftly the group is working, your next step is to determine whether progress is being made toward the development of competitive strengths based on the skills, assets, and systems you use to compete.

Measuring Emerging Competence

Since strategically useful competences often emerge and manifest themselves in unexpected ways, our major challenge was to come up with a measure that would apply universally. Such a measure is a tall order in a world in which it is precisely the uniqueness and idiosyncrasy of each firm's competences that are expected to yield competitive advantages in the future.

We took our cue from evolutionary economics.[6] The literature asserts that although the content of competences can vary a lot, they do have a common effect. Just as a skilled person can reliably and consistently achieve desired results and avoid undesirable ones, a competent project group can reliably and consistently achieve desired results and avoid undesirable ones. One proxy measure for emerging competence is the degree of convergence between what you tried to achieve and what you actually did.[7] Achievement in a project group is measured by identifying ten generic objectives of most business projects and asking your group to score progress (figure 11-4). A score of 1 indicates that results are far worse than expected; a score of 5 indicates results far better than expected.

We can't guarantee that increasingly closing in on these objectives will give you a winning project. What we can promise is that unless this eventually happens, the results derive more from luck than from strategy.[8] If your team isn't becoming increasingly able to do what it is trying to do, it isn't building competence. It works as long as you stay lucky, but this is unlikely in an increasingly turbulent, competitive environment.

One interesting pattern that often emerges from analyzing the competence measure reflects an imbalance in emphasis. It's easier to meet deadlines, for instance, if you blow the budget and let quality

FIGURE 11-4

EMERGING COMPETENCE

Assess project performance over the last two months on each of the following dimensions.

Objective	Results Far Worse than Expected			Results Far Better than Expected		N/A
1. Meeting budget	1	2	3	4	5	____
2. Meeting staffing needs	1	2	3	4	5	____
3. Meeting major deadlines	1	2	3	4	5	____
4. Meeting quality standards	1	2	3	4	5	____
5. Meeting reliability standards	1	2	3	4	5	____
6. Meeting costs	1	2	3	4	5	____
7. Meeting efficiency standards	1	2	3	4	5	____
8. Meeting user/client satisfaction objectives	1	2	3	4	5	____
9. Meeting service objectives	1	2	3	4	5	____
10. Meeting objectives overall	1	2	3	4	5	____

slip. It's similarly convenient to focus on the hard numbers—cost, deadlines, and efficiency—while sacrificing the softer but more important measures of client satisfaction and client service. Often, survey results show that the numbers- and deadline-oriented objectives are being favored over technical-oriented ones. This is not acceptable: business success generally requires that all these objectives be met with some level of proficiency.

Measuring Distinctiveness

As discussed, there is a big difference between simply being competent and being distinctively competent. Distinctiveness is a measure of how well you are identifying possible differentiating and exciting attributes, or are eliminating the dissatisfying and tolerable attributes. Distinctiveness makes a competitive difference in two circumstances: when you add more value for selected customer segments than the competition can, and when you operate with greater efficiency than the competition does. Managing either one or both yields the opportunity to generate better margins than competitors.

Projects are typically begun with one or the other form of distinctiveness in mind. Value-adding projects are usually intended to generate new revenue streams and growth, whereas cost-reduction projects are usually targeted at improving productivity. In either case, the question is whether the team is confident of establishing value in the target markets, improving efficiency, or, in the best of all worlds, doing both.

We measure whether your project is leading to distinctive customer value, with the statements in figure 11-5. If your project is not intended to garner revenues from customers, decide with your group to fill it out from the perspective of an internal client, or just go on to figure 11-6.

We use the items in figure 11-5 as part of an ongoing monitoring process. Slippage (which occurs when formerly high scores start to drop) indicates that new information has revealed that the market impact may not be as profound as the team once believed. If there is little market impact for a project (or at least evidence that you are building the potential to have impact in the marketplace), the project may not be moving in a positive direction.

When you evaluate the responses to figure 11-5, look at two issues. First, look for items with high variation of the scores. This means that people don't agree on the value in the project. It's worthwhile to air the reasons for these differences in opinion, because those with different ideas may have insights that no one else thought about. It also clears the air of wishful thinking if the nonbelievers provide credible evidence in support of their low scores.

Second, look at items with high average scores (say, 3.5 or more). For these high-scoring items, decide how progress on these fronts will be measured and monitored. In our experience, a big gap usually exists between the potential for achieving customer value added and the reality of what is being accomplished, unless there is a concerted effort to make sure that the value added is actually occurring. The opportunity to build added value slips away in the hot pace of implementation.

FIGURE 11-5

POTENTIAL FOR DISTINCTIVE VALUE

To what extent do you agree with each of the following statements?

	Strongly Disagree			Strongly Agree		N/A
As a result of this team's activities, customers/clients will get more value from our offerings than they have in the past	1	2	3	4	5	____
As a result of this project, customers/clients will get more value from our offerings than from competitive offerings	1	2	3	4	5	____
As a result of this project, we will be able to meet customer needs we have never served before	1	2	3	4	5	____
As a result of this project, we will be able to create offerings for an entirely new set of customers/clients	1	2	3	4	5	____
As a result of this project, customers/clients will be willing to pay a premium price for our offerings	1	2	3	4	5	____
This project will significantly improve our responsiveness to customers/clients compared with past performance	1	2	3	4	5	____
This project will make us more responsive to customers/clients than our competitors	1	2	3	4	5	____
This project will significantly improve the quality of our offerings compared with past quality levels	1	2	3	4	5	____
This project will allow us to produce a higher-quality offering than our competitors or other organizations like ours	1	2	3	4	5	____

A powerful and simple way to make sure you're measuring real value added is to decide on a way to measure it. Then, appoint someone (often a promising junior person) to simply measure and report at every meeting what progress has been made on the measure. Having a measure developed and consistently attended to dramatically improves the chances that the opportunity will not slip away. For example, if one area in which you assume value will be added lies in bringing on new customer segments, someone can be asked to keep track of whether representative customers from the new segments are actually buying and ordering, and to estimate whether they are as profitable and as satisfied as was originally assumed.

Figure 11-5 assesses potential distinctive value, but what about potential distinctive efficiency? Figure 11-6 addresses this issue. Even in high-value-added products and services, it is the rare firm that escapes the imperative to contain costs and improve efficiency. Over the long run, efficiency concerns always arise and projects to improve efficiency abound.[9]

For some projects, however, the issue is not efficiency at all. If your team agrees that this is so, do not use figure 11-6. Again, go through the table with your team and agree to delete irrelevant items.

When you evaluate the responses to figure 11-6, look again at high-variation items and high-score (3.5 or more) items and carry out the same exercises suggested for figure 11-5. In particular, make sure that someone is appointed to monitor and report progress on accomplishing efficiency gains. Very often, existing systems are not set up in such a way that you can accurately measure increases in systemwide efficiency, so creating the measurement structure to do this may be a project in itself.

Obviously, in the initial stages of a project, we cannot expect high scores on either value or efficiency. The team's understanding of the business drivers will tend to be low, a new team will find it hard to operate deftly, and competences will not have had enough time to develop. If low scores on market impact and operational efficiency persist, however, the manager in charge ought to question whether the team is actually creating the distinctiveness that is a precursor to later competitive advantage.

The core lesson is that unless you are building distinctiveness, all your efforts at new business development will be for naught. So, while the results of the surveys presented in this section can't perfectly predict whether your project will be a winner, the results can give you a strong indication of the project's progress (or lack thereof).

Also of interest is whether your group has identified ways beyond the current project's charter to capitalize on its upside poten-

FIGURE 11-6

DISTINCTIVE OPERATIONAL EFFICIENCY

To what extent do you agree with each of the following statements?

Undertaking This Project Will Accomplish the Following	Strongly Disagree			Strongly Agree		N/A
Allow us to do more work without increasing headcount	1	2	3	4	5	____
Allow us to gain economies of scale	1	2	3	4	5	____
Reduce the number of steps required to complete a transaction	1	2	3	4	5	____
Reduce our turnaround time	1	2	3	4	5	____
Allow us to make better use of assets we already own	1	2	3	4	5	____
Reduce the amount or cost of input resources	1	2	3	4	5	____
Lower our cost per unit of output	1	2	3	4	5	____
Eliminate or reduce postsales service requirements	1	2	3	4	5	____
Lower our fixed costs	1	2	3	4	5	____
Reduce our costs of distribution	1	2	3	4	5	____
Reduce our costs for storage or inventory	1	2	3	4	5	____
Reduce our costs of operations	1	2	3	4	5	____

tial. If so, you will be seeing indications of emerging option value. Use the statements in figure 11-7 to find out whether some of the value of a project derives from its upside potential.

In other words, Figure 11-7 helps you gauge option value. As with figures 11-5 and 11-6, use the group to discuss high variation of scores and high average scores. The critical problem with option value is that unless someone in your firm is proactively looking to capitalize on option potential, it can be overlooked in the hubbub of getting the new initiative implemented. The key issue here is deciding how to measure whether option value is emerging, and who will be responsible for designing an approach to capitalizing on emerging

FIGURE 11-7

EMERGING OPTION VALUE

To what extent do you agree with each of the following statements?

Undertaking This Project Will Accomplish the Following	Strongly Disagree			Strongly Agree		N/A
Help us learn new manufacturing, production, or operations skills	1	2	3	4	5	____
Help us learn about new market segments	1	2	3	4	5	____
Help us learn about international market opportunities	1	2	3	4	5	____
Help us learn what product features and attributes our customers really care about	1	2	3	4	5	____
Help leverage our existing distribution capacity	1	2	3	4	5	____
Help utilize excess operations capacity	1	2	3	4	5	____
Leverage our skills in design and customization	1	2	3	4	5	____
Leverage our skills in operations	1	2	3	4	5	____
Leverage our skills in service and distribution	1	2	3	4	5	____
Leverage our skills in sourcing	1	2	3	4	5	____
Extend the reach of our products and services	1	2	3	4	5	____
Extend brand awareness of our offering	1	2	3	4	5	____
Provide a new source of differentiation for our company	1	2	3	4	5	____
Capitalize on brand loyalty	1	2	3	4	5	____
Leverage our advertising	1	2	3	4	5	____
Build our reputation in a new business area	1	2	3	4	5	____
Put us in a favorable position with respect to future industry standards	1	2	3	4	5	____
Allow us to gather better information on customers and competitiveness	1	2	3	4	5	____
Develop new sources of supply	1	2	3	4	5	____
Enhance our image	1	2	3	4	5	____
Provide ideas for new products or services	1	2	3	4	5	____
Give us an advantage in sourcing from suppliers	1	2	3	4	5	____
Give us an advantage in accessing distributors	1	2	3	4	5	____

option value as it becomes clear. We like to make the discussion of option value a regular agenda item at performance reviews and major project management meetings.

Closing In on Competitive Advantage

Finally, we can now make some judgments about emerging competitive advantage. We do this by asking respondents to estimate the probability of the future advantage of the project with respect to profits, margins, and revenues, and estimate the likely duration of the advantage. You will find that these questions will be much easier to answer for your launch projects than for your options projects. This is natural; at the stage that they are only options, you will not be expecting them to create major advantages. The questions we ask are listed in figure 11-8. While these are obviously fairly crude measures, we have found them to correlate quite well with actual outcomes in a study that compared early responses to the questionnaire with later "hard" data from business plans and performance reports for a sample of high-technology ventures.

Our heuristic is that any project with an average advantage score below 60 percent is a candidate for serious reevaluation. The business concept aside, a team that responds with low scores in figure 11-8 is a team without great confidence in the future, a clear signal that all is not well. If your team has scores like this, it may be time to stop and get to the bottom of what's going on.

Figure 11-8 has proven to be helpful to managers who must face up to the difficult decision of whether to persist with a project or to end or redirect it. Distinguishing between necessary persistence and dangerous obstinacy is not always easy, but scores that drag on with low probability of eventual success are indicators that it may well be time to redirect. In particular, be alert to cases for which the score for the overall success of the project is high but none of the items tapping competitive superiority have been assigned high probabilities. If things are going well with some aspects of the business (for instance, its technical accomplishments) but the project shows little promise of improving competitive position (value or margin), you may want to consider deploying the team's talent to another project in your portfolio.

FIGURE 11-8

EMERGENCE OF COMPETITIVE ADVANTAGE

Indicate the probabilities you would assign in the spaces below, using a scale of 0 to 100. If any question does not apply to your project (because, for example, it is not intended to contribute to profit) check the "not applicable" (N/A) column.

	Probability on Scale of 0 to 100	N/A
What is the probability of success for the project at the moment?	____	____
What is the probability that the project will contribute to unusually high profits when it achieves market potential?	____	____
What is the probability that the project will contribute to higher profits than what your competitors obtain with a similar offering?	____	____
What is the probability that the project will significantly improve the margin (revenues less expenses) that your firm obtains from your offerings?	____	____
What is the probability that the project will improve the margin that your firm obtains relative to competitors?	____	____
What is the probability that the project will significantly increase your firm's revenues?	____	____
What is the probability that the project will increase your firm's revenues relative to competitors?	____	____

Score: _____

The last important piece of data emerges from figure 11-9, which addresses the durability of competitive advantage. Responses to these statements suggest how urgently and aggressively to drive the project. They should be evaluated along with the questions about competitive insulation, which we looked at in chapter 8.

It's important to effect a rapid launch for offerings with short-lived advantages. A slow launch not only gives competitors more time to catch up but also truncates the time during which you reap the rewards.[10] Once this advantage comes to an end, someone needs to be thinking about where the next one is coming from. The duration

FIGURE 11-9

DURABILITY OF COMPETITIVE ADVANTAGE

Indicate in the right-hand column the number representing the length of time you believe you have before competitive erosion will weaken your position.

Responses

1. We will maintain higher profits than our competitors do,   _____
   for the following time frame:
   1 = 0–3 months; 2 = 4–6 months; 3 = 7–12 months;
   4 = 13–24 months; 5 = 24+ months

2. We will maintain higher margins than our competitors do,   _____
   for the following time frame:
   1 = 0–3 months; 2 = 4–6 months; 3 = 7–12 months;
   4 = 13–24 months; 5 = 24+ months

3. We will maintain higher revenues than our competitors do,   _____
   for the following time frame:
   1 = 0–3 months; 2 = 4–6 months; 3 = 7–12 months;
   4 = 13–24 months; 5 = 24+ months

statements also help you think through how urgent the project is. Finally, the statements can yield some ideas about how much to invest in creating the advantage. If duration is short, the time to get returns on the investment is also short, which suggests that extreme parsimony in executing the project may be called for.

INTERPRETING THE DATA AND USING IT TO FORMULATE ACTION PLANS

Our recommendation is to use the ACE survey instruments (figures 11-2 through 11-9) in conjunction with discovery-driven planning. One way is to have the team fill out the surveys as you reach each major milestone, and then look at the results when you meet to discuss your assumption and milestone checklist (see figures 10-2, 10-4, and 10-5). This allows you to consider both what you are doing (assumption and milestone checklist) and how you are doing it (ACE surveys) at the same time.

Use the decisions you reached during discovery-driven planning in conjunction with the ACE survey results to formulate an action plan. Have the team talk about the patterns they see, focusing on how to improve the lowest scores and how to reduce the extent of any undesirable disagreements, as reflected by the variation in responses to an item. Using a trained process consultant or facilitator can be helpful, particularly when the team is newly formed or if there are deeply contentious issues.

To illustrate how this works, consider the analysis of business drivers presented in figure 11-10. The figure expands figure 11-2, with actual results from a project in our database.

The project was an ambitious and well-funded effort made by a highly innovative banking organization to enter a brand-new arena—namely, the capture of point-of-sale data from consumers. When we conducted the analysis, the project had been under way for about a year. Although considerable investment had been made by then, senior management was concerned about the venture's slow progress in a business for which they considered rapid entry to be an important competitive advantage. The preceding manager (who had initiated and launched the project) had left the company, and we were invited to comment on the project by the new division head. All members of the management team, as well as some operating personnel, completed the ACE surveys.

The first thing that struck us about their responses was a general lack of clarity on virtually all the characteristics that related to the basic revenue model. As you can see, the responses to items 1–7 are all quite low, suggesting that the team had not figured out how it was going to appeal to customers and gain value from them. The very identity of customers, the ways in which the offering would be used, and pricing strategies were unclear. Scores for items 9 and 11–16 were somewhat higher. These items refer to internal operating issues, such as resource cost, operations, and bottlenecks. Even here, however, the team's scores were not all that high. Moreover, the high standard deviations for item 9 (regarding risk to the firm) and item 16 (regarding major bottlenecks) indicated significant disagreement in these areas.

During a meeting to discuss the results, we considered what might improve the understanding of business drivers for this team. As part of the diagnosis, we prepared a discovery-driven plan. How the firm was going to extract revenue from the information it was

FIGURE 11-10

SAMPLE ANALYSIS: BUSINESS DRIVERS

To what extent do you believe that your team understands each of the following aspects of your project?

Projects Intended to Generate Revenues Directly	Mean	Standard Deviation	Projects Not Intended to Generate Revenues Directly
1. Key sources of revenue	2.50	1.0	Key sources of revenue
2. Who key customers are	2.75	0.86	Who key clients or users are
3. The customers' needs being satisfied	2.75	0.79	The clients' or users' needs being satisfied
4. The competition you face in filling these needs	2.25	0.86	The competition you face in filling this need
5. Where, when, and how customers will use your offering	2.75	0.86	Where, when, and how clients will use your offering
6. Risks to the customers buying your offering	2.50	0.92	The risks to the clients using your offering
7. How to price your offering	2.25	0.86	How to assess the value of your contribution
8. Legal or regulatory matters affecting your business	3.25	0.97	Legal or regulatory matters affecting your business
9. The main sources of risk to your firm	3.80	1.4	The main sources of risk to your firm
10. Support services that must be provided	2.75	0.92	Support services that must be provided
11. The cost of revenues	3.00	0.86	The cost of revenues
12. How key operations need to be carried out	3.25	0.79	How key operations need to be carried out
13. Factors that interfere with operations reliability	3.25	0.79	Factors that interfere with operations reliability
14. Factors that interfere with output quality	3.50	1.1	Factors that interfere with output quality
15. Costs of your operations	3.75	0.79	Costs of your operations
16. Major bottlenecks preventing improved operations	3.25	1.2	Major bottlenecks preventing improved operations
Grand Average	2.8		

collecting at the point of sale was poorly understood. Some team members thought they would contract with owners of retail outlets to use the information for local marketing. Others thought they would sell the household-identified transaction data to major packaged-goods manufacturers. Still others believed that the ultimate objective of the venture should be to end up as a supplier of payment and payment-processing systems, which the retailers could then out-source to them.

In short, there was very little agreement on the basic business model or unit of business, creating significant disagreement among team members. The resulting confusion then extended to the operating aspects of the fledgling business—after all, different business models with different units of business suggest totally different operating and pricing conditions. Lack of clarity on one item often correlates with lack of clarity on the other. The high standard deviations regarding risk to the firm (item 9) and bottlenecks (item 16) were similarly related to different points of view regarding the ultimate business result.

The data collected for the survey became the basis for a fundamental review of the entire business proposition. First, the new senior executive put on hold any further development of the technology and an ambitious hiring and ramp-up program until a credible business model could be identified. Next, he insisted on a careful review of all the assumptions the team had made with respect to costs, geographic penetration of the business, and appeal to initial customer sets. Finally, he established some definitive financial objectives and a schedule with firm deadlines for the business.

Unfortunately, assumption after assumption made during the first year of the project proved to be in error in the light of this careful review of the discovery-driven plan. The new senior executive decided to shut the project down and stem the huge losses that it was incurring at that point.

Although in this case, the story did not have a happy ending, the executive in charge felt that the company had learned a great deal from the project, in particular a lesson about how expensive it can be not to take time out to measure progress in the process of competence development. "All in all," he observed, "using the surveys probably saved us another six months and as much as $20 million more in investment before we would have figured out the seriousness of the problems with the project."

Managing the Emergence of Competitive Advantage

The only limit to the use of the diagnostic surveys seems to be imagination in how they are applied. They have been used to look at differences by level in the organizational hierarchy, where it quickly became clear that more senior people were a lot more sanguine about progress than the people on the front lines. The surveys have helped iron out differences in perspectives of people from different functional specializations, when understandable differences in point of view can be blown into major conflicts if not handled well. Teams working on mergers, joint ventures, and alliances have also put the surveys to good use to tease out differences in perceptions among the players. On other occasions, parts of the survey have been administered to a firm's distributors, customers, bankers, brokers, and suppliers, bringing to the surface illuminating differences between the results as seen by the project team and those seen by other stakeholders.

Using a tool like this is particularly useful for uncertain projects, for several reasons. First, the process requires everyone to think about the same set of competitive and strategic issues in a comprehensive and shared way. This happens less than one might think, because people tend to get wrapped up in their piece of the process and forget what is going on elsewhere. Second, the information is captured undiluted, confidentially, and quickly. This gives the process credibility—it's not a consultant telling the people in the firm what's going on; it's the people in the firm telling themselves. Third, these tools allow issues to surface early and get dealt with rather than fester unresolved. Fourth, and perhaps most important, the process requires people to stop and take stock not only of what they are doing but of how they are working together. Unfortunately, in these days of high-pressure schedules and tight deadlines, the time needed to take stock is hard to come by. Some companies have learned the hard way the value of building a regular time-out session around meetings to discuss the surveys.

We believe that as the business world becomes more competitive and less certain, successful strategies will derive from a combination of disciplined analysis, experimentation, and discovery. The trouble is that while we have many useful tools to help us understand the analytical part of the equation, far fewer are available to help us with the discovery-oriented part. Our work on how new business models emerge, change, and sometimes drive competitive advantage is an attempt to develop such a tool.

By focusing on the process by which the competences are emerging, progress can be measured, monitored, and, therefore, managed. Treating new business development projects as strategic experiments is consistent with an entrepreneurial, discovery-driven orientation. People must learn to recognize initially unintended competences and how these competences can better serve the company's goals. A further benefit is that opponents have difficulty matching such competences because they have not gone through the experiences or learned the lessons that the experimenting firm has.

Our approach does depart from some of the usual metrics used to handle the analytical side of competence creation. This is necessary because in a new project, such unusual measures are the only ones you have to work with. Under high uncertainty, you are literally managing your way down a path whose final destination is unknown. There is no clear, crisp map of the new terrain. Instead, you have indicators of progress, captured in the answers to five sets of questions. Are we coming to understand the business? Are we working more effectively together? Are we increasingly able to do new things with reliability? Are at least some of these likely to give us a measure of distinction? And how likely are we to succeed?

Admittedly, the measures are fuzzy. The difficulty is that we are trying to measure what is going on today and likely to occur in the future—not the hard, objective, easily obtained information about what has already happened.[11] What we want is information that we can use to make decisions and changes rather than information about things beyond our ability to change. We are unabashedly more interested in fuzzy leading indicators than crisp lagging ones.

SUMMARY OF ACTION STEPS

The action steps that follow are meant to get you started on the concepts and processes discussed in the chapter. Feel free to elaborate in a way that works for your company.

STEP 1: Identify members of the project team—all the people with major responsibility for allocating resources to and executing the project.

STEP 2: Sit down with your project team and reach agreement on which surveys are relevant to the project and how the statements will be interpreted—for instance, who is "the customer" or "the client." Delete items and sections not relevant to your project.

STEP 3: At a kickoff meeting and thereafter at each major project milestone, complete the surveys and send them to someone who can process them confidentially.

STEP 4: Compile the results: Calculate team averages for each item, and flag the items with the lowest scores. Calculate variation in responses—either the standard deviation or the range—for each item, and flag the items with the highest variation

STEP 5: For the surveys tapping distinctive value, distinctive efficiency, and option potential, decide on measures you will use to monitor progress for high-score items. Appoint someone to monitor them and report at each major project review meeting.

STEP 6: Discuss results with the team at a meeting or in a conference call. Focus on a frank discussion of items in each survey with low average scores and high variation. Work through the suggestions in the chapter pertaining to each survey.

STEP 7: Discuss with the team what must be done to continue improving on the measures that tap the high-scoring items for distinctive value, efficiency, or option potential.

STEP 8: Repeat the process at each major milestone in your discovery-driven plan.

CHAPTER 12

THE MOST

IMPORTANT JOB

Entrepreneurial Leadership

YOUR MOST IMPORTANT JOB AS AN ENTREPRENEURIAL LEADER is not to find new opportunities or to identify the critical competitive insights. Your task is to create an organization that does these things for you as a matter of course. You will have succeeded when everyone in the organization takes it for granted that business success is about a continual search for new opportunities and a continual letting go of less productive activities. You will have succeeded when everyone feels that he or she has not only the right but the obligation to seek out new opportunities and to make them happen. You will have succeeded when the hallways buzz with energy, when people come to work excited, and when they are proud to be associated with your dynamic organization. And, of course, you will have succeeded when the value you create within your organization translates into stakeholder wealth.

This chapter focuses on how your behavior as an entrepreneurial leader impacts the search for opportunity in your organization. What distinguishes leaders who are capable of sustained and significant business revitalization from other managers is their personal practices on the job. These practices fall into three broad categories: practices that set the work climate, practices that orchestrate the process of seeking and realizing opportunities to grow the business, and hands-on practices that involve problem solving with the people at work on a particular venture. We'll discuss each in turn, but before doing so we stress that these practices are important for creating an entrepreneurial mindset in general—irrespective of whether a specific new business model is being created. The practices we describe below are important for establishing a pervasive spirit and a willingness to seek out and grasp entrepreneurial initiative throughout your business.

The problem with launching new business models is that everything about a new business model is likely to be out of whack with the business model of your existing core business. The more the new business opportunities differ from the model in your base business, the more difficult it will be for people used to the existing model to understand them. Unless, and only unless, you pay attention to resolving the discontinuities between the new models and the base business, the very forces that made the old business model successful will tend to preserve it to the detriment of the business models you are creating (or reinventing, in the case of a major reconfiguration of your existing models).

Although the General Electric Company may be overused as an example these days, the reason is probably that it is one of the best examples of a leading team's having systematically created an entrepreneurial mindset at every level. GE's Jack Welch has proven to be a master at this in the two decades that he has been at the head of the company. He reduces the paralyzing effects of uncertainty through leadership. He isn't afraid to tell people what they should focus on. At the same time, his organization frees people to capitalize on new opportunities through structures that encourage entrepreneurial behavior and the tools and training to make entrepreneurial behavior effective. Does it work? We think so. Take a look at table 12-1, which evidences the value GE has created since Welch took the helm in 1981.[1]

Welch summarizes his philosophy for managing in today's world as follows: "You can't predict anymore. But that doesn't matter—what is important is that you must be able to adapt and exploit—

TABLE 12-1

VALUE CREATION AT GE

	1982	1987	1999
Sales	$22 billion	$44 billion	$100 billion
Employees	435,000	285,000	293,000
Market value	$21 billion	$53 billion	$372 billion

be agile enough to guess where the value is going and position your-self to exploit it if it does."[2] Let's move on to what you'll need to do.

CLIMATE-SETTING PRACTICES

The goal behind climate setting is to create for everyone in the business a pervasive sense of urgency to be working on the next new business initiative. Everyone, from the CEO to the shipping room staff, must be clear that searching for entrepreneurial opportunities is urgent and is everyone's responsibility. Profitable growth becomes everyone's charter.

To foster such a climate, the most important thing you can do is behave as you would like your people to behave, and to model this behavior consistently, predictably, and relentlessly. Not everyone can be charismatic. Anyone can, however, learn to be doggedly persistent in modeling the behavior he or she wants others to adopt. This is a timeless principle, taught in every historically great school for leadership—people will heed your behavior and follow your example, but they will not change what they do on the basis of words alone.

The most important behavior on your part involves dedicating a disproportionate share of your own time, attention, and discretionary resources to creating new business models. Existing businesses, and the leaders in charge of them, face little difficulty in articulating their needs, building a case for their support, and attracting people. Entrepreneurial initiatives, on the other hand, are usually seen as marginal or unimportant in their early stages. Unless you personally allocate to them disproportionate attention, disproportionate resources, and disproportionate talent, they will get squeezed by the existing business to the extent that they never have a chance to take off. Your challenge is to provide counterpressure to the inertial forces that lead your people to constantly attend to the demands of today's business.

Disproportionate Attention

A major theme of this book is how the advent of uncertainty, unpredictability, and entrepreneurial opportunity has made the sensible management practices we learned to use in more stable situations useless, even dangerous. One of these traditional practices, which has a lot of face validity, is that leaders should focus largely on the most substantial lines of business, the most important clients, and the most profitable products. To some extent, this makes sense (as we discussed in chapter 7). It can lead you seriously astray, however, when your focus on what is most important today causes you to neglect tomorrow's opportunities.

A vital ingredient for the success of your new business development program is that your very best people want to work on new initiatives. They will look to you for signals that new businesses are important to you and to their future careers. So, when the often-small, untried, and risky (in the sense that returns are unpredictable) initiative gets space on your managerial agenda and is taken seriously, talented and ambitious people in the company are much more inclined to see them as development opportunities rather than career quagmires. In far too many companies, taking risks is perceived as fatal, especially if results were not as anticipated.[3]

A powerful symbolic and practical lever for communicating the importance you attach to new business development is how you manage your own agenda. Consider GEFS (GE Financial Services). Though it is a huge operation today, it started from modest beginnings—with a portfolio of installment loans supporting the GE appliance business. The former head of this operation, Gary Wendt, who is credited with much of the enormous success of GEFS, used his personal agenda as a simple but inordinately powerful tool for growing the business into ever new entrepreneurial arenas.

Over the years, he used his personal agenda to make it unequivocally clear that he expected entrepreneurial business growth from every member of management. At every major meeting, the topic of business development was on the agenda (usually in the number one spot). In every annual review, managers were asked to demonstrate the revenues they had created from businesses that did not exist five years before. From division heads to newly hired analysts, everyone was held accountable for some set of activities having to do with creating entrepreneurial revenue and profit streams. In short, no one who worked in the organization could avoid the unremitting focus on new business development.

You need to make sure that you are similarly consistent, predictable, and focused, and that you sustain this emphasis over a long period. Pressure applied only once is soon forgotten, and alternating pressure (as in flavor-of-the-month management) will cause people to be confused, disillusioned, or angry. Wendt's consistent, visible, and predictable attention to business development created a pressure in GEFS for entrepreneurial business growth that took it from the $300 million installment loan portfolio we looked at in chapter 6 to a financial services behemoth with $250 billion in assets under management when he left in 1998.

Examples of Wendt's single-minded determination to drive growth through entrepreneurial transformation at GEFS are numerous. Years ago, for instance, he was asked whether his agenda would change if someone rushed in and told him that the computer room was on fire (implying that his business could be completely destroyed). Wendt replied that he employed firefighters to handle such emergencies. As the leader, his most important job was to keep people focused on business development. Since business development is an uncomfortable and unpredictable process, Wendt knew that if he allowed it to appear to be a low priority for him, all those working for him would heave a sigh of relief and go back to business as usual, with new businesses struggling to find a place on the priority list. In fact, as he remarked, even if he did try to get involved in putting out the fire, he would probably only interfere with the efforts of the highly competent people employed to do so.

We can't stress enough how important it is for you to visibly demonstrate your commitment to new business initiatives and sustain this commitment in everything that you do. Only you can make your associates realize that no other issues are important enough to drive new business initiatives from the agenda.

We do not mean to imply that focusing on new business initiatives rather than on your existing businesses comes at no cost. Disproportionate attention should not be allocated lightly. No matter how smart or determined, no entrepreneurial leader is dealt more than twenty-four hours in a day. Time spent on entrepreneurial activity is time denied to the existing business, which may also need as much attention as it can get from you. This reinforces the importance of setting priorities and making strategic trade-offs between the entrepreneurial projects you decide to pursue (as discussed in chapter 8).

Disproportionate Allocation of Resources

Though critically important, properly managing your own agenda and personally leading the drive for entrepreneurial opportunities is not enough. Management of the agenda needs to be reinforced by the allocation of resources to entrepreneurial initiatives that are disproportionately large relative to their ability to deliver revenues or profits in the near term.

By disproportionate resources, we mean budget, access to operating capacity or operating assets, and, most vitally, the very best people. Ironically, these are the very resources that are highly desired by managers of the existing business, who are apt to hotly contest any other claim on them. Like the payment of disproportionate attention, the disproportionate allocation of resources to new business models has its costs. Every dollar and every hour of operations capacity allocated disproportionately to entrepreneurial initiatives is money and time denied the existing business. Disproportionate allocation must be a deliberate process, with commitment of resources being visibly recognized as a matter of strategic choice, not a struggle between long- and short-term goals. Both are important, and both need resources. For this reason, your strategy must visibly dictate how many of your resources will be devoted to the different types of projects in your portfolio (see figure 8-3). Establishing resource commitments to new business initiatives in this way creates an explicit recognition of their option value.

You need not personally decide which fledgling opportunity is most deserving. An approach that some very successful firms have followed is to create structures in which entrepreneurial initiatives have a legitimate claim on getting the resources they need without being entirely at the mercy of the managers in charge of major divisions. For example, 3M's well-known 15 percent rule dictates that (with no questions asked) 15 percent of an individual's time can be spent in pursuit of ideas that the person thinks are promising or important to the future of the company.

In other companies, the same effect is created by allocating budget to smaller, separate entities that can afford to pay attention to new initiatives. For instance, a central development fund, often run by the equivalent of an internal board, can push resources at promising opportunities. Joint ventures and research consortia can provide the separation and focus that entrepreneurial initiatives need. In pharmaceuticals, for example, a lot of product development is actually done by small start-ups (e.g., in biotechnology), which then partner with the more established firms to get access to their resources, experience with the regulatory approval process, and marketing clout.

The rise of the stock market and the liquidity of the IPO market of late have created still another mechanism for releasing disproportionate resources to entrepreneurial initiatives—namely, allowing them to wholly or partially spin off from their parent (which may or may not retain an equity interest). Lucent Technologies (itself a spin-off from AT&T) and Hewlett-Packard have been exploring this way of funding entrepreneurial ideas.

Disproportionate Allocation of Talent

Finally, you must be prepared for your organization's top talent to work on entrepreneurial initiatives. This can create a painful dilemma. When top talent works on an entrepreneurial initiative, the current business is weakened accordingly. However, if only mediocre talent is assigned to the difficult task of new business development, the ventures are doomed. Furthermore, allowing ventures to be run by mediocre people sends an even stronger signal to the rest of the business about your real priorities. The smart people in the firm will recognize that business development is not truly a priority for you, and they will organize their own priorities accordingly. The message: If you don't walk the talk, only the dumb people will listen.

Orchestrating Practices

People find uncertainty much more manageable if it can be framed, better understood, and simplified. One of your challenges as an entrepreneurial leader is to help your associates cope with the difficulty of determining what to focus on and how their priorities should be set. You do this by taking full burden of uncertainty from them. Well-meaning managers trying to become more entrepreneurial can easily go wrong in how they approach the management of uncertainty. They mistakenly believe that imposing any discipline on entrepreneurial development will kill off creativity and smother initiative.

Nothing could be further from the truth. As we have argued throughout the book, what is needed instead is considerable discipline, albeit a different kind of discipline—the kind used by habitual entrepreneurs. They realize that many entrepreneurial ideas will not lead to business success. They realize that to have enough resources to explore the options that may ultimately open an opportunity, they must exercise parsimony. They realize that creativity that doesn't lead to products and services that meet real customer needs at a sensible price does not increase the value of the firm. They realize, at the same time, that most people are more effective if they don't have to cope with the paralyzing effects of uncertainty.

Ballparking

One way to reduce uncertainty for people is to specify what type of entrepreneurial opportunities you expect people to be seeking. Drawing on an American idiom, we call this ballparking. A ballpark is a place where baseball is played. To come up with a ballpark estimate, therefore, is to show people a big-picture, rough definition. In ballparking, you roughly specify the arenas in which you want your people to play and how they should try to play them.

Ballparking involves defining the entrepreneurial directions that can be taken and, just as important, those directions that are not to be pursued. To beef up your opportunity register, give people room to come up with many entrepreneurial ideas. At the same time, there are limits to how many ideas you can pursue and how many you can genuinely excel in pursuing.

Defining a ballpark is particularly important for established businesses moving into a new business model and away from deeply embedded old ones. The business press is full of stories of large companies that have powerfully dominant positions in their markets and considerable resources, but that have not communicated a clearly thought-through plan for driving growth and increasing shareholder wealth. To illustrate just how challenging—and how important—ballparking can be, let's look at some large companies: AT&T (box 12-1), Sears (box 12-2), Coca-Cola (box 12-3), and Citibank (box 12-4). We will compare how senior managers struggled to delineate ballparks for them. In closely studying the examples of these firms, we have also found that the definition of a ballpark can be remarkably useful to the individual units of a business—departments or branches. All that you need to do is narrow your scope when defining the ballpark. Ballparking is also useful to the smaller firm, as we discuss in an example below.

The art of ballparking is to decide, preferably with key people in your company, in which arenas you will play and what new arenas will be pursued. You then let the people get on with playing the game. A simple statement of vision and mission is not enough. This is a myth. Vision, which we believe to be vitally important, has to do with what the business holds dear—its purpose, what makes working there more than just a job, what values bind employees together, what they want to accomplish as a group. Ballparking is a more focused idea. It is much more actionable, and it delineates the arenas in which the business will be competing if the company is to achieve its vision. To effectively take entrepreneurial initiative, people need something much more specific than a vision statement; they need to know what business directions to pursue in order to deliver on that vision.

BOX 12-1

"ALL SIZE AND NO FOCUS" AT AT&T

In 1984, Judge Harold Green launched a telecommunications revolution by mandating the breakup of AT&T's monopoly over telecommunications businesses in the United States. This initiated years of floundering, during which the telecommunications giant tried to create a new and compelling identity for itself. Foreseeing the convergence of voice and data communication, as well as the growing importance of computers, some managers argued that AT&T should move aggressively into the computer business. This move initiated a costly, failed venture into computing, which was followed by the hostile takeover of NCR, a computing and related-product company. At the time of the acquisition, NCR revenues were $7 billion. Six short years later, revenues had dropped to $4 billion. Moreover, even though the hardware side of the business was doing well, its managers found themselves increasingly hampered in their efforts to grow by their customers' reluctance to do business with a competitor from the core telecommunications business. Eventually, in CEO Robert E. Allen's own words, line management realized that the firm was "all size and no focus." The subsequent trivestiture of NCR and Lucent Technologies and the later withdrawal from a number of experimental markets and services have basically left AT&T as a long-distance telephone-operating company. Today, as the former Bell operating companies and new entrants begin to muscle into this business, Allen is no longer at the helm.

It is therefore one of your primary responsibilities to demarcate the acceptable arena for entrepreneurial development by setting up the parameters that define which business initiatives are acceptable to you and which are not. The challenge of ballparking is to think through which entrepreneurial initiatives the organization is capable of deploying and which initiatives it cannot.

BOX 12-2

SEARS: "A COMPELLING PLACE TO SHOP"

Managers at Sears are no strangers to the demands of changing business models. From its origins as the virtual creator of catalog-based merchandising aimed at customers too far away to shop in person to its now-ubiquitous presence in the suburban mall, Sears managers have provided several generations of U.S. consumers superlative value. By the 1970s, however, the old model had begun to lose its luster. Aggressive competitors such as Kmart and Wal-Mart were capturing significant shares in the consumer retail business, and the traditional operating procedures at Sears put it at a competitive disadvantage relative to its more technologically advanced rivals. Moreover, retailing in general was regarded as an increasingly competitive and unattractive industry. Throughout the 1970s and much of the 1980s, Sears managers shifted their emphasis from retailing to several alternative business models, diversifying into banking, insurance, real estate sales and development, credit cards, eye care centers, mutual funds, and auto supplies, while still trying to maintain the company's core retail and catalog businesses.

The resulting conglomerate was judged by many observers to be a chaotic mess. In trying to turn Sears around, CEO Arthur C. Martinez made a conscious decision to leverage future new business opportunities from the company's core strengths, which he judged to stem from its strong brand-name recognition with consumers. Martinez began his turnaround effort in 1992 by redefining the ballpark. The revitalized Sears organization has forged a retailing core devoted to the "Three C's: Sears as a Compelling place to shop, a Compelling place to work, and a Compelling place to invest." This ballpark was reinforced by what he termed the Three P's: Passion for the customer, the value added by the People, and the passion for Performance leadership. Businesses that didn't belong in this ballpark—such as financial services—were divested.

BOX 12-3

"A COKE SHOULD ALWAYS BE WITHIN ARM'S REACH OF DESIRE"

The late Roberto C. Goizueta has been given credit for recognizing the strategic implications of the insight that soft-drink consumption is largely a function of availability. In light of this observation, he determined that it was only through aggressive promotion of its global brand, and the logistics to back it up, that Coca-Cola could hope to hang on to its share of the soft-drink market. Instead of pursuing a business model that relied on the manufacture of relatively inexpensive syrup, to be distributed by independent, separate bottling companies, Goizueta designed a new business model in which the global distribution of the product created important profit flows. He thus expanded Coca-Cola's ballpark. At huge cost, he invested in purchasing and, as necessary, building global bottling and distribution capacity, thereby creating an integrated global soft-drink distribution business. In so doing, he established strong central controls and processes to ensure that the brand was used consistently everywhere in the world. He captured additional profitability throughout the chain and positioned Coke for major global expansion.[a]

a. Today, Goizueta's global strategy is being carefully redirected by newly appointed president Douglas N. Daft, who takes the position that the next wave of growth for Coca-Cola will come from increasing focus on tailoring the company's products to local needs and decreasing the tight control from its Atlanta headquarters. See Constance L. Hays, "Learning to Think Smaller at Coke," *New York Times*, February 6, 2000.

In trying to establish your firm's ballpark, you may find the following exercise helpful. First, articulate a number of criteria for the least desirable entrepreneurial extensions of your existing business. What types of businesses do you not want to participate in? You should list many types of businesses that are undesirable to your organization. It's important to articulate these criteria in terms specific to the way your business operates—anybody can say, "We don't

---

BOX 12-4

WALTER WRISTON'S "FIVE I'S" MOVE CITIBANK INTO THE FUTURE

A recognized visionary and statesman for the industry, Walter Wriston built for Citibank in the early 1980s a new ballpark that propelled not only Citibank but the entire U.S. banking industry into previously unforeseen directions. This bank, declared Wriston, could no longer continue to rely on traditional services, which were coming under increasing margin pressure, and it could ill afford to rest on its considerable success in the institutional and investment banking arenas. Instead, he told his managers, he wanted new business in every one of what he termed the "Five I" arenas: individual, information, insurance, institutional banking, and investment banking.

Although not all of the moves in entrepreneurial directions worked out, the vision propelled massive growth and development in such brand new (to Citibank) businesses as ATM-supported branch banking, consumer credit cards, and insurance annuities sold near bank branches. It also foreshadowed the merger of Citibank with Travelers Insurance in 1998, which created a massive financial services powerhouse.

---

want to develop businesses in low-profit, high-fixed-cost markets." Say instead, "We don't want to develop any businesses in which the value perceived by the customer is under the control of another firm and we are simply a component supplier." Then explain why you've made these choices. What are the qualities of these businesses that render them unattractive? You want to establish, eventually, a set of criteria for screening out entrepreneurial ideas that may be generally attractive, but are not a good fit for your business.

Delineating unattractive business arenas provides a realistic backdrop against which you can now begin fleshing out the qualities that make a business initiative attractive to you. What aspects of these opportunities make you believe you can profitably manage them?

Having profiled the criteria that make potential entrepreneurial developments attractive, your next step is to specify the underlying logic of the criteria. In other words, make a connection between what makes the selected business criteria attractive and what it takes to succeed in those types of markets.

Try to develop some short, simple statements that rapidly convey the kinds of businesses you want to go into. For instance, when we were working with Texas Instruments' radio frequency identification business (TIRIS), one criterion that came out of our ballparking session was "Is it smart?" The rationale behind this question was that the company did not wish to enter application areas in which the particular advantages of their technology would not be well utilized (and consequently not recognized by customers as a basis for price premiums).

The final challenge is to develop, if you can, a powerful image to communicate your ballpark estimate.

Let's illustrate with the example of an acquaintance, a Scandinavian entrepreneur we shall call Peter, whom we consider adept at starting up businesses. His record bears him out: He and his two brothers have orchestrated the launch of more than two dozen entrepreneurial businesses. Peter's philosophy is to create entrepreneurial businesses that can be spun off to the start-up team or sold off to large companies seeking new business opportunities. Over the years, the real strengths of his companies have been in applying computer-aided design and computer-aided manufacturing technologies to settings in which these techniques had previously not been used. This meant consolidating fragmented industries or creating new niches within previously existing industries.

Peter is very disciplined with respect to his least desired businesses. He is not interested in businesses which do not solve a demonstrable problem that customers really want solved. He doesn't consider businesses that are likely to attract the attention of major global players, such as Japanese and Korean companies. Neither is he interested in businesses limited only to his domestic market in Scandinavia: Because Scandinavia is a small market, its growth potential is limited.

As a result of carefully considering the kinds of businesses he doesn't want, Peter has derived a very crisp articulation of his "most wanted" businesses. He sums up his criteria in a rule he calls "50 to the power of 4." By "50 to the power of 4," he means that he's interested in any business proposal that has the potential to deliver 50 million kronor ($8 million) in profits in each market by capturing 50 percent market share with 50 percent margins in each of 50 different countries. The "50 to the power of 4" rule saves his organization a lot of time by letting his people quickly screen out a lot of business ideas that their boss would see as having insufficient upside potential. The 50 percent market-share potential directs his associates to only those businesses that plan to attend to a real and well-understood customer need or problem. The 50 percent margin potential means that customers will be willing to pay him very well to solve the problem; by solving real problems for customers who are painfully aware of them, he knows he can charge a premium and capture a differentiated position. And the 50-country potential means that he can establish a highly profitable position, and can do so in niche markets that are unlikely to attract massive competitive response from large global competitors.

Peter does not hold his people strictly to each "50"—it is the basic principles that concern him. If there is a compelling argument to justify bending the "50 to the power of 4" rule, he can be persuaded. The image of what he's after, however, is crystal clear. His ballpark specification provides room for his employees to come up with many ideas to develop entrepreneurial initiatives at the same time that it lets them quickly reject those that they know will not measure up to his requirements.

The origin of his "50 to the power of 4" rule resides in his understanding of the conditions under which his firm's strategic strengths will allow him to succeed in gaining a large market share at a high margin. These strengths include the following:

- He can draw off his deep skills in CAD/CAM (computer-assisted design/computer-assisted manufacturing) by entering fragmented industries and using CAD/CAM technology to consolidate the industry.

- He can deploy the advantages that Scandinavian companies have in that they are accepted in parts of the world where many other nations' citizens are viewed with dislike or suspicion.

- He can capitalize on the centuries-long Scandinavian tradition of doing business in many countries outside their small home markets, using, among other things, their renowned multilingualism.

The above example responds to the first three steps that we suggest you think through—first defining the least-wanted businesses; then defining the most-wanted businesses, being clear about what will drive future success and capturing the key points in short, simple phrases; and finally, creating an idiom or image to symbolize your idea, which will help to give your ballpark specification staying power. The "50 to the power of 4" symbol used by our Scandinavian entrepreneur, the Three-C's/Three-P's of Martinez, and the Five I's of Wriston are great examples.

Reducing the concept of the ballpark to a simple, powerful image can be a daunting task. It requires insight and discipline to decide on the core drivers for future entrepreneurial development. But if you can do it, you'll be providing everyone in your company with a single beacon that illuminates where your business's destiny lies.

Once you've specified the ballpark, which shows people the acceptable arenas in which entrepreneurial initiatives may be pursued, your next task is to lay the ground rules that will tell people just how these initiatives should be developed. This is where all that we have covered in the book comes together, where the management processes that we have described so far become part of everyday life as you create an entrepreneurial mindset.

Real Options Reasoning and the Discipline of Parsimony

As we have argued throughout the book, the right way to play the business development game is by using real options reasoning. This means starting in such a way that investments and launch costs are minimized until the upside potential is demonstrated.

Try to make parsimony with respect to resource expenditures a way of life. Try to get people to look for entry strategies in which the focus is on earning the right to invest in assets or to incur fixed costs by demonstrating revenue potential ahead of such investment.[4] Left to their own devices, people will seldom willingly impose the discipline of resource parsimony on themselves. They find it much easier to spend their way out of problems (especially if it's not their own money they are spending).

How do you accomplish this? Just as you create the urgency to pursue new businesses, your own behavior will communicate to people the right way to launch them. Real options reasoning is reinforced by your practices. If every time a project is proposed, its proponents know that you will challenge them to demonstrate that they have spent their imagination instead of, or ahead of, your money and resources, they will be motivated to develop the project like a resource-constrained entrepreneur. They will learn, for instance, to reduce investment wherever they can. They will avoid incurring assets, fixed costs, and start-up expenses unless the returns justify them. They will think twice before making a decision that could be expensive. On the upside, they will be genuinely focused on early wins that pave the way to successes.

Discovery-Driven Planning, Discovery-Driven Philosophy

Discovery-driven planning, discussed at length in chapter 10, is a way of planning that corresponds to a philosophy about running new initiatives. In this philosophy, it is not a crime to fail, only to fail expensively and without learning. It is not a crime to miss deadlines, only not to know why. And it is not a crime to admit that you were wrong, only to be unable to articulate the logical basis for your original assumptions. Although habitual entrepreneurs think and manage this way intuitively, a discovery-driven philosophy runs counter to what many people have been taught about good management.

Some concrete expectations that you can set involve the way that discovery-driven planning will be used in your organization. First, it must be used as a dynamic management tool rather than a static exercise. People need to realize that this isn't a rote exercise that they go through to get projects approved, but a powerful way of learning what the true business opportunity is and how to capture it. Second, people need to pay attention to all the aspects of the plan. They need to understand the market and competitive benchmarks, their organizational deliverables, the logic underlying their assumptions, how they will move from milestone to milestone, and, most importantly, how they will test assumptions at the lowest possible cost. Unless you, as a leader, make it clear that you expect to see assumptions checked and validated, the reverse financial statements updated, and the business model reassessed at key milestones, people soon stop paying attention to these activities.

A further, crucial role you play as the champion for the entrepreneurial mindset in your firm is to communicate a discovery-driven philosophy to senior executives and external stakeholders (such as stock analysts). The pressure that these people place upon those trying to develop new businesses can lead their reversion to more conventional methods. You need to consistently explain the logic behind a discovery-driven philosophy, to be prepared to offer evidence in support of its effectiveness, and if necessary, to bear the blame for those well-managed efforts that don't turn out as expected.

HANDS-ON LEADERSHIP PRACTICES

The final set of leadership practices we'll discuss are those in which you actively champion initiatives. As a leader, when you do become actively involved in identifying and developing new ventures (as opposed to creating a climate and orchestrating the behavior of others), you personally can have enormous impact. In a small organization, this will be a routine part of your job. In a larger one, you'll want to conserve your energies to focus on those initiatives that you believe are the most important for the future of the organization and for which your skills and talents will offer the greatest return.

The first and most important role that you will play is to use the perspectives that you have developed through the application of techniques like those in this book—namely, to uncover entrepreneurial insights with the potential of forming the basis for major market breakthroughs that are uniquely accessible to you and your firm. We'll focus on four distinct activities: First is the identification of these insights. Second is the conversion of each insight into an actionable business description that is easily comprehended by everyone responsible for its execution. Third is the building of pervasive organizational resolve to pursue this business proposition. Fourth is the discharge of entrepreneurial leadership obligations. It is your job to build the "speed, simplicity, and self-confidence" (to use Jack Welch's famous phrase) needed to assure rapid and effective execution.

Identifying Entrepreneurial Insights

The analytical processes described in this book will help you spot opportunities for business growth that your competitors are less likely to see. You will also be able to execute entrepreneurial strategies that they can't copy, simply because they aren't you—they don't see things from your perspective. As you revisit your opportunity register, consider whether any ideas there may represent entrepreneurial insights with high breakthrough potential. In particular, look for opportunities in the following situations:

- Formerly tolerable attributes of the industry are showing signs of becoming more dissatisfying to segments of the market, especially lead-steer segments, as discussed in chapter 9. Lead-steer segments are opinion leaders whom others will follow, the way a herd follows the leading animal.

- Your analysis of the consumption and value chains suggests that new technologies, infrastructures, or data systems could be deployed to remove or reconfigure links in these chains.

- An entire industry is operating on the basis of assumptions that you may be able to challenge (examples of mistaken assumptions: Xerox patents are unassailable; the piano industry is mature; nobody wants black-and-white TVs anymore).

- Well-established business models in an industry may soon succumb to a force for change that you have identified and are positioned to capitalize on. For instance, the ability to create huge aggregate markets by consolidating needs across many small players is a force that predictably will disrupt business models in many industries. Similarly, advances in manufacturing technology now make it feasible and cost-effective to create custom-tailored products for ever-smaller market sizes, a force that promises to revolutionize not only the way products are made, but the way they are sold and positioned.

- Your organization is developing capabilities that can attend to the needs of customers in another industry (e.g., digital versus chemical processing of images in photographic applications).

- The variance of performance across firms in an observed industry is low, but there are signs that some major change is pending (e.g., formerly regulated industries going private, industries that never used to be competitive seeing a surge of new competition).

- A new kind of problem category is becoming big enough to generate increasing attention and you see a way in which your firm might attend to this problem. For instance, with more and more women in the workforce, the traditional role they played in family and community comes under stress, creating new needs. Examples of the kinds of new problems are arranging transportation, medical care, and other services for children during working hours; managing the care of the home; and staffing volunteer organizations. Some of these problems might represent business opportunities for the firms prepared to capitalize on them.

- New technologies are coming into a market by serving segments currently at the fringes. Often, major technological discontinuities first enter a market in applications that initially appeal to only a few specialized segments seeking extreme values of the attribute that the technology delivers.

- In the shorter term, you see the delayed effects of discontinuous change beginning to appear in an industry. When a major change event occurs in an industry, the effects of various organizations' responses to it may have major lags. For instance, firms that have changed their purchasing policies will not feel the effects of the change for some months. Similarly, firms that have revised their budgeting policies will not feel the full effects of the changes for perhaps a year. In these circumstances, you can be prepared to address the lagging need by seeing its emergence before your future customers do.

In working through this process, you may identify a set (not too big a set, though) of opportunities that your firm is in a unique position to capitalize on. The next step is to qualify these insights.

Converting Entrepreneurial Insights to Business Propositions

Having identified a few core insights that you think may be key to future breakthroughs, your next challenge is to convert each one into a powerful, actionable, business proposition. To be powerful, a business proposition must have three properties: it must be simple, it must be actionable, and it must resonate with those responsible for its execution.

When it comes to simplicity, our acid test is whether you can write the proposition on a business card and still convey your meaning. This kind of simplicity makes the business proposition easy to comprehend and to communicate. Canon's business proposition for its personal copier business was completely unambiguous: "to sell a copier that is small, inexpensive, and reliable enough for personal use on a secretary's desk." Yamaha, too, broadened the horizons of what had been strictly a piano company with its business proposition "to sell keyboards." A good way to start a business proposition is to link it to the market with the opening phrase: "Customers should pay good money for . . ." or "Customers should embrace . . ." Note the use of the word *should*, which indicates that we are still talking about a proposition—not a fact as yet.

As with ballparking, the power of the business proposition increases if it can be reduced to a simple, powerful, and actionable image. Consider the clarity, simplicity, and actionability behind Priceline.com's "Name your price" business proposition. Once you have that image in mind, the operational challenges required to make it happen will crystallize. People can mobilize around it, can focus on it, can talk about it. Actionable images can be pictures, symbols, metaphors, analogies—anything that makes it easy for people to instantly understand and resonate with the basic operational challenges.

Building Resolve

Once you have put together the business proposition, your next step is to get people to commit to the launching of a new business initiative. This requires a commitment and resolve from others in your organization.

Resolve starts with a business purpose that has visceral meaning for the implementers. The more your venture appeals to personal sentiments, the more prepared people will be to make inordinate efforts to get it done. For this reason, you should try to build personal meaning into the venture. You increase resolve when you can sketch out the benefits of meeting the challenge in ways that appeal to your people: to their values, their competitive spirit, their sense of accomplishment, their professional pride. In short, you want to connect the outcome of the venture to something that the implementers themselves intrinsically value.

Another way to get people to commit to an initiative is to involve them in the process early on so that they can play a part in shaping it. People are more likely to devote their energy to something that they have helped to create. Another advantage of giving people a voice early in the process is to get different perspectives on the business proposition. Since you are not infallible, it is possible (given the amount of uncertainty most managers face) that adjustments to the business proposition will have to be made because your initial underlying assumptions are not supported. Because you have the same cognitive limitations and biases that everyone else does, it is important to put the emerging business proposition to critical test by engaging in constructive debate with those whose opinions may be different from yours. You and those responsible for execution need to have confidence that you aren't deluding yourselves. This, too, helps build people's resolve to stay with the project.

Yet another way to build resolve is to refrain from proposing lofty long-term goals that appear impossible to achieve. Break them down into shorter-term, more easily accomplished goals that set the longer-term trajectory. This will give people a confidence-boosting sense of accomplishment early on, despite a long road ahead. For example, the manager of a venture into the publishing business was faced with exhorting the sales force to go out and increase market share by 20 percent in two years. She faced a seemingly impossible task by converting it into something much more manageable. She showed the sales force that to accomplish this goal, all that they needed to do was to each capture ten new orders per month. The sales force was able to mentally picture the challenge of capturing ten orders per month much more easily than they could the enormous long-term goal.

Finally, find ways to recognize and celebrate the short-term successes as they occur along the way. In the preceding example, the sales manager called the entire sales force together with the support staff each month to celebrate the big sales and the progress toward the target, building a community of purpose that drove everyone in the business to increased effort.

Discharging Entrepreneurial Leadership Responsibility

As the business proposition takes shape, people will depend on you to assume some important leadership responsibilities, which we discuss below. As mentioned earlier, the assumption of these responsibilities is characteristic of the entrepreneurial leader. It is important that you exercise them religiously if you are to instill in everyone in your organization the desire to take entrepreneurial initiative.

Framing   As we discussed in chapter 2, the way you get a new business initiative going is by establishing a challenging frame. It's important to realize that other kinds of framing can be essential as well. For instance, the reverse financials and benchmark specifications discussed in chapter 10 can be used to set the frame for the technical and organizational challenges to be overcome. You can then unleash the engineering and scientific talent in the firm upon these clearly specified challenges.

We learned the importance of framing the technical challenges in an initiative when we spoke with Keizo Yamaji of Canon, who has been credited with transforming Canon from an average-performing photographic company into the printing, imaging, and computer-based powerhouse it is today. The inspiration for the business came from a consulting report he read, which said that Xerox's patents were unassailable. Most managers would have given up at that point. Instead, Yamaji reasoned that if this were widely known, it would keep competitors out; if he, then, could crack the patent problem, he could have the market to himself. He spent a long time in the field observing how people interact with copiers and noticed a set of needs that were completely underserved by incumbent Xerox. This was the market for just a few copies of short documents. Xerox offered great, big machines designed to produce hundreds of copies.

Next he carefully assessed the skills of his engineering staff and stacked up these talents against what he thought would be the characteristics of a so-called personal copier. Then he called in the engineers:

[I told them,] "I want you to make me a copier. It can be no bigger than a large breadbox. It can't retail for more than $1,200 in the USA. It mustn't ever need servicing. And I want it in eighteen months."

As he put it, "At first the engineers did what engineers always do—they whined! But then, guess what happened—they went out and they did it. It was a little bigger, it cost a bit more. While it did need servicing, it needed servicing very seldom, and it took just under two years to build instead of eighteen months. But I got my copier and the multibillion dollar business that it represented."

Now imagine the difference if he had told them, "I want you to build me a small, cheap, reliable copier—soon."

Yamaji framed the project, but he didn't micromanage it. As he explained to us how he went about creating the personal copier, he observed that his biggest challenge was to set up a challenge for engineering that would push people to the limits of their capabilities without pushing them over their limits. This is where your personal judgment is deeply needed by the organization.

As Yamaji realized, his obligation as a manager launching an entrepreneurial business was to frame the challenge for his people clearly enough and then get out of their way. "It was not my job to do it," he said. "My job was to frame what the outcome should be in terms specific enough to let them go do it."

Absorbing Uncertainty It is particularly important to help your people cope with uncertainty by circumscribing the number of risks they perceive. Failure to do so can seriously hamper the progress of the entrepreneurial business, because most people, faced with massive uncertainty, find it very hard to take decisive action. Afraid of being wrong, they freeze in the headlights. The problem is that we are increasingly working in a world in which it is more expensive to be slow than it is to be wrong—provided that you have pushed your people to operate with parsimony, you can probably afford a whole lot of learning-rich setbacks as people figure out what the future opportunity will be.

As a leader, your task is to make uncertainty less daunting. The idea is to create among your colleagues the self-confidence that lets them act on opportunities without seeking managerial permission. Employees must not be overwhelmed by the complexity inherent in many business situations.

How do you accomplish this? By taking the uncertainty out of the situation. They need to hear you say, "Assume that X, Y, and Z are going to happen. If you execute on these assumptions and I'm wrong, its not your problem, its my problem. Your problem is to execute assuming that I am right. I may come to you later and say that I was wrong and we now have to assume A, B, and C are going to happen. But for now, assume that I am right." We can't stress enough how important this is—or how liberating it is for people to hear, as the following example shows.

We were working with a project team in the insurance industry, a team on the brink of launching its major new product nationwide. To appreciate this story, it is important to know that in the United States, insurance is regulated on a state-by-state basis. In essence, before you can know where a product is to be sold, you have to know how many state regulatory authorities have approved the product for issue in their state. The project manager was interrogating his main operations person:

"Are you ready?" he asked.

"I think so," came the obviously reluctant reply.

"Well, is it yes or is it no?"

"If I can use Therese for some of the training, and we don't run into too many computer glitches, and the West Side team manages to make the right transfers over ... " and on and on burbled the operations manager.

It became pretty clear to both of us what was going on—the operations manager simply couldn't answer the question! He was being asked to account not only for whether his team was operationally ready but also to anticipate the level of challenge he would be up against, given varying levels of regulatory approval.

We intervened at this point and got the project manager off in a corner. His job, we argued, was to first tell the operations guy how many states he had to be ready for. Without this information, the operations guy was simply frozen by the inability to know whether he really would be ready, we said. The project manager, obviously intrigued, said that he would try it. We went back to the group, and the project manager asked, "So, if we assume approval in fifteen states on day one, do you think you are ready?"

The change in atmosphere and confidence was palpable. "Oh, absolutely, fifteen won't be a problem at all—in fact I have backup capacity lined up in case it's a few more than that!" came the forceful, confident, liberated reply. Reflecting on this afterward, we concluded that the source of all the hesitancy had been a basic uncertainty about the level of the challenge. Until this uncertainty was resolved by a more senior executive, the question simply couldn't be answered with confidence by someone at an operating level. This is what senior managers are often there for—to help people box and bound otherwise paralyzing uncertainties.

This does leave you with the problem of coping with your own uncertainty, but, after all, the business of thinking entrepreneurially is all about coping with uncertain situations. Remember that you don't have to be 100 percent right all the time, just right enough often enough. Furthermore, a competent, confident, and therefore resilient team can usually cope with the differences between the frame you set and the real-world shots as they are called. What is crucial is to recognize when you must absorb the uncertainty so that others can get on with implementation; this uncertainty can often only be credibly absorbed at a senior level—by you, the one who can most afford to be wrong.

Often managers fail to take the uncertainty load off their team's back because the need to do it is not obvious to them. A real contradiction of modern management is the manager's duty to be clear about expectations without resorting to the old style of telling people exactly what to do.

At times, your ability to absorb uncertainty will immensely accelerate the business development process. Specifically, make sure that your people have been given guidelines for setting their own priorities—what is really important and what can wait. Make sure people know what you are expecting them to prepare for—how soon, how big, with what level of aggressiveness. The better you can prepare them by giving them best-guess directions until more information becomes available, the more effective they will be.

Defining Gravity   Another leadership task is to define the "laws of gravity"—that is, what must be accepted and what cannot be accepted. The term *gravity* is used to represent the things people accept as limiting conditions. Sure, there is gravity on the earth, but that doesn't mean we have to let it dominate our lives. If we can be freed from the psychological cage of believing that gravity makes flying impossible, we can use our creativity to invent an airplane. This is what successful entrepreneurs do—they see opportunities where others see barriers and limits.

Take John MacCormack of Visible Changes. He twice put his company on *Inc.* magazine's list of the fastest-growing businesses in the United States. What is it, you might ask, a high-tech start-up? A breakthrough manufacturer? Not at all. It's a chain of southwestern hairdressing salons—a tough, low-margin business if ever there was one. And it gets even worse in a recession, because people get their hair cut less frequently. So the last time Texas went into a recession, McCormack could have accepted it as an explanation for poor performance. Instead, he challenged his managers to think creatively about the coming recession: "Are we going to participate in this recession, or are we going to beat it?" Recognizing that opting out of recessionary times was not something they should succumb to without a struggle helped people come to grips with what they could do, even in the face of limiting conditions.

The job was defined as making sure those customers who did get haircuts came to his salons, Visible Changes. The managers proactively contacted customers and offered promotions. They used their knowledge of customers to target special events in the customers' lives, such as anniversaries and holidays. They went out of their way to make sure that their salon stayed uppermost in customers' minds. The result? Customers averaged one visit every five weeks (as opposed to a pre-recession four weeks), but they didn't wait six weeks, and they didn't switch salons. McCormack challenged people to the limits of their potential without pushing them beyond it.

One of your responsibilities is to define gravity for those who will implement the business proposition. You need to review the barriers listed in your opportunity register and define for your team what limits must be accepted as given (their gravity) and what barriers will not be tolerated as constraints (Go build an airplane!) as they move forward with implementation. This calls for judgment that reflects your understanding of the limits of your people's capabilities and how far they can be pushed to expand those limits without falling apart.

Path Clearing Yet another challenge of entrepreneurial leadership involves clearing obstacles that arise as a result of internal competition for resources. This can be a problem especially when the entrepreneurial business is beginning to undergo significant growth. A growing business will often find itself for the first time pitted squarely against other (often established) businesses in the firm in the fierce internal competition for funds and staff. The competition thus earns your venture the displeasure of the line managers of other divisions and sometimes even those in your own division, who may have an urgent need for those resources they are no longer getting.[5] If these managers are not checked, they may deploy all their organizational power and historical track record to deny the new venture the resources it desperately needs, or they may delay their allocation long enough to give competitors time to come in and take up the slack.

There may be a real need for you to intervene and, if necessary, prompt the reworking of the entire budget for your organization. Staffing plans may need to be revamped to attend to the rapidly escalating needs of the entrepreneurial business.

The necessity of this type of intervention increases as the resource requirements of the preexisting divisions increase. Consider the case of a venture in a division of an electronics firm that we studied. The venture had developed a technology with long-run revenue potential in the billions of dollars. Unfortunately, just as a critical mass of major applications for the technology were becoming clear, demand for the company's core business also began to take off. The division heads of the core businesses desperately needed huge amounts of funds to expand capacity. Since the firm's top managers came from the core business, understood the core business, and could bank on the revenues from investment in that business, there was enormous pressure to withhold resources from the entrepreneurial business. In this case, growth was slowed, the senior managers of the original venture management team quit in frustration, and the firm probably lost about a year in bringing the new application to market. Fortunately, competitors were even farther behind and the business has since become a considerable success, but the story might just as easily have had an unhappy ending.

Underwriting   Entrepreneurial ventures often labor under a significant problem—skeptical potential customers and suppliers. Their attitude is likely to be "Why should we support a venture that's still not viable and might get shut down?" Your role is to find a way to allay these concerns by getting someone with sufficient credibility to underwrite the business, promising to stick with the venture even if significant initial losses are incurred. If you do not have that credibility, you may have to seek it from your manager, or even your manager's manager. Without it, you don't have a business.

Consider the firm we talked about in chapter 11. It was pursuing a database venture that involved capturing specific information about the purchasing behavior of consumers buying packaged goods and then selling the information to the manufacturers of those goods and to their retailers. The difficulty was that the key customers for this information were likely to be the major packaged-goods players—firms such as Procter & Gamble, Unilever, General Foods, General Mills, and so on. Unless they could be persuaded that the database added value, the venture would never achieve its optimistic revenue projections.

These key customers were skeptical. Although the concept was intriguing, given the vast amounts they expend on direct-mail advertising and promotion, our client had little credibility. The division launching the business was part of a financial services company with no foothold in retail merchandising or database marketing. The large manufacturers were thus worried about making major investments in the new technology and its utilization, including training and systems development, only to find that the parent firm of the new venture firm would fail to aggressively support the business. To assuage their fears, it would have been helpful for the very senior managers of the parent firm to personally assure these customers of their commitment to the venture. Unfortunately, that never happened.

So the customers never signed on to support the business. What eventually transpired was precisely what they had anticipated: The firm terminated the entrepreneurial business after it had incurred losses for several years. The reaction of the customers was a predictable "I told you so!" These customers had never believed that the host would persist in the first place, and now their skepticism had been justified. Two years later the same concept was very successfully launched by a competitor, and the entire category of services involving identification of individual purchasing patterns is now a high-growth market.

Deciding whether and when to underwrite an uncertain entrepreneurial business is by no means easy. You simply cannot bet the ranch on every venture that comes along, and you must exercise careful judgment to decide when to step in and sever a vicious circle. Although you need to be confident that the business will succeed before betting the ranch, the business cannot move forward until the ranch is bet.

KEEPING A FINGER ON THE PULSE

As the venture moves toward implementation and others begin to take charge, your role as an entrepreneurial leader largely involves constructive monitoring and control of the developing opportunity. We've listed some issues that are likely to continue to require your attention as the venture unfolds.

CONSTANTLY CHECK FOR MARKET ACCEPTANCE. The lowest-cost route to successful implementation is to probe constantly for evidence that the market you have envisioned accepts the business proposition of the venture. As we stressed in chapter 9 when discussing entry strategies, there is no better evidence that the business proposition is valid than securing orders ahead of investments in the venture. Understandably, this may be very difficult to pull off, but again as we said earlier, if you can't get orders, can you get letters of intent? If you can't get letters of intent, can you get letters expressing interest? If you can't even get someone to write a letter expressing interest, then the basic business proposition should be viewed with alarm.

PUSH TO SECURE DEALS WITH KEY STAKEHOLDERS. The success of virtually every venture is dependent on being able to cut about three to five critical deals with key stakeholders whose initial commitment is crucial to the venture. Push those running the venture to identify the deals that will make or break the venture, and then make sure they are making progress on these deals well ahead of major investment commitments. Typically, such deals may be agreements with key suppliers, distributors, funding sources, employees, or customers. If their support cannot be secured, the entire project is at risk. Furthermore, if you can't get the right deal, why risk the fate of your venture team? Little can be gained, for instance, by making an acquisition or by consummating an exclusive purchase license if you vastly overpay for it. Other ventures will surface—the people on your team need to know that they can walk away from this project, if necessary, and that you will support them in their decision to do so.

CHALLENGE THE TEAM NOT TO SPEND MONEY UNTIL IT KNOWS IT CAN MAKE MONEY. You should promote the principle that entrepreneurial ventures are not entitled to assets and fixed-cost burdens until they have revenue streams to justify them. Push team members hard to get initial investment down as close to zero as possible. Minimize initial assets by buying them second-hand rather than new or, better yet, by leasing rather than buying, or, still better, by subcontracting manufacture rather than leasing. Best of all is "tin-cupping" existing manufacturing rather than subcontracting.

PUSH YOUR TEAM HARD TO INITIATE REVENUE FLOWS AHEAD OF COST FLOWS. You do this by securing advance payments and by postponing cash outflows, such as remuneration. Drive them to avoid incurring fixed costs—incur cost on a variable-per-usage basis rather than committing to a fixed cost. All these tactics reduce the burden on the project to generate return on investment.

PUSH THE TEAM TO BE REALISTIC IN IDENTIFYING SKILL DEFICIENCIES. Particularly when the skills that may be needed to make the project successful are new to you or, worse, new to the world, there is a temptation to severely underestimate the difficulty you will have in securing them and/or developing and deploying them. Lack of these skills virtually guarantees that the initial quality delivered to the marketplace will be inadequate, with the result that the first few brave souls who order from you will be disappointed. You cannot allow this to happen. Make sure that the right skills are developed and reliably in use before inflicting your offering on an unsuspecting market.

ORCHESTRATE MARKET ENTRY. Do not allow the team to rush a half-baked product to market or to tinker endlessly to "perfect" a product that has never been tested in the market. Ensure that you have identified lead users who are recognized and rewarded for taking on the role of a beta site.

KEEP THE FOCUS ON LEARNING. To repeat, ensure that team members practice the discipline of discovery-driven planning. Document assumptions and test them before making major investments. Systematically redirect your project as you convert assumptions into knowledge. In particular, learn from surprises as well as mistakes. A surprise is what occurs when you do better than expected. Even so, you did something wrong! Often, the result won't be analyzed, because it was positive. But because surprises stem from incorrect assumptions, you need to check out those assumptions to make sure that you continue to be surprised.

MAKE SURE THE TEAM CONTINUES TO MONITOR CRITICAL SENSITIVITIES. Occasionally, small changes in key assumptions or variables presage large dislocations in performance. There is also a natural propensity to spend time checking what is easy to check, not what is important to check. Make sure that someone is watching for early warning signals that high-impact variables may be heading for a cliff.

MANAGING FAILURE

The trouble with any venture is that it runs a real risk of failure for all the reasons we just enumerated. It is all very well for managers to exhort people to innovate, but when failure occurs, your entire business stops to see what you are going to do. This pause is testing time, and your reaction sets the standard for all future commitment to entrepreneurial development on the part of your people.

We have found that entrepreneurial leaders employ three important practices when confronted with a failure: constructive postmortems, recouping, and spotting entrapment.

Constructive Postmortems

No one should be rewarded for making bad decisions, and so entrepreneurial leaders of successful programs do not forgive foolish failure. On the other hand, projects in which the team has consistently made good decisions but that failed as a result of circumstances beyond their control deserve recognition and reward. Entrepreneurial leaders who are successful at promoting deep commitment to continuous entrepreneurial development typically conduct constructive postmortems to distinguish projects that have failed because of bad luck from those that failed because of bad decision making. If you have all along been tracking assumptions and deviations from assumptions through a discovery-driven plan, the distinction between bad management and bad luck is an easy one. Postmortems also lead to the second practice, recouping.

Recouping

Often there is much to be learned and deployed elsewhere, even from a business launch that failed. For instance, in our study of the financial service company that ventured into capturing consumer data, the firm had developed very powerful data compression technology that could have been used elsewhere in the firm, but this opportunity was lost in the recriminations that followed the decision to shut down the project. No attention was paid to the prospect of recouping all the positive benefits of the failed business. Furthermore, recouping helps convey to those on the venture team—valuable talent whom the firm could ill afford to have crippled by a feeling of failure—that it was the venture that failed, not them.

Spotting Entrapment

Often it is necessary for you to detect that the business development team is entrapped in a welter of optimism that precludes them from recognizing that the business is doomed. This occurs for many reasons—it is difficult not to be falsely optimistic about exciting projects or to fear the consequences of failing so much as to deny imminent failure. However, entrapment may also occur because the business development manager cannot bear to recognize that all those team members who left solid career tracks to join the venture have done so in vain, and so the manager plows on in the hope that things will turn around. In other cases, the pressure to resist recognizing failure comes from outside forces. We observed that powerful distributors were pressuring a development manager to carry on with a project that they wanted continued despite the poor results for the firm. Thus it is important to be alert to the signs of entrapment. If a venture seems to be trapped in any of these signs of poor business logic, you may personally have to shut down the project.

SUMMARY OF KEY QUESTIONS

We conclude with some key questions for you to ask yourself to make sure you're doing everything you can to promote entrepreneurial initiative in your organization.

Am I paying consistent, predictable, and disproportionate attention to entrepreneurial thinking among team members?

Are entrepreneurial initiatives consistently high on my agenda?

Am I visibly allocating disproportionate resources to entrepreneurial initiatives?

Am I consciously allocating disproportionate talent to them?

Is this widely recognized throughout the organization? How would I know?

Do I have enough new business initiatives in my portfolio of opportunities to support my strategy, distributed in various stages of development?

Am I consciously orchestrating an entrepreneurial development process?

Have I articulated a clear and logically compelling ballpark?

Has this been captured in an engaging, memorable image?

Am I mandating options thinking and the discipline of parsimony on proposals?

Am I imposing the appropriate planning, monitoring, and control of initiatives we are pursuing?

Am I preparing to make appropriate interventions in initiatives already under way?

Am I alert to and prepared for occasions on which my intervention, or that of my boss, may be needed?

Have initiatives been framed adequately?

For each specific initiative, especially new business ventures, might we need internal path clearing?

How well prepared am I to clear the path, if needed? How well prepared is my boss to do so?

For each specific initiative, might we need external underwriting?

How well prepared am I to underwrite or to secure support elsewhere in the firm, if needed?

For each specific initiative, have I defined gravity—specifying the possible parameters of what must be accomplished?

For each specific initiative, will I need to absorb uncertainty?

Do I have a system of constructive postmortems in place?

Do I give deliberate attention to recouping from initiatives that are unsuccessful?

Am I on the alert for entrapment?

CHAPTER 13

THE

ENTREPRENEURIAL EDGE

When Strategy is Discovery

WE HAVE BOTH STARTED BUSINESSES. WE WERE BOTH TRAINED as strategists. In the ten years that we have worked together, we have seen the boundaries between entrepreneurship and strategy blur. This is because in today's business environment, we no longer have the option of holding on to yesterday's business model; we must create entrepreneurial organizations that continuously come up with new models. An organization incapable of constant innovation and change will in short order lose its franchise and be acquired at best, dispersed at worst. Managers who seek to act strategically have no choice but to embrace the entrepreneurial mindset. In so doing, they will have to leave behind some of the comforting premises under which strategy, the "art of generalship," has long been practiced. In this chapter, we summarize what this means for managers and strategists as individuals, and why practices such as reducing complexity and observing uncertainty to make things simple are so crucial.

An entrepreneurial mindset invokes a far more dynamic view of competitive advantage than is typically used in strategy. When the old rules—about share advantages, scale economies, and decreasing returns, for instance—stop working, we lose time-honored guide-posts through our competitive landscape. Levinthal's research suggests what this means. People and organizations, he argues, can only deal with a limited amount of complexity; systematically dysfunctional behavior results when they are confronted with rapid change in their competitive and technological landscape. The ray of hope he offers is that if you can capture the main features of these landscapes, you can reduce complexity to a level that an organization can absorb, increasing its adaptive capacity.

In other words, though the world is getting more complicated and uncertain, there are ways in which you can simplify it enough to function in it. If you can pick out the few most salient features of a rapidly shifting landscape, you'll be better able to cope than if you try to capture every last wrinkle and ridge. In this book, we have offered some simple ways to think about complicated things; our goal is not to pretend that the world isn't a complex place but to help you to understand enough to take action in spite of complexity and uncertainty.

Besides overwhelming complexity and increasing uncertainty, a second kind of pressure we increasingly see has to do with how people are coping with the flood of issues and events demanding their attention. In the companies we study and work with, there is a noticeable increase in the stress that managers are feeling. They desperately need better tools to manage their own agendas, to tame the flood of messages and inputs seeking their attention, to husband the scarce resources of time and energy, and to make space for other things that are important to them.

This is why, throughout the book, we have tried to emphasize focusing, setting priorities, making choices, and having the discipline to let things go, as well as taking on new things. The things you elect not to do are as much a part of your entrepreneurial mindset as the things you elect to do.

CORE GUIDELINES FOR MANAGING WITH AN ENTREPRENEURIAL MINDSET

Below we provide some key guidelines for managing with an entrepreneurial mindset—in effect highlighting again some of the points we made in the book.

In a world of great uncertainty, you can be as right as anyone else. Using the tools in this book, you can influence, if not shape, your destiny, just like habitual entrepreneur Bob Goergen, who built a billion-dollar candle enterprise in an industry that had been in slow decline for 300 years, and John MacCormack, who turned a chain of hairdressing salons into one of the fastest-growing businesses in the United States.

We say that you can shape your destiny, but we agree that only a fool believes that it can be dictated. Throughout the book, therefore, we have suggested generous injections of reality into the way you should think about strategy. Whether it is a reality check on the reactions of customers to a new attribute, the use of benchmarks to critically evaluate your advantages in a discovery-driven plan, a ruthless reassessment of progress at major milestones, or our insistence that you act parsimoniously and take our options, we recommend that you find ways of minimizing the impact of competitive reality. The first reality to recognize is to remember that a business is simply a mechanism to capture value by using its competences to deliver an offering that satisfies a customer's needs better than do competitors' offerings. To win, you need to understand customers' experiences almost better than they do, and certainly better than the competitors do. You need to get into customers' heads, experience the effects of your offering on their needs, and figure out what they will be willing to pay for, not just what they would like you to do. This leads to the final guidelines.

DEVELOP INSIGHT INTO THE CUSTOMERS' BEHAVIORAL CONTEXT. This is a powerful weapon in your entrepreneurial arsenal. It's fashionable to talk about looking outside the box. It's much harder to find anyone who can show you how this translates into opportunities to redesign, resegment, reconfigure, redifferentiate—after all, the boxes that people try to look beyond are there in the first place because they made business sense at the time. Successful entrepreneurs often don't have to have a revolutionary product. What they have instead is a revolutionary insight into the context in which their customers live and an idea on how they might solve an important problem for the customers within that context. We have emphasized customer and competitive context—

the consumption chain, attribute map, and segmentation and reconfiguration ideas—to help you structure your out-of-the-box thinking.

IN AN ENTREPRENEURIAL MINDSET, EVERYBODY PLAYS. We stress that you do
not need to use these tools alone. Besides, no matter how brilliant
you are, you can rarely be as brilliant alone as a competitor who has
learned to mobilize the entire organization. The act of bringing
other people into the entrepreneurial process is essential, and you
can use the tools we have provided to engage all your people to generate opportunities. They must believe that any and all new ideas are
welcome, but also understand that not all opportunities are economically feasible even if they are good. They must feel strongly that
execution, not analysis, is what will make a real difference to the
company.

EXPERIMENT INTELLIGENTLY. You can't analyze your way to competitive
advantage. If you could simply think rationally about creating advantage to make it happen, so could your competitors. Strategy today is
more about strategic experimentation and trial-and-error learning
than it is about analysis and forecasting. How do companies experiment? Companies experiment, and therefore execute their strategies,
using real options reasoning: by continually starting, selecting, pursuing, and dropping projects and businesses before launching aggressively in those projects whose value is finally revealed. In an uncertain
world, real options give you flexibility, the potential to learn, and a way
of hedging bets. They allow you to learn at minimum possible cost.

One of the key managerial tasks of the years beyond 2000 will
be to manage the company's portfolio of options, just as a key role for
future strategists will be maximizing the learning from real options
investments.

EXERCISE DISCIPLINE. Manage the experimental process with the rock-
ribbed discipline of successful, habitual entrepreneurs. They can't
rely on surplus resources to buffer them from big, expensive mistakes. We have described the techniques they use to achieve the necessary discipline and showed you how it can be used. The opportunity register, your options portfolio, your discovery-driven plans, and

the responses to the questions we ask throughout the book are all ways of imposing discipline and constructive control on new business creation for your firm.

SPEND IMAGINATION INSTEAD OF MONEY. Many of the ideas presented here are not expensive to implement. They have little downside and represent few risks. They spend creativity and imagination instead of funds. In a world of increasingly ruthless competition for shareholder returns, parsimony is essential. As you continue to build your own entrepreneurial arsenal, look for ways in which people can be encouraged to utilize their own creativity before asking for material resources. If you are working with the right group of colleagues, they will welcome the challenge.

FRAMING IS CRUCIAL TO THE ENTREPRENEURIAL LEADER. Without a frame to work with, people freeze in the headlights of oncoming uncertainty. Your job, your most solemn responsibility as a leader in an entrepreneurial context, is to provide the frame within which people can meet the challenges of the future. You may find yourself framing what a product should look like, as Keizo Yamaji did when he launched the personal copier business; framing what constitutes a legitimate business through the establishment of a ballpark, as did Peter with his "50 to the power of 4" rule; framing the specific challenge a business must meet, as we do in discovery-driven planning; or framing a business around a focused set of priorities, as Thomas Engibous did when he propelled Texas Instruments into a focus on digital-signal-processing technology.

BE RUTHLESS WITH RESPECT TO PRIORITIES. Trying to do too many things has sunk many an entrepreneurial business, and it can sink yours, too. We have offered some rules of thumb. Whether you use them or not, it's important that you understand your company's capacity. Trying to do more than the firm is capable of handling is tantamount to doing nothing. Dropping things that don't merit your attention or the attention of co-workers is every bit as important as starting things that might lead you to a brighter future. You need to specify clearly what is not going to be done, or will no longer be done, and act on it.

USING FUZZY MEASURES EARLY ON IS BETTER THAN USING PRECISE ONES TOO LATE.
As a manager, you want two things from measures: forewarning (so you'll see the warning signs of a problem before it becomes too serious to handle) and actionability. Measures should serve as your guide. The better access people have to measures, the better they are able to link their job to something that drives strategy, and the better they can control their own actions and help create an attractive future. Make sure your measures are operational—not "increase market share by 20 percent" but "sell fifty more this week than we did the same week last year." This gives people the basis for acting in a consistent way.

PAY ATTENTION TO THE COST—NOT THE RATE—OF FAILURE.   As we have emphasized throughout, you will sometimes fail. If you are doing the experimental, options-oriented job that you should be doing, you could fail a lot. Becoming comfortable with real or potential failure is one of the most difficult challenges for a manager trained in the old school of infallible, numbers-oriented leadership. We've made this point throughout, and we'll make it again now. In conditions of significant uncertainty, you are likely to have very little control over your rate of failure. Indeed, failure is often the tuition fee you pay to access new opportunities. What you can control is the cost of those failures. Using the disciplines in this book—validating assumptions prior to investment, operating with parsimony, redirecting, keeping your priorities straight—will help you do this.

THE UPSIDE

We have spoken a good deal about the pressure of operating under uncertainty. The risks, the visible downside, and the constant change are, understandably, hard to cope with. The long hours spent grappling with new information, the intense discussions to try to understand what's going on, and the genuine personal effort it takes on your part as the leader to embody what you want the organization to be is at times exhausting.

What we haven't spent nearly enough time on is the exhilaration of winning in an entrepreneurial environment. It's a lot of fun to create something new and see it develop. It's a lot of fun to outwit and outmaneuver your competitors. It's a lot of fun to see customers genuinely respond to your efforts to add exciters and eliminate tolerables. It's a lot of fun to be vindicated after experiencing disappointment but sticking with it. It's also a lot of fun to make a lot of money for your firm or for yourself. It's a lot of fun to win.

So this is our encouragement to you. Use what seems to be helpful to you here. Start simple, skip the complicated parts until your team has built some confidence, and then perhaps come back to the book and revisit the more challenging sections. Get more and more comfortable with your emerging role as an entrepreneurial leader. And when you and the people who are working alongside you win, enjoy the celebration you deserve so much.

NOTES

PREFACE

1. The topic of how entrepreneurs succeed in creating wealth in the face of fundamental uncertainty has figured prominently in the work of Kirzner (1973, 1997), Knight (1921); Hayek (1945); and of course Schumpeter (1950). Venkataraman (1997) has suggested that a focus on markets of the future is a distinctive contribution of the study of entrepreneurship. We would argue that creating future new businesses is the distinctive focus of an entrepreneurial mindset.

2. The Citibank study represents our first major collaboration. Called Citiventures, the project was a three-year field study of dozens of corporate ventures started in the bank. During the study, we observed many attempts at new business creation within a single firm. We conducted over three hundred interviews for this project, involving managers at every organizational level and in most parts of the business. Insights from earlier studies of the corporate venturing process can be found in Block and MacMillan (1993); and Starr and MacMillan (1990).

3. McGrath (1997); McGrath (1996); McGrath (1999); McGrath and MacMillan (2000). See also McGrath, MacMillan, and Tushman (1992); MacMillan and McGrath (1994).

4. McGrath (1993); McGrath, MacMillan, and Venkataraman (1995); McGrath et al. (1996); Nerkar, McGrath, and MacMillan (1996); McGrath (1998).

5. MacMillan, Zemann, and SubbaNarasimha (1987); Hambrick, Mac-Millan, and Day (1982); Hambrick and MacMillan (1984); MacMillan, Siegel, and SubbaNarasimha (1985); Macmillan, Block, and SubbaNarasimha (1986).

6. MacMillan and Day (1987); MacMillan, McCaffery, and Van Wijk (1985); Chen and MacMillan (1992); MacMillan (1988); McGrath, Chen, and MacMillan (1998); D'Aveni (1994).

7. McGrath and MacMillan (1995); Block and MacMillan (1985). See also Low and MacMillan (1988).

8. MacMillan (1987); MacMillan (1983); Guth and MacMillan (1986); MacMillan (1986); McGrath, Venkataraman, and MacMillan (1992); Venkataraman, MacMillan, and McGrath (1992); McGrath (1995).

Chapter 1: Needed: An Entrepreneurial Mindset

1. Henry Schacht, former CEO of Lucent Technologies, gave us this phrase.

2. MacMillan first made this argument well over a decade ago. The importance of understanding habitual entrepreneurs is now being recognized by the academic community (MacMillan 1986; Birley and Westhead 1993; Wright, Westhead, and Sohl 1999).

Chapter 2: Framing the Challenge

1. Christensen (1997).

2. An excellent description of visions that work can be found in Collins and Porras (1994).

3. For instance, Garud and Nayyar (1994) make the point that it is the organization's ability to recall technologies and ideas over time that often leads to substantial competitive advantages.

Chapter 3: Building Blockbuster Products and Services

1. Drucker (1973).

2. The attribute map and its use were first described in MacMillan and McGrath (1996). For additional reading on marketing, attributes, and positioning in general, a good place to start is Kotler (1994). See also Day (1990) on marketing and strategy. For attributes of information goods, see Shapiro and Varian (1998).

3. Dos Santos and Peffers (1995).

4. See the Web sites www.mindspring.net/aboutms/history.html and http://www.hoovers.com.

5. Hart and Milstein (1999).

6. Clark and Fujimoto (1991).

7. Reichheld (1996).

8. Silverman and Osterland (1999).

9. For a great description of sorting out what customers would like from what they will pay for, see Greg Brenneman's (1998) description of deciding what services Continental Airlines would offer after its turnaround.

10. The data in this example is drawn from a Harvard Business School case, "Progressive Corporation" [N9-797-109].

11. Brenneman (1998).

12. See Brown and Eisenhardt (1998) for additional descriptions of how this works.

13. Abernathy and Clark (1985); Christensen (1997).

14. Dana Canedy and Reed Abelson, "Can Kellogg Break Out of the Box?" *New York Times*, January 24, 1999.

15. Porter (1980).

16. Schoemaker and van der Heijden (1992); Schoemaker (1992).

17. Van der Heijden (1996).

CHAPTER 4: REDIFFERENTIATING PRODUCTS AND SERVICES

1. MacMillan (1975).

2. Conversation with Bernie Gunther, a principal at MMG, October 4, 1999.

3. McGrath and MacMillan (1997).

4. Jamie Beckett, "Oral-B Polishes Sales with Blue Dye," *San Francisco Chronicle*, January 2, 1992.

5. "Popular Science Awards Energizer 'Best of What's New' Title," PR Newswire Association, Inc., November 12, 1996.

6. For intriguing ideas about how smart, widely dispersed, and interconnected machine intelligence may create huge opportunities, see Kelly (1997) and Evans and Wurster (1997). The information on "smart trucks" was taken from Tapscott (1995).

7. Brock Yates, "I'll Trade You Two Camels for One New Car," *Washington Post Magazine*, Sunday final ed., September 6, 1987, 237.

8. "Mobile Speedpass Surpasses Three Million Users—Innovative Payment Technology Sets Standard for the Next Millennium," *Business Wire*, August 31, 1999.

9. Aldo Morri, "Wireless to Monitor Elevators," *Wireless Week*, July 20, 1998.

10. Paul Kemezis and Jim Cowhie, "Industrial Gases: Prospects Brighten in '95," *Chemical Week*, February 22, 1995.

11. Lucio Guerrero, "E-Tailer's Return Policies Critical," *Chicago Sun-Times*, December 26, 1999; Eric Wieffering, "Dayton Hudson to Roll Out New Target Web Site Return Policy" *Minneapolis Star Tribune*, August 28, 1999.

12. This segment actually exists—MacMillan and his wife buy cars in this way. This type of buyer is the automaker's dream, as long as it is your make of auto they are buying!

CHAPTER 5: DISRUPTING THE RULES OF THE GAME

1. As of this writing, Amazon.com is alive and well—whether the business model works is yet to be seen.

2. This section builds on McGrath, MacMillan, and Tushman (1992) and MacMillan and McGrath (1994).

3. Tushman and Anderson (1986); Christensen (1997); Utterback (1994).

4. Porter (1998).

5. Go to the e-STEEL.com Web site. Two other excellent sites for obtaining news of developments like this can be found at estats.com and DeepCanyon.com, both focused on information industries.

6. *Business Week*, June 1, 1999.

7. Aldrich and Fiol (1994) highlight many of the difficulties facing firms attempting to compete in brand new industry spaces that are not yet taken for granted. Among them are difficulties in getting transaction partners to sign up, difficulties with regulatory and other authorities, and a general lack of legitimacy that can cause the business to have trouble acquiring resources.

8. Actual trade-offs of multiple attributes can be tackled using conjoint analysis techniques like those in the Bundopt software package developed by Green and Krieger at Wharton in 1996. Conjoint analysis is an analytical technique in which respondents choose among different combinations of attributes. The combinations are selected and presented so as to allow a statistical analysis that identifies the combination of attributes that is most attractive to the respondents.

9. This assumes, of course, that the evolution of existing products (such as the increasingly ubiquitous PALM handheld devices) doesn't satisfy these needs well enough.

10. For an excellent discussion of how to build world-class, breakthrough value chains by forming alliances, see Doz and Hamel (1998).

CHAPTER 6: BUILDING BREAKTHROUGH COMPETENCES

1. The implications of firms' dependency on external resource providers for their survival are forcefully laid out in Pfeffer and Salancik (1978).

2. See, for example, Vasconcellos and Hambrick (1989).

3. This does not imply that the organizational components delivering the numbers are simple. Indeed, most highly successful organizations deliver their key ratios through a mutually reinforcing complex of interrelated practices, one reason that traditional benchmarking has so often led to disappointment. See Nadler and Tushman (1988); Porter (1996); and Levinthal (1997) for academic perspectives on this.

4. See Reichheld (1996) for some excellent ideas on how to get at the essentials of this kind of negative customer assessment. He outlines useful ideas for assessing the reasons for customer defection and for doing something about it.

5. This sort of response by people in the company is to be expected at first, because it is usually hard for people working in one area to see systemic problems. Addressing this tendency created enormous demand a few years back for systemwide approaches, such as business process reengineering. Our major reservation with business-process-reengineering-like approaches is that in the zeal to eliminate redundant or inefficient operations, many

good and innovative ideas also get eliminated, leaving companies lean but unable to generate new businesses. See Levinthal and March (1993) for a theoretical analysis of dilemmas of this sort.

6. McGrath et al. (1996).

7. McGrath (1998).

8. We can use this example because these competences have since diffused and are now commonplace in the industry.

9. Conversation with GEFS manager, 1993.

10. This is one reason, we believe, that fewer companies are looking to strategies based on products alone as opposed to bundling products with processes and services. It is much easier to imitate and improve on a product because the innovators' insights are already codified into definable functionality. It is much harder to imitate a complex product plus service plus information transaction. Witness the success of Japanese and other Asian firms in product innovation versus their struggles with competing in services, such as international banking. This is a further reason for the decline of patenting as a source of competitive protection in all but a few industries (such as pharmaceuticals and advanced materials).

11. This, by the way, can account for disappointing results from a benchmarking effort—benchmarking the outcomes of a competence creation effort often leaves out the actual drivers of why it works in the first place.

12. Among our personal favorites are the books by Slywotsky and associates, such as *Value Migration* and *The Profit Zone*.

13. The periodical *Value Line Investment Survey* is available in most public libraries and on-line.

14. Fuld (1995) is a good reference on intelligence capabilities and offers a wealth of ideas for sources of data.

15. The idea that group-level comprehension of the relationships between actions and desired firm-level outcomes is a critical driver of performance can be traced to Weick and Roberts (1993). The importance of this relationship to organizational efforts to create new distinctive competences (and subsequent competitive advantages) was empirically tested in McGrath's dissertation (McGrath 1993) and subsequent articles drawing from this conceptual base.

CHAPTER 7: SELECTING YOUR COMPETITIVE TERRAIN

1. This is the well-known trade-off between exploring new knowledge and exploiting existing knowledge (March 1991).

2. The idea of a strategic terrain and competing for arenas within this terrain is derived from Kauffman's (1993) concept of a fitness landscape in biology and is applied to problems of strategy by scholars such as Levinthal (1997).

3. This is one reason that the pursuit of large market shares is not always the best way to win from a strategic point of view.

4. Singh (1986).

5. Garud and Kumaraswamy (1993).

6. Multiple-business companies can also stratify their different divisions, to help think through portfolio decisions.

7. At this stage, in the interest of simplicity, we have not discussed new businesses, or corporate ventures. We will get to corporate ventures in chapter 12. Meanwhile, if your register contains such ventures, they should also be categorized as arena building.

8. So, we have had Porter's justly famous "five forces" model (1980); the Boston Consulting Group's product/portfolio matrix (Henderson 1980); and the GE business attractiveness matrix and various other influential ideas for measuring attractiveness. These were useful tools when they were developed, and they remain useful today. As with any tool, however, one needs to be careful about the conditions under which they work. Under increasing uncertainty, many core premises of these models (e.g., stable value chains and relatively clear industry boundaries) fail to hold.

9. McGrath (1997); MacMillan, Siegel, and SubbaNarasimha (1985).

10. Data from www.pfizer.com.

11. This is a point made by Christensen (1997).

12. "Genetically Modified Food: Food for Thought," *Economist*, June 19, 1999, 19–21.

13. Lieberman and Montgomery (1988).

14. Saba (1999).

15. We use surveys to capture the information, using a 1-to-7 scale, in which a score of 1 is low (disagree completely) and a score of 7 is high (agree completely). For us to consider a score high or low, the average has to be above 5. If we have data from a team, we average the individual responses to obtain a team score. See McGrath and MacMillan (2000).

16. See Harrigan (1980).

17. Today, Gillette's new CEO is about to embark on a similar process of rigorously evaluating the contributions made by some of the underperforming divisions (such as Waterman pens) in the company, with the possible result that they will be sold.

18. A seminal book on the topic of resource allocation is Bower (1970), whose framework was applied to the corporate venturing process by Burgelman (1983; 1988; 1991).

19. McGrath, Venkataraman, and MacMillan (1992).

20. Schon (1963); Chakrabarti (1974); Day (1994); Ginsberg and Abrahamson (1991).

21. See Itami (1987). See also chapter 6 in Block and MacMillan (1993) on locating new business development efforts.

22. For an extensive discussion of managing the politics involved with new business development strategies, see Block and MacMillan (1993), chapters 10 and 11.

23. There are several excellent references available on how to manage internal politics. See Pfeffer, *Managing With Power* (1992); Tushman and O'Reilly, *Winning through Innovation* (1997); and MacMillan and Jones,

Strategy Formulation: Political Concepts (1986). For a detailed look at the use of power and its consequences, a classic remains Robert Caro's biography of Robert Moses, *The Power Broker* (1974).

24. *The Economist*, June 19, 1999.

CHAPTER 8: ASSEMBLING YOUR OPPORTUNITY PORTFOLIO

1. Brown and Eisenhardt (1998) observe that a distinguishing characteristic of firms able to cope with high-velocity change is that the development priorities are clear throughout the company.

2. Bowman and Hurry (1993); Kogut (1991); McGrath (1997).

3. Black and Scholes (1973).

4. Coy (1999); Belanger (1999).

5. Scouting options have been called "probes" as well (see Brown and Eisenhardt 1998).

6. For the sacrificial product, see Lynn, Morone, and Paulson (1997). For the probe, see Brown and Eisenhardt (1998).

7. McGrath and MacMillan (1995). See also Block and MacMillan (1985). We pursue this in detail next in chapter 8.

8. McGrath and Boisot (1998); Ashby (1956).

9. Or what the late Ned Bowman dubbed "a bundle" of options.

10. Information on AT&T from Hoovers' on-line company profile at www.hoovers.com.

11. Baldwin and Clark (1997).

12. This approach is consistent with Wheelwright and Clark's (1995) approach to getting a handle on what products are in the pipeline—we extend this concept to look broadly at the business ideas you might explore.

13. Galbraith (1973) long ago observed that when faced with overload and no way to increase the processing capacity, a system has few choices other than to buy itself time by lowered performance.

CHAPTER 9: SELECTING AND EXECUTING YOUR ENTRY STRATEGY

1. D'Aveni (1994) has a book full of wonderful examples of hypercompetitive interchanges in a variety of different industries.

2. Venkataraman (1989) was one of the first to explicitly recognize the importance of the transaction set—the set of initial customers, suppliers, buyers and others with whom a fledgling venture interacts. He found that when partners left the transaction set of a fledgling business, its vulnerability increased dramatically, as the founding team had to scramble to replace defections from the set of transaction partners.

3. See Christiansen (1997) for more on this. His main thesis is that attending to the needs of good current customers can systematically inhibit a business from understanding the needs of new customers.

4. Von Hippel (1988) calls these *lead users*.

5. Stinchcombe (1965) first drew scholarly attention to this issue with a famous treatise on the liabilities of newness. Among these liabilities are a

lack of legitimacy and reputation with which to persuade potential customers (and other allies) that new, young businesses will be sustainable and trustworthy and will fulfill their obligations. Endorsement of what a new business is doing by high-status individuals and firms is a potent way of overcoming these liabilities. This is borne out by recent empirical research. Stuart, Hoang, and Hybels (1999), for instance, find that new biotech firms endorsed by high-prestige partners were more successful at attracting investment and other forms of support.

6. This may seem trivial, but it isn't. We have seen quite a few business propositions that made sense for the customer company as a whole that were resisted because the benefits would accrue to some group in the company other than the one making the purchasing decision. This is a case of the reward and incentive structures in the company being misaligned with what is good for it. This happens more than you might think.

7. See, for instance, Chen and MacMillan (1992).

8. Chen (1996).

9. The core theory behind much of this discussion began with Edwards's (1955) discussion of "mutual forbearance."

10. The formal term for this is "resource diversion"—see McGrath, Chen, and MacMillan (1998).

11. Grove (1996).

12. Intel subsequently diverted its resources to its then modest—but later spectacularly successful—microprocessor chip business.

13. Mao Zedung (1966).

14. MacMillan (1985).

15. To protect the business, we have used a fictitious product in this discussion.

16. This kind of competitive signaling is thought to lead to the establishment of stable *spheres of influence* among multiple-point competitors, in which they practice mutual forbearance and refrain from attacking one another directly in important arenas. See Edwards (1955) and Bernheim and Whinston (1990).

17. Myron Levin, "Targeting Foreign Smokers," *Los Angeles Times,* November 17, 1994.

18. This discussion also draws on the ideas of Richard D'Aveni, who discusses the pet food industry at length in a teaching note prepared for the Harvard case.

CHAPTER 10: PUTTING DISCOVERY-DRIVEN PLANNING TO WORK

1. People also tend to ignore evidence that contradicts previous assumptions (Kiesler and Sproull 1982). In addition, assumptions may be hard to remember. A famous study by Russ Ackoff (1981), formerly of the Wharton School, found that after six weeks, managers in a typical organization can't recall half of the assumptions underlying key decisions they had made. This study is a useful analysis of planning pathologies and what can be done about them.

2. Winter (1995) offers an insightful discussion of the role of replication in capturing profits from a strategy.

3. This characterization of the learning process stems from a long stream of research into behavioral learning theory (Cyert and March 1963; March and Simon 1993).

4. See Weick (1979) for a discussion of the concept of enactment and Cheng and Van de Ven (1996) for a discussion of the application of this idea to entrepreneurial behavior. McGrath (forthcoming) also found empirical evidence of the importance of creating variance for learning in a sample of corporate new business ventures.

5. Maister (1982); see also Maister (1993).

6. For a detailed exposition of many different business models we refer you to Slywotsky and Morrison (1997).

7. In the academic literature, the idea that complex combinations of skills, assets, and systems can be a powerful source of competitive insulation is prevalent in both evolutionary economics (Nelson and Winter 1982) and the resource-based view of the firm (Wernerfelt 1984; Teece, Pisano, and Shuen 1997).

8. The concept of assumption-based milestone planning was first articulated by Block and MacMillan (1985).

9. We are grateful to Professor Shuichi Matsuda of Waseda University in Tokyo, Japan, for data on Kao's floppy-disk venture. We have never had a consulting relationship with the company (indeed, we met representatives only after the illustrative reconstruction of the case was published in the *Harvard Business Review*).

10. The sections on documenting assumptions and learning from milestones draw heavily from the work of Zenas Block—see Block and MacMillan (1985).

11. The work of Ming Jer Chen shows that competitors are often willing to depress prices to hold share, particularly in the face of irreversible investments (Chen and MacMillan 1992).

12. If Monte Carlo simulations seem like too much work, there is a simple alternative. Run a series of "what if" analyses that take on the upper and lower range of each assumption to find the variables that most affect the outcome.

13. We wish to thank Yasu Kitahara for this insight, which he has incorporated in a software package developed specifically for discovery-driven planning. If you are interested, he is reachable at kitahara@integratto.co.jp.

CHAPTER 11: MANAGING PROJECTS WITH UNCERTAIN OUTCOMES

1. The research on which this chapter was based stems from McGrath's doctoral dissertation (McGrath 1993). It owes much to the intellectual engagement of her doctoral committee, comprising the late Ned Bowman, Harbir Singh, Jitendra Singh, George Day, and S. Venkataraman. Oh, and MacMillan helped too.

2. Meyer (1999).

3. McGrath (1993); McGrath, MacMillan, and Venkatraman (1995); McGrath et al. (1996).

4. Wageman (1995).

5. *Merriam-Webster's Collegiate Dictionary*, 10th ed., on-line version.

6. Nelson and Winter (1982).

7. One issue with this measure is that people do tend to adjust aspirations based on previous results. We avoid contamination of our results by controlling for this in our research. We included data on the ambitiousness and difficulty of goals over time, in order to avoid being mislead by increases in convergence produced by decreases in ambitiousness of goals (Lant 1992). From a practical point of view, just make sure that people are not being too easy on themselves.

8. Barney (1986).

9. Williamson (1991).

10. MacMillan, McCaffery, and Van Wijk (1985).

11. See Meyer (1999).

CHAPTER 12: THE MOST IMPORTANT JOB: ENTREPRENEURIAL LEADERSHIP

1. Our appreciation of Welch's accomplishments at GE arise from many years of working with the company as it went through a transformation from being the best-run exemplar of traditional approaches to strategy to being an exemplar of a firm with an entrepreneurial mindset.

2. Jack Welch, speaking at the Zweig Lecture Series at the Wharton School, University of Pennsylvania, February 17, 1999.

3. March and Shapira (1987).

4. Hambrick and MacMillan (1984).

5. We have found that a particular time when entrepreneurial efforts incur intense displeasure is when the reward system for undertaking the risk of starting the entrepreneurial business takes off as a result of the success of the start up, and the internal entrepreneurs begin to generate more rewards than the incumbents of the established businesses.

BIBLIOGRAPHY

Abernathy, W. J., and K. Clark. 1985. "Innovation: Mapping the Winds of Creative Destruction." *Research Policy* 14:3–22.

Ackoff, R. 1981. *Creating the Corporate Future: Plan or Be Planned For.* New York: John Wiley and Sons.

Adler, P. S. 1989. "Technology Strategy: A Guide to the Literature." In *Research in Technological Innovation, Management and Policy,* edited by R. Rosenbloom and R. Burgelman. Volume 4: 25–151. Greenwich, Conn.: JAI Press.

Aldrich, H. E. 1979. *Organizations and Environments.* Englewood Cliffs, N.J.: Prentice-Hall.

Aldrich, H. E., and C. M. Fiol. 1994. "Fools Rush In? The Institutional Context of Industry Creation." *Academy of Management Review* 19:645–670.

Amburgey, T. L., D. Kelly, and W. P. Barnett. 1993. "Resetting the Clock: The Dynamics of Organizational Change and Failure." *Administrative Science Quarterly* 38:51–73.

Amit, R., and P. Schoemaker. 1993. "Strategic Assets and Organizational Rent." *Strategic Management Journal* 14:33–46.

Ashby, W. R. 1956. *An Introduction to Cybernetics.* London: Chapman and Hall.

Bain, J. S. 1959. *Industrial Organization.* New York: John Wiley and Sons.

Baldwin, C., and K. B. Clark. 1997. "Managing in an Age of Modularity." *Harvard Business Review* 75:84–93.

Barney, J. B. 1991. "Firm Resources and Sustained Competitive Advantage." *Journal of Management* 17:99–120.

————. 1986. "Strategic Factor Markets: Expectations, Luck, and Business Strategy." *Management Science* 32:1231–1241.

Belanger, K. 1999. "Strategic Investing in Schumpeterian Environments: The Case of Enron." Paper presented at the 1999 Babson College–Kauffman Foundation Entrepreneurship Research Conference at Columbia, S.C., May 12–15, 1999.

Bernheim, B. D., and M. D. Whinston. 1990. "Multimarket Contact and Collusive Behavior." *Rand Journal of Economics* 21:1–26.

Birley, S., and P. Westhead. 1993. "A Comparison of New Businesses Established by 'Novice' and 'Habitual' Founders in Great Britain." *International Small Business Journal* 12:38–60.

Birnbaum-More, P. H., and A. R. Weiss. 1990. "Discovering the Basis of Competition in Thirteen Industries: Computerized Content Analysis of Interview Data from the U. S. and Europe." In *Mapping Strategic Thought*, edited by A. Huff. New York: John Wiley and Sons.

Birnbaum-More, P. H., A. R. Weiss, and R. Wright. 1994. "How Do Rivals Compete: Strategy, Technology and Tactics." *Research Policy* 23:249–265.

Black, F., and M. Scholes. 1973. "The Pricing of Options and Corporate Liabilities." *Journal of Political Economy* 81:637–654.

Block, Z., and I. C. MacMillan. 1985. "Milestones for Successful Venture Planning." *Harvard Business Review* 62:4–8.

————. 1993. *Corporate Venturing: Creating New Business within the Firm*. Boston: Harvard Business School Press.

Bower, J. L. 1970. *Managing the Resource Allocation Process*. Boston: Harvard Business School Press.

Bowman, E. H. 1980. "A Risk/Return Paradox for Strategic Management." *Sloan Management Review* 21:17–31.

Bowman, E. H., and D. Hurry. 1993. "Strategy through the Option Lens: An Integrated View of Resource Investments and the Incremental-Choice Process." *Academy of Management Review* 18:760–782.

Brenneman, G. 1998. "Right Away and All at Once: How We Saved Continental." *Harvard Business Review* 76:162–179.

Brown, S., and K. Eisenhardt. 1998. *Competing on the Edge*. Boston: Harvard Business School Press.

Burgelman, R. A. 1996. "A Process Model of Strategic Business Exit: Implications for an Evolutionary Perspective on Strategy." *Strategic Management Journal* 17:193–214.

————. 1991. "Intraorganizational Ecology of Strategy Making and Organizational Adaptation: Theory and Field Research." *Organization Science* 2:239–262.

————. 1988. "Strategy Making as a Social Learning Process: The Case of Internal Corporate Venturing." *Interfaces* 18:74–85.

————. 1983. "A Process Model of Internal Corporate Venturing in the Diversified Major Firm." *Administrative Science Quarterly* 18:223–244.

Caro, R. A. 1974. *The Power Broker*. New York: Knopf.

Carroll, G. R. 1993. "A Sociological View on Why Firms Differ." *Strategic Management Journal* 14:237–249.

Chakrabarti, A. 1974. "The Role of Champion in Product Innovation." *California Management Review* 17:58–62.

Chandler, A. D. 1962. *Strategy and Structure*. Garden City, N.Y.: Doubleday.

Chen, M-J. 1996. "Competitor Analysis and Interfirm Rivalry: Toward a Theoretical Integration." *Academy of Management Review* 21:100–134.

Chen, M-J., and I. C. MacMillan. 1992. "Nonresponse and Delayed Response to Competitive Moves: The Roles of Competitor Dependence and Action Irreversibility." *Academy of Management Journal* 35:359–370.

Cheng, Y., and A. H. Van de Ven. 1996. "Learning the Innovation Journey: Order Out of Chaos?" *Organization Science* 7:593–614.

Christensen, C. 1997. *The Innovator's Dilemma: When New Technologies Cause Great Firms to Fail*. Boston: Harvard Business School Press.

Clark, K. B., and T. Fujimoto. 1991. *Product Development Performance: Strategy, Organization and Management in the World Auto Industry*. Boston: Harvard Business School Press.

Cohen, W. M., and D. A. Levinthal. 1994. "Fortune Favors the Prepared Firm." *Management Science* 40:227–251.

———. 1990. "Absorptive Capacity: A New Perspective on Learning and Innovation." *Administrative Science Quarterly* 35:128–152.

Collins, J. C., and J. I. Porras. 1994. *Built to Last: Successful Habits of Visionary Companies*. New York: HarperBusiness.

Coser, L. A. 1956. *The Functions of Social Conflict*. New York: Free Press.

Coy, P. 1999. "Exploiting Uncertainty: The Real Options Revolution in Decision Making." *Business Week* (June 7):118–124.

Crockett, R. O., and P. Elstrom. 1998. "How Motorola Lost Its Way." *Business Week* (May 4):140–148.

Cyert, R. M., and J. G. March. 1963. *A Behavioral Theory of the Firm*. Englewood Cliffs, N.J.: Prentice-Hall.

D'Aveni, R. A. 1994. *Hypercompetition: The Dynamics of Strategic Maneuvering*. New York: Free Press.

D'Aveni, R. A., and I. C. MacMillan. 1990. "Crisis and the Content of Managerial Communications: A Study of the Focus of Attention of Top Managers in Surviving and Failing Firms." *Administrative Science Quarterly* 35:634–657.

Day, D. L. 1994. "Raising Radicals: Different Processes for Championing Innovative Corporate Ventures." *Organization Science* 5:148–172.

Day, G. 1990. *Market Driven Strategy*. New York: Free Press.

Dierickx, I., and K. Cool. 1989. "Asset Stock Accumulation and Sustainability of Competitive Advantage." *Management Science* 35:1504–1513.

Dos Santos, B. L., and K. Peffers. 1995. "Rewards to Investors in Innovative Information Technology Applications: First Movers and Early Followers in ATMs." *Organization Science* 6:241–259.

Doz, Y., and G. Hamel. 1998. *Alliance Advantage: The Art of Creating Value through Partnering.* Boston: Harvard Business School Press.

Drucker, P. 1973. *Management Tasks, Responsibilities, Practices.* New York: Harper and Row.

Edwards, C. D. 1955. "Conglomerate Bigness as a Source of Power." In *Business Concentration and Price Policy* (The National Bureau of Economics Research conference report). Princeton: Princeton University Press, 331–352.

Eisenhardt, K. 1989. "Agency Theory: An Assessment and Review." *Academy of Management Review* 14:57–74.

Evans, P. B., and T. S. Wurster. 1997. "Strategy and the New Economics of Information." *Harvard Business Review* 75:71–82.

Fuld, L. 1995. *The New Competitor Intelligence: The Complete Resource for Finding, Analyzing, and Using Information about Your Competitors.* New York: John Wiley and Sons.

Galbraith, J. 1973. *Designing Complex Organizations.* Reading, Mass.: Addison-Wesley.

Garud, R., and A. Kumaraswamy. 1995. "Technological and Organizational Designs for Realizing Economies of Substitution." *Strategic Management Journal* 16:93–109.

———. 1993. "Changing Competitive Dynamics in Network Industries: An Exploration of Sun Microsystems' Open Systems Strategy." *Strategic Management Journal* 14:351–369.

Garud, R., and P. R. Nayyar. 1994. "Transformative Capacity: Continual Structuring by Intertemporal Technology Transfer." *Strategic Management Journal* 15:365–385.

Gersick, C. J. G. 1991. "Revolutionary Change Theories: A Multi-Level Exploration of the Punctuated Equilibrium Paradigm." *Academy of Management Review* 16:10–36.

Ginsberg, A., and E. Abrahamson. 1991. "Champions of Change and Strategic Shifts: The Role of Internal and External Change Advocates." *Journal of Management Studies* 28:173–190.

Grove, A. 1996. *Only the Paranoid Survive: How to Exploit the Crisis Points That Challenge Every Company and Career.* New York: Doubleday.

Guth, W. D., and I. C. MacMillan. 1986. "Strategy Implementation versus Middle Management Self-interest." *Strategic Management Journal* 7:313–327.

Hambrick, D. C., and I. C. MacMillan. 1984. "Asset Parsimony: Managing Assets to Manage Profits." *Sloan Management Review* 25:67–74.

Hambrick, D. C., I. C. MacMillan, and D. L. Day. 1982. "Strategic Attributes and Performance in the BCG Matrix: A PIMS-Based Analysis of Industrial Product Businesses." *Academy of Management Journal* 25:510–531.

Hannan, M. T., and J. Freeman. 1977. "The Population Ecology of Organizations." *American Journal of Sociology* 82:929–964.

Harrigan, K. R. 1981. "Deterrents to Divestiture." *Academy of Management Journal* 24:306–323.

————. 1980. *Strategies for Declining Businesses*. Lexington, Mass.: Lexington Books.

Hart, S. L., and M. B. Milstein. 1999. "Global Sustainability and the Creative Destruction of Industries." *Sloan Management Review* 41:23–33.

Harvey, J. B. 1974. "The Abilene Paradox: The Management of Agreement." *Organizational Dynamics* 3:63–80.

Haveman, H. 1992. "Between a Rock and a Hard Place: Organizational Change and Performance under Conditions of Fundamental Environmental Transformation." *Administrative Science Quarterly* 37:48–75.

Hayek, F. 1945. "The Use of Knowledge in Society." *American Economic Review* 35:519–530.

Henderson, B. D. 1980. *The Experience Curve Revisited*. Perspective No. 229. Boston: The Boston Consulting Group.

Henderson, R., and I. Cockburn. 1994. "Measuring Competence? Exploring Firm Effects in Pharmaceutical Research." *Strategic Management Journal* 15:63–84.

Herbert, R. F., and A. N. Link. 1988. *The Entrepreneur*. New York: Praeger.

Itami, H. 1987. *Mobilizing Invisible Assets*. Cambridge, Mass.: Harvard University Press.

Janis, I. L. 1972. *Victims of Groupthink*. Boston: Houghton Mifflin.

Kamien, M., and N. Schwartz. 1975. "Market Structure and Innovation: A Survey." *Journal of Economic Literature* 13:1–37.

Kauffman, S. 1993. *The Origins of Order*. Oxford: Oxford University Press.

Kelly, K.. 1997. "New Rules for the New Economy: Twelve Dependable Principles for Thriving in a Turbulent World." *Wired Magazine* (September): 140–197.

Kemezis, P., and J. Cowhie. 1995. "Industrial Gases: Prospects Brighten in '95." *Chemical Week*, February 22.

Kiesler, S., and L. Sproull. 1982. "Managerial Responses to Changing Environments: Perspectives on Problem Sensing from Social Cognition." *Administrative Science Quarterly* 27:548–570.

Kirzner, I. 1997. "Entrepreneurial Discovery and the Competitive Market Process: An Austrian Approach." *Journal of Economic Literature* 35:60–85.

————. 1973. *Competition and Entrepreneurship*. Chicago: University of Chicago Press.

Knight, F. H. 1921. *Risk, Uncertainty and Profit*. Midway reprint 1971. Chicago: University of Chicago Press.

Kogut, B. 1991. "Joint Ventures and the Option to Expand and Acquire." *Management Science* 37:19–33.

Kotler, P. 1994. *Marketing Management: Analysis, Planning, Implementation and Control*. 8th ed. Englewood Cliffs, N.J.: Prentice-Hall.

Lant, T. K. 1992. "Aspiration Level Adaptation: An Empirical Exploration." *Management Science* 38:623–644.

Leonard Barton, D. 1992. "Core Capabilities and Core Rigidities: A Paradox in Managing New Product Development." *Strategic Management Journal* 13:111–126.

Levinthal, D. 1997. "Adaptation on Rugged Landscapes." *Management Science* 43:934–950.

Levinthal, D., and J. G. March. 1993. "The Myopia of Learning." *Strategic Management Journal* 14:95–112.

Levitt, B., and J. G. March. 1988. "Organizational Learning." *Annual Review of Sociology* 14:319–340.

Lieberman, M. B., and D. B. Montgomery. 1988. "First Mover Advantages." *Strategic Management Journal* 9:41–58.

Low, M. B., and I. C. MacMillan. 1988. "Entrepreneurship: Past Research and Future Challenges." *Journal of Management* 14:139–161.

Lynn, G. S., J. G. Morone, and A. S. Paulson. 1997. "Marketing and Discontinuous Innovation: The Probe and Learn Process." In *Managing Strategic Innovation and Change*, edited by M. L. Tushman and P. Anderson. New York: Oxford University Press.

MacMillan, I. C. 1988. "Controlling Competitive Dynamics by Taking Strategic Initiative." *Academy of Management Executive* 2:111–118.

———.1987. "New Business Development: A Challenge for Transformational Leadership." *Human Resource Management* 26: 439–454.

———. 1986. "To Really Learn about Entrepreneurship, Let's Study Habitual Entrepreneurs." *Journal of Business Venturing* 1:241–243.

———. 1985. "How Business Strategists Can Use Guerrilla Warfare Tactics." *Journal of Business Strategy* 1:63–66.

———. 1983. "The Politics of New Venture Management." *Harvard Business Review* 62:8–13.

———. 1975. "The Classification of Buyers into 'Behavioural Sets' in Order to Refine Industrial Marketing Efforts." *Business Management* (South Africa) 6:19–27.

MacMillan, I. C., Z. Block, and P. N. SubbaNarasimha. 1986. "Corporate Venturing: Alternatives, Obstacles Encountered, and Experience Effects." *Journal of Business Venturing* 1:177–191.

MacMillan, I. C., and D. Day. 1987. "Corporate Ventures into Industrial Markets: Dynamics of Aggressive Entry." *Journal of Business Venturing* 2:19–39.

MacMillan, I. C., and P. Jones. 1986. *Strategy Formulation: Power and Politics.* 2d ed. St. Paul, Minn.: West Publishing Company.

MacMillan, I. C., M. L. McCaffery, and G. Van Wijk. 1985. "Competitors' Responses to Easily Imitated New Products: Exploring Commercial Banking Product Introductions." *Strategic Management Journal* 6:75–86.

MacMillan, I. C., and R. G. McGrath. 1996. "Discover Your Products' Hidden Potential." *Harvard Business Review* 74:58–73.

———. 1994. "Technology Strategy." In *Advances in Global High-Technology Management*, edited by M. W. Lawless and L. R. Gomez-Mejia. Volume 4: 27–66. Greenwich, Conn.: JAI Press.

MacMillan, I. C., R. Siegel, and P. N. SubbaNarasimha. 1985. "Criteria Used by Venture Capitalists to Evaluate New Venture Proposals." *Journal of Business Venturing* 1:119–128.

MacMillan, I. C., L. Zemann, and P. N. SubbaNarasimha. 1987. "Criteria Distinguishing Successful from Unsuccessful Ventures in the Venture Screening Process." *Journal of Business Venturing* 2:123–138.

Maister, D. 1993. *Managing the Professional Service Firm.* New York: Macmillan.

———. 1982. "Balancing the Professional Service Firm." *Sloan Management Review* 24:15–29.

Mao Zedung. 1964. *Selected Military Writings of Mao Zedung.* Peking: Peking Press.

March, J. G. 1991. "Exploration and Exploitation in Organizational Learning." *Organization Science* 2:71–87.

March, J. G., and Z. Shapira. 1987. "Managerial Perspectives on Risk and Risk Taking." *Management Science* 33 (11):1404–1418.

March, J. G., and H. Simon. 1993. *Organizations.* New York: John Wiley and Sons.

McGrath, R. G. Forthcoming. "Exploratory Learning, Innovative Capacity and the Role of Managerial Oversight." *Academy of Management Journal.*

———. 1999. "Falling Forward: Real Options Reasoning and Entrepreneurial Failure." *Academy of Management Review* 24:13–30.

———. 1998. "Discovering Strategy: Competitive Advantage from Idiosyncratic Experimentation." In *Strategic Flexibility: Managing in a Turbulent Economy*, edited by G. Hamel et al. New York: John Wiley and Sons.

———. 1997. "A Real Options Logic for Initiating Technology Positioning Investments." *Academy of Management Review* 22:974–996.

———. 1996. "Options and the Entrepreneur: Towards a Strategic Theory of Entrepreneurial Wealth Creation." *Best Papers, Academy of Management Proceedings*, Cincinnati, Ohio, August 1996.

———. 1993. "The Development of New Competence in Established Organizations: An Empirical Investigation." Doctoral dissertation, University of Pennsylvania.

McGrath, R. G., and M. Boisot. 1998. "Corporate Level Real Options: The Strategic Equivalent to Requisite Variety." Paper presented at the Strategic Management Society's annual meeting, Orlando, Fl., November 1998.

McGrath, R. G., and I. C. MacMillan. 2000. "Assessing Technology Projects Using Real Options Reasoning: The STAR Approach." *Research-Technology Management.* Forthcoming.

———. 1997. "Discovering New Points of Differentiation." *Harvard Business Review* 75:133–145.

———. 1995. "Discovery Driven Planning." *Harvard Business Review* 73:44–54.

McGrath, R. G., M-J Chen, and I. C. MacMillan. 1998. "Multimarket Maneuvering in Uncertain Spheres of Influence: Resource Diversion Strategies." *Academy of Management Review* 23:724–740.

McGrath, R. G., I. C. MacMillan, and M. L. Tushman. 1992. "The Role of Executive Team Actions in Shaping Dominant Designs: Towards the

Strategic Shaping of Technological Progress." *Strategic Management Journal* 13:137–161.

McGrath, R. G., I. C. MacMillan, and S. Venkataraman. 1995. "Defining and Developing Competence: A Strategic Process Paradigm." *Strategic Management Journal* 16:251–275.

McGrath, R. G., S. Venkataraman, and I. C. MacMillan. 1992. "Outcomes of Corporate Venturing: An Alternative Perspective." *Best Papers, Academy of Management Proceedings*, Las Vegas, Nev., August 1992.

McGrath, R. G., et al. 1996. "Innovation, Competitive Advantage and Rent: A Model and Test." *Management Science* 42:389–403.

Meyer, M. 2000. *Finding Performance*. Boston: Harvard Business School Press, forthcoming.

Miles, R. E., and C. C. Snow. 1978. *Organizational Strategy, Structure and Process*. New York: McGraw-Hill.

Miller, D. 1993. "The Architecture of Simplicity." *Academy of Management Review* 18:116–138.

Morri, Aldo. 1998. "Wireless to Monitor Elevators." *Wireless Week*, July 20.

Mowery, D. C., and N. Rosenberg. 1982. "The Influence of Market Demand upon Innovation: A Critical Review of Some Recent Empirical Studies." In *Inside the Black Box: Technology and Economics*, edited by N. Rosenberg. Cambridge, UK: Cambridge University Press.

Myers, S., and D. G. Marquis. 1969. *Successful Industrial Innovations: A Study of Factors Underlying Innovation in Selected Firms*. No. NSF 69 17. Washington, D.C.: National Science Foundation.

National Commission on Space. 1986. *Pioneering the Space Frontier*. New York: Bantam Books.

Nelson, R. R., and S. J. Winter. 1982. *An Evolutionary Theory of Economic Change*. Cambridge, Mass.: Harvard University Press.

Nerkar, A., R. G. McGrath, and I. C. MacMillan. 1996. "Three Facets of Satisfaction and Their Influence on the Performance of Innovation Teams." *Journal of Business Venturing* 11:167–188.

Penrose, E. 1959. *The Theory of the Growth of the Firm*. New York: John Wiley and Sons.

Pfeffer, J. 1992. *Managing with Power*. Boston: Harvard Business School Press.

Pfeffer, J., and G. Salancik. 1978. *The External Control of Organizations: A Resource Dependence Perspective*. New York: Harper and Row.

Porter, M. E. 1998. "Clusters and the New Economics of Competition." *Harvard Business Review* 76:77–90.

———. 1990. *The Competitive Advantage of Nations*. New York: Free Press.

———. 1985. *Competitive Advantage*. New York: Free Press.

———. 1980. *Competitive Strategy*. New York: Free Press.

Reichheld, F. F. 1996. *The Loyalty Effect*. Boston: Harvard Business School Press.

Reinhardt, A., and C. Yang. 1999. "Risks Soar, the Rockets Don't." *Business Week* (May 31): 44.

Romanelli, E., and M. L. Tushman. 1994. "Organizational Transformation as Punctuated Equilibrium: An Empirical Test." *Academy of Management Journal* 37:1141–1166.

Ross, J., and B. M. Staw. 1993. "Organizational Escalation and Exit: Lessons from the Shoreham Nuclear Power Plant." *Academy of Management Journal* 36:701–732.

———. 1986. "Expo 86: An Escalation Protoype." *Administrative Science Quarterly* 31:274–297.

Rumelt, R. P. 1987. "Theory, Strategy and Entrepreneurship." In *The Competitive Challenge: Strategies for Industrial Innovation and Renewal*, edited by D. J. Teece. New York: Harper and Row.

Saba J. 1999. "Casebook No. 39." *MC Technology Marketing Intelligence* 19:42 –45.

Scherer, F. M. 1979. *Industrial Market Structure and Economic Performance*. Chicago: Rand McNally.

Schmookler, J. 1966. *Invention and Economic Growth*. Cambridge, Mass.: Harvard University Press.

Schoemaker, P. 1992. "How to Link Strategic Vision to Core Capabilities." *Sloan Management Review* 34:67–81.

Schoemaker, P., and C. A. J. M. van der Heijden. 1992. "Integrating Scenarios into Strategic Planning at Royal Dutch/Shell." *Planning Review* (May/June): 41–46.

Schon, D. A. 1963. "Champions for Radical New Inventions." *Harvard Business Review* 41:77–86.

Schumpeter, J. 1950. *Capitalism, Socialism, and Democracy*. 3d ed. New York: Harper and Row.

Selznick, P. 1957. *Leadership in Administration: A Sociological Interpretation*. New York: Harper and Row.

Shapiro, C., and H. R. Varian. 1998. *Information Rules: A Strategic Guide to the Network Economy*. Boston: Harvard Business School Press.

Silverman, G., and A. Osterland. 1999. "A Panic over Plastic: Consumers Are Wising Up about Pricey Late Fees." *Business Week* (September 6): 32–33.

Singh, J. V. 1986. "Performance, Slack and Risk Taking in Organizational Decision Making." *Academy of Management Journal* 29:562–585.

Sitkin, S. B. 1992. "Learning through Failure: The Strategy of Small Losses." In *Research in Organizational Behavior*, edited by B. M. Staw and L. L. Cummings. Volume 14: 231–266. Greenwich, Conn.: JAI Press.

Slywotzky, A. J., and D. J. Morrison. 1997. *The Profit Zone*. New York: Random House.

Starr, J. A., and I. C. MacMillan. 1990. "Resource Cooptation and Social Contracting: Resource Acquisition Strategies for New Ventures." *Strategic Management Journal* 11:79–92.

Staw, B. M., L. E. Sandelands, and J. E. Dutton. 1981. "Threat-Rigidity Effects in Organizational Behavior: A Multilevel Analysis." *Administrative Science Quarterly* 26:501–524.

Stinchcombe, A. L. 1965. "Organizations and Social Structure." In *Handbook of Organizations*, edited by J. G. March. Chicago: Rand McNally.

Stuart, T., H. Hoang, and R. C. Hybels. 1999. "Interorganizational Endorsements and the Performance of Entrepreneurial Ventures." *Administrative Science Quarterly* 44:315–349.

Tapscott, D. 1995. *The Digital Economy: Promise and Peril in the Age of Networked Intelligence.* New York: McGraw-Hill.

Teece, D. J., G. Pisano, and A. Shuen. 1997. "Dynamic Capabilities and Strategic Management." *Strategic Management Journal* 18:509–533.

Tushman, M. L., and P. Anderson. 1986. "Technological Discontinuities and Organizational Environments." *Administrative Science Quarterly* 31:439–465.

Tushman, M. L., and C. A. O'Reilly III. 1997. *Winning Through Innovation: Leading Organizational Change and Renewal.* Boston: Harvard Business School Press.

Tushman, M. L., and E. Romanelli. 1985. "Organizational Evolution: A Metamorphosis Model of Convergence and Reorientation." In *Research in Organizational Behavior,* edited by L. L. Cummings and B. M. Staw. Volume 7: 171–122. Greenwich, Conn.: JAI Press.

Utterback, J. M. 1994. *Mastering the Dynamics of Innovation: How Companies Can Seize Opportunities in the Face of Technological Change.* Boston: Harvard Business School Press.

Utterback, J. M., and W. J. Abernathy. 1975. "A Dynamic Model of Process and Product Innovation." *Omega* 3:639–656.

Van der Heijden, K. 1996. *Scenarios: The Art of Strategic Conversations.* New York: John Wiley and Sons.

Vasconcellos, J. A. S., and D. Hambrick. 1989. "Key Success Factors: Test of a General Theory in the Mature Industrial-Product Sector." *Strategic Management Journal* 10:367–382.

Venkataraman, S. 1997. "The Distinctive Domain of Entrepreneurship Research." In *Advances in Entrepreneurship, Firm Emergence, and Growth,* edited by J. Katz and R. Brockhaus. Volume 3: 119–138. Greenwich, Conn.: JAI Press.

———. 1989. "Problems of Small Venture Start Up Survival and Growth: A Transaction Set Approach." Ph.D. dissertation, University of Minnesota.

Venkataraman, S., I. C. MacMillan, and R. G. McGrath. 1992. "Progress in Research on Corporate Venturing." Chap. 19 in *State of the Art of Entrepreneurship Research,* edited by D. L. Sexton and J. D. Kasarda. Boston: PWS-Kent Publishing.

Venkataraman, S., and A. H. Van de Ven. 1993. "Hostile Environmental Jolts, Transaction Set, and New Business." *Journal of Business Venturing* 13:231–255.

von Hippel, E. 1988. *The Sources of Innovation.* New York: Oxford University Press.

Wageman, R. 1995. "Interdependence and Group Effectiveness." *Administrative Science Quarterly* 40:145–180.

Weick, K. E. 1979. *The Social Psychology of Organizing.* Reading, Mass.: Addison-Wesley.

Weick, K. E., and K. H. Roberts. 1993. "Collective Mind in Organizations: Heedful Interrelating on Flight Decks." *Administrative Science Quarterly* 38:357–381.

Wernerfelt, B. 1984. "A Resource-Based View of the Firm." *Strategic Management Journal* 5:171–180.

Wheelwright, S. C. and K. B. Clark. 1995. *Leading Product Development: The Senior Managers' Guide to Creating and Shaping the Enterprise.* New York: Free Press.

Williamson, O. E. 1991. "Comparative Economic Organization: The Analysis of Discrete Structural Alternatives." *Administrative Science Quarterly* 36:269–296.

Winter, S. 1995. "Four Rs of Profitability: Rents, Resources, Routines and Replication." In *Resource-Based and Evolutionary Theories of the Firm: Towards a Synthesis,* edited by C. Montgomery. Boston: Kluwer Academic Publishers.

Wright, M., P. Westhead, and J. Sohl. 1999. "Editor's Introduction: Habitual Entrepreneurs and Angel Investors." *Entrepreneurship, Theory and Practice* 22:5–21.

INDEX

ABOUT
THE
AUTHORS

RITA GUNTHER MCGRATH is an Associate Professor in the Management Division of the Columbia University Graduate School of Business. She is the recipient of the *Entrepreneurship Theory and Practice* Award for the best conceptual paper submitted to the 1996 and 1992 Academy of Management Meetings, Entrepreneurship Division, as well as of the inaugural (1992) Kauffman Foundation Fellowship in Entrepreneurship.

Prior to her life in academia, she managed major information technology projects, worked in the political arena, and founded two start-ups. In her research and consulting, she has worked with companies such as Hewlett-Packard, Intel, DuPont, Citigroup (formerly Citibank), Chubb & Son, Texas Instruments, Ericsson, Fluor Daniel, Inc., and many others. She is also active in Columbia's executive education programs and is faculty director for its program on leading entrepreneurial change in organizations.

McGrath is a co-editor of the Special Research Forum on "New and Emerging Organizational Forms," forthcoming from the *Academy of Management Journal*, and the author of many book chapters and scholarly articles. Her articles have appeared in the *Harvard Business Review, Strategic Management Journal, Management Science, Academy of Management Review, Research-Technology Management,* and *Academy of Management Journal.* She serves on the editorial boards of the *Academy of Management Journal, Strategic Management Journal,* and *Journal of Business Venturing.*

IAN MACMILLAN is the Academic Director of the Sol C. Snider Entrepreneurial Research Programs at the Wharton School, University of Pennsylvania. He is also the Fred Sullivan Professor in the Management Department. Formerly he was Director of the Entrepreneurship Center at New York University and a teacher at Columbia and Northwestern Universities and the University of South Africa. In 1999 he was awarded the Swedish Foundation for Small Business Research Prize for his contribution to research in entrepreneurship.

Prior to joining the academic world, MacMillan was a chemical engineer and gained experience in gold and uranium mining, chemical and explosives manufacturing, oil refining, soap and food production, and the South African Atomic Energy Board. He has been a director of several companies in the travel, import/export, and pharmaceutical industries. He also has extensive consulting experience, having worked with such companies as DuPont, General Electric, GTE, IBM, Citibank, Metropolitan Life, Chubb & Son, American Re-Insurance, Texas Instruments, KPMG, Hewlett-Packard, Intel, Fluor Daniel, Matsushita (Japan), Olympus (Japan), and L. G. Group (Korea), among others.

MacMillan's articles have appeared in the *Harvard Business Review, Sloan Management Review, Journal of Business Venturing, Administrative Science Quarterly, Academy of Management Journal, Academy of Management Review, Academy of Management Executive, Management Science,* and *Strategic Management Journal,* among others.